P9-ASF-386

Becoming a
FASHION DESIGNER

Lisa J. Springsteel

WILEY

Front Cover Illustration by Izak Zenou
Represented by Trafficnyc.com

Back Cover Photographs and Illustration: (top left) Spring 2010 watercolor handbag painting by Raquel Caruso, (top right) Red Dalilah "2056 Collection" from the Kara Saun 2006 runway presentation, (bottom) Sketch entitled "Romantic Rhythm" by fashion designer Emily Tischler.

This book is printed on acid-free paper. ∞

Copyright © 2013 by John Wiley & Sons, Inc. All rights reserved

Published by John Wiley & Sons, Inc., Hoboken, New Jersey

Published simultaneously in Canada

No part of this publication may be reproduced, stored in a retrieval system, or transmitted in any form or by any means, electronic, mechanical, photocopying, recording, scanning, or otherwise, except as permitted under Section 107 or 108 of the 1976 United States Copyright Act, without either the prior written permission of the Publisher, or authorization through payment of the appropriate per-copy fee to the Copyright Clearance Center, Inc., 222 Rosewood Drive, Danvers, MA 01923, 978-750-8400, fax 978-646-8600, or on the web at www.copyright.com. Requests to the Publisher for permission should be addressed to the Permissions Department, John Wiley & Sons, Inc., 111 River Street, Hoboken, NJ 07030, 201-748-6011, fax 201-748-6008, or online at www.wiley.com/go/permissions.

Limit of Liability/Disclaimer of Warranty: While the publisher and author have used their best efforts in preparing this book, they make no representations or warranties with the respect to the accuracy or completeness of the contents of this book and specifically disclaim any implied warranties of merchantability or fitness for a particular purpose. No warranty may be created or extended by sales representatives or written sales materials. The advice and strategies contained herein may not be suitable for your situation. You should consult with a professional where appropriate. Neither the publisher nor the author shall be liable for damages arising herefrom.

For general information on our other products and services, or technical support, please contact our Customer Care Department within the United States at 800-762-2974, outside the United States at 317-572-3993 or fax 317-572-4002.

Wiley publishes in a variety of print and electronic formats and by print-on-demand. Some material included with standard print versions of this book may not be included in e-books or in print-on-demand. If this book refers to media such as a CD or DVD that is not included in the version you purchased, you may download this material at http://booksupport.wiley.com.

For more information about Wiley products, visit our Web site at www.wiley.com.

Library of Congress Cataloging-in-Publication Data:

Springsteel, Lisa J.-
  Becoming a fashion designer / Lisa J. Springsteel
      p. cm.
  Includes index.
  ISBN 978-1-118-14382-7 (pbk. : alk. paper); 978-1-118-41916-8 (ebk); 978-1-118-42098-0 (ebk); 978-1-118-43373-7 (ebk); 978-1-118-48701-3 (ebk); 978-1-118-48703-7 (ebk)

1. Fashion design—Vocational guidance. I. Title
  TT507.S735 2013
  746.9'2023—dc23

                                               2012026251

Printed in the United States of America

10 9 8 7 6 5 4 3 2 1

To all future fashion designers on your
triumphant journey to creative success

"Good clothes open all doors."

—THOMAS FULLER

CONTENTS

FOREWORD

EMBARKING ON A CAREER IN FASHION DESIGN CAN BE DAUNTING. But if you have a passion and a love of fashion, you should never let anything hold you back. *Becoming a Fashion Designer* is so exhilarating because it details the successes and failures that so many of us in fashion have had to endure to create and maintain our businesses. You can learn as much from someone's mistakes as you can from their triumphs. Our collective experience as designers will likely be the best information you receive. That is why this book will be so important to you.

When I started, there was no formula for success. Now, I see that becoming a designer required not only passion, but also a lot of essential know-how. One of the most significant insights I discovered along the way was that I could manufacture my clothes in New York City's Garment Center. If it hadn't been for the small factories that nurtured me without judgment or minimums, I wouldn't be where I am today. These factories still operate here in New York and can help you get off the ground and guide you through the ups and downs ahead.

Becoming a Fashion Designer is so valuable because it chronicles how we as designers made our big mistakes and where we seized our most vital opportunities. Our stories can help you avoid the setbacks and seize your moment. This book reveals the most imperative lessons for success, including how to survive when things aren't going well and how to behave when they are. In fact, I envy you. I wish I had these insider tips when I was just starting out. But now that you have all the information and resources you need from *Becoming a Fashion Designer*, the pressure is on you to step up and fulfill your dreams. Now it's your turn. Are you ready to become a fashion designer?

Nanette Lepore

PREFACE

AS A HIGH SCHOOL STUDENT, I narrowed down my career paths to two possibilities, and interned in both fashion and child psychology to determine which field was the best fit. Although I possessed an extraordinary adoration of children and a knack for helping people, I felt my true passion was in fashion. I did question if having such a specific degree might hinder me if I ever decided at some point in my career that it was just not for me. I remember having a conversation with my grandmother about my concern, and from the next room my grandfather, who had overheard our conversation, said, "Lisa, do you love fashion?" I said, "Oh yes, yes, grandpa, I do." He said, "Then major in fashion. Do what you love." After receiving his straightforward advice, I was further convinced fashion was indeed the right choice for me, and I have never looked back since.

Having had a clearly defined idea of what I wanted to major in during high school allowed me to focus on my fashion program selection. I wound up attending Florida State University, a school whose renowned fashion program ranked fifth in the United States at the time. Part of the curriculum included a mandatory internship, which took place during my senior year of college. I headed off to Neiman Marcus, located in Bal Harbour, an upscale coastal beach village in Miami, Florida. I worked in visual merchandising, and it was exciting to be in such a luxurious environment working for a specialty retailer of that magnitude. I remember consistently getting the urge to sketch concepts that came to me as I sat day after day in that wonderfully inspiring environment. I was surrounded by stunningly gorgeous designer gowns, exquisite visual displays, a clearly affluent clientele, and a beyond talented staff.

Shortly after I graduated from college, I decided to move to New York to pursue my fashion career. I arrived in the summer of 1994, and it was one of the best decisions I have ever made. Over the span of my 20-year fashion career, I have experienced the most exciting and wondrous journey of a lifetime. I have participated in design meetings with Mr. Ralph Lauren, selected fabric for the wardrobes of celebrities attending the Emmy Awards and appearing on the front cover of magazines, worked alongside Sean Combs to globally source all of the luxurious fabrics for his Fall 2008 menswear runway show for Mercedes-Benz Fashion Week in New York (while simultaneously being filmed for an MTV documentary), attended star-studded black tie events, and have met many famous fashion insiders. I learned through experience what to do and what not to do in every imaginable situation and became an expert on the ins and outs of the fashion industry. Knowing firsthand how difficult it was to learn the tricks of the trade of fashion, I became passionate about sharing my knowledge with others who were setting out on the same path. I wanted the information to be presented in an authentic and no-nonsense format, giving aspiring fashion designers an unmistakably solid idea of what the fashion industry is like and what will be expected.

Becoming a Fashion Designer is a dynamic and comprehensive book imparting unprecedented insider tips from top fashion designers, industry insiders and prominent executives, and expert advice on establishing a fashion design career. It will take you step-by-step through the process and will become your go-to reference. Whether you are exploring a career in fashion design or are certain you want to become a designer, you will learn all the information necessary to realize your dream. If you're already working as a fashion designer, but are interested in taking your design career to the next level, or if you're ready to launch your own collection, you will be provided with information to help facilitate your career dreams. Anyone who has ever tried to launch a fashion design career knows how grueling it can be. The fashion industry is a highly prominent field, which creates a decidedly competitive environment that is greatly guarded, secretive, and difficult to infiltrate and navigate. Of the various job opportunities available in the fashion industry, the job of fashion designer ranks as the most popular position, making the competition even stronger. The book pays special attention to this and demonstrates several ways in which an aspiring fashion designer can stand out from the competition.

Chapter 1, "An Introduction to a Career in Fashion Design," provides the reader with a comprehensive overview of a career in fashion design. It defines fashion design and what designers do. Original interviews with legendary fashion designers and executives are presented, in which they discuss their education, apprenticeships, and career rise, and also offer insider advice. Various fashion designers, at all levels, discuss the different tasks they carry out on a daily basis. A history of fashion design is provided, including an extensive account on the founding father of fashion, Charles Frederick Worth and the growth of fashion houses in Paris, highlighting the original couturiers who formed the basis of the fashion industry. The extent of worldwide media coverage and the effect as it relates to fashion design is discussed. This chapter also delves into the magnitude of the fashion industry on a global scale, including statistics as to the number of people working in the fashion industry, both globally and in the United States, as well as the volume of sales that the fashion industry produces. A highlight of this chapter is a detailed description of the inner workings of the fashion industry, from how the industry operates to how to successfully adapt to the work culture. Prominent fashion designers and executives from around the world give invaluable advice specifically geared to an aspiring fashion designer. Unique to most fashion design books is the section on finding balance to live a more stress-free life.

Chapter 2, "The Education for a Fashion Design Career," describes the educational requirements for becoming a fashion designer. College requirements are outlined, including a comparison between a two-year and four-year design degree program. Various fashion designers discuss why they chose the university they attended for their fashion design studies. Interviews with a fashion design educator, fashion design students, and interns are presented. The importance of interning is highlighted, as well as ways in which one can turn an internship into a permanent job. The benefits of studying abroad are discussed. Postgraduate degree programs and the value of taking continuing education courses are addressed.

Chapter 3, "The Job Market," walks the reader through the steps needed to determine his or her own individual design specialty. This chapter also describes the various types of jobs available in the fashion design sector, with corresponding job descriptions. Special attention is paid to the importance of personal branding and creating a personal branding statement. This chapter explains how to successfully land a fashion design job, offering guidelines for portfolio development and résumé creation. A variety of professionals in the field discuss what every fashion designer should include in his or her portfolio. The importance of networking and building a business network is detailed. Also provided is an all-inclusive listing of tried-and-true job search methods specific to fashion designers seeking work in the fashion industry. Interview tips and guidelines for negotiating the job offer and securing the ultimate job offer package are revealed. Human resources, employment agency, and fashion design executives advise on the skills they seek when hiring a fashion designer.

Chapter 4, "The Fashion Design Process," takes the reader through the entire design process on a step-by-step basis, from conceptual development to sample approval through to production hand-off.

Chapter 5, "Launching Your Own Fashion Collection," presents a thorough description of starting a fashion design business. It offers the reader a true depiction of the intense amount of work and skill required to successfully establish, manage, and grow one's business. Steps to write a business plan are offered. We learn from various fashion design business owners what was the most challenging aspect of launching their own collection. Types of business ownerships are outlined. Steps to define your brand are discussed. Original interviews with fashion designers are presented. An intellectual property checklist is provided. We will hear from copyright attorneys regarding the best ways for fashion designers to protect their work from unauthorized copying and infringement. Also included is information related to creating an accounting, budgeting, and bookkeeping system; hiring employees, contractors, and interns; developing a marketing plan, including a special section on unlocking the keys to a successful public relations strategy, and establishing a sales and order fulfillment strategy. Interviews with a celebrity stylist and television personality, the creator of New York Fashion Week, and a fashion director are included in this chapter.

Chapter 6, "Strategic Business Trends in the Fashion Industry," provides information regarding the trends toward outsourcing and globalization, as well as the importance and growing awareness of corporate social responsibility (CSR). Examples of innovative fashion company initiatives in CSR are profiled as cases in point. The head of CSR of a clothing company discusses his CSR program and the importance of incorporating it into his corporate structure. An environmentally friendly apparel company and an accessories company are profiled. We will learn from various designers about the role that sustainable fabrics play in their overall design philosophy, as well as the eco-friendly fabrics they use in their collections.

The Appendix includes an extensive list of resources tailored to a fashion design professional. Included are professional organizations, associations, and councils; fashion industry networking websites, professional networking websites, and social networking websites; professional trade publications; online portfolio websites; color and trend forecasting companies; broadcast and cable television programming, full-feature movies, and documentaries with a fashion theme, as well as a listing of major fashion magazines.

Self-Evaluation: Is Fashion Design for You?

Place a checkmark in the YES or NO columns after each of the following questions to get a sense if fashion design is the right career path for you.

	YES	NO
Do you like to make and wear your own clothes?		
Were you born with a sense of style?		
Are you inspired by the objects, landscapes, pop culture, and people around you?		
Do you have a refined color sense?		
Do you possess an artistic edge?		
Do you pay close attention to every single detail in every design or mock sketch that you create?		
Do you constantly re-sketch your illustrations until you get them just right?		
Do you love reading fashion magazines and have one or more subscriptions that you look forward to receiving each month?		
Do you go to a bookstore or magazine shop just to read through the fashion magazines?		
Do you get excited thinking about designing a fashion collection for an apparel manufacturer or design house?		
Do you dream of launching your own label one day?		
Do design concepts come to you out of the blue, and do you find yourself excited to make them come to life on your sketchpad?		
Can you quote and recite Tim Gunn's hysterically funny one-liners from *Project Runway*?		
Do you enter all the fashion design contests that are open to emerging fashion designers?		
Do you have the ability to articulate your design vision, and to engage and influence others to help you carry it out?		
Does multi-tasking like no other, in a high-pressure environment, scare you?		
Are you open to doing administrative tasks in order to pay your dues?		
Would it be unusual for you to be standing amongst hundreds of people on line for an Open See at Henri Bendel in New York?		
Are you considered by your friends, family, and peers to be a trendsetter?		
Do you take criticism well?		
Are you prepared to have your designs critiqued and changed?		
Are you ready, willing, and able to work long hours, including weekends, especially before fashion or market weeks?		
Do you possess both a creative and business mindset?		
Do you truly believe that Anna Wintour should, at the very least, be ruler of the *Kingdom of Fashion*?		

If you answered "yes" to most of these questions, you just may have found your ideal career fit!

ACKNOWLEDGMENTS

I would like to offer sincere thanks to the fashion designers, costume designers, stylists, and executives, many of whom I know personally, who provided interviews for the book, and in doing so, devoted countless hours of their precious time and showed such care for this project. They include Reem Acra, Dennis Basso, Manolo Blahnik, Guy Bradford, Randolph Duke, Daymond John, Chris Knott, Nanette Lepore, Deborah Lloyd, Fern Mallis, Bibhu Mohapatra, Maggie Norris, Pamella Roland, Ralph Rucci, Peter Som, Anna Sui, Todd Thomas, Zang Toi, Kay Unger, Robert Verdi, Stuart Weitzman, and Stephanie Winston Wolkoff. I would also like to acknowledge their agents, managers, publicists and public relations executives for their support, dedication, and unwavering efforts.

I wish to express tremendous appreciation to the renowned photographers, artists, and illustrators whose visual contributions made this book come to life, including Deborah Anderson, Nigel Barker, Claire Benoist, Fidel Berisha, Ivan Clemente, Joseph Dolderer, Mariah Do Vale, Mark Drew, Jodie Edom, Nicky Emmerson, Yoshikazu Enomoto, Steve Exum, Richard Gleason, Timothy Greenfield-Sanders, Rick Guidotti, Eka Halim, Bernard Hunt, Joseph Hunwick, Greg Kadel, Anna Kiper, Lennart Knab, Dan and Corina Lecca, Elizabeth Lippman, Adrian Lourie, Giovanni Martins, Anders Overgaard, Michael Roberts, Udo Spreitzenbarth, Hannah Thomson, Maria Valentina, Adam Weiss, and painter Nelson Shanks, for your stunning interpretation. Special thanks to Izak Zenou for providing such strikingly gorgeous and wonderfully eye-catching illustrations, both for the cover and throughout the book. To Izak Zenou's manager, Michelle Edelman of Traffic Creative Management in New York, I am eternally grateful for all that you have done.

I also want to give thanks to all the fashion designers, fashion executives, attorneys, educators, students, freelancers and interns who provided interviews and contributions, and shared their inspirational knowledge, talent, and expertise.

Gracious thanks to my editor, Paul Drougas, for his expertise in leading me through the process, with his calm demeanor and sense of humor always intact. Many thanks to everyone at Wiley who had a hand in the making of this book, including senior production editor Nancy Cintron, marketing manager Penny Makras, copyeditor Devra Kunin from Foxxe Editorial Services, and Mike New. Overwhelming appreciation to my publisher, John Wiley & Sons; it is an honor to be included in your family of authors.

The unconditional support and love of my parents, Warren and Bess, and of my sister, Amy, has been just as priceless to me growing up as it is today. I am eternally indebted to you, and love all of you so much. I know my grandparents are looking down with such pride and joy. They had a huge presence in my life, and I miss and love them more than words can express. Brayden: there is no greater love.

I would like to convey my heartfelt gratitude to Anne Bradstreet (1612–1672) who, in 1650, became the first female published writer in America, opening the doors and creating a voice for female writers everywhere.

› Becoming a
FASHION DESIGNER

Illustrated by Izak Zenou
for Lancôme. COURTESY
OF IZAK ZENOU.

1 An Introduction to a Career in Fashion Design

"Fashion is not something that exists in dresses only. Fashion is something in the air. It's the wind that blows in the new fashion; you feel it coming, you smell it, in the sky, in the street; fashion has to do with ideas, the way we live, what is happening."

— Coco Chanel

SOMEHOW, AT SOME POINT IN YOUR LIFE, SOMETHING INSPIRED A CREATIVE SPARK INSIDE OF YOU. Perhaps when you were a child, you discarded the original outfit that your Barbie™ doll came in and created a much more elaborate one. Or when you were growing up, you were completely enamored with how stunning your mother looked as you watched her get dressed up for a night on the town—her dress, her shoes, her jewelry, her hair! No matter how you arrived at your decision, welcome.

There is nothing quite as rewarding as being a fashion designer: a creative visionary who, from a mere brainstorming concept, creates a fully saleable collection seen on runways, in stores and catalogs, and on people around the world. From idea to finished product, fashion designers do a lot more than just design. During a typical workday, a designer can cast models for an upcoming fashion show, meet with the public relations director to discuss international press, troubleshoot a fit issue with the technical design team, seek counsel from the legal department to ensure the hangtag meets government regulations, and discuss last season's bestsellers with merchandising.

Look 34 of the Spring 2012 Peter Som Runway Collection.
PHOTOGRAPHER: DAN LECCA. COURTESY OF PETER SOM.

As a fashion designer who dreams of launching your very own collection, you will have the opportunity to express not only your own unique design aesthetic to the world, but also your personal viewpoints on societal issues and life-changing moments in history, ranging from politics and world peace to charitable and philanthropic causes, gay rights, and environmental sustainability. Renowned fashion designer Kenneth Cole is famous for expressing his strong personal opinions in his advertising campaigns. This is only one of the many thrilling ways that you can use your innate sense of style, refined color sense, individual creativity, and artistic talent to influence people, lifestyles, and trends. So, in essence, fashion designers hold the key not only to creating innovations in fashion, but also to relaying a message that is important to them.

Fashion is not just a product; it is an extension of who people are, how they embody, perceive, portray, and conduct themselves, and how they live. Fashion is a mood lifter; it can enhance our life and lift our spirits—and, most of all, it can bring us joy. Many people take pride in expressing their personal aesthetic through what they wear and how they wear it, from head to toe. There is a psychological aspect to fashion that can have a profound effect on the consumer (for example, a sense of confidence or an overwhelming feeling of power) when he or she puts on a specific garment, shoe, accessory, or even fragrance, and a good designer will always keep this in mind when designing for their target customer.

On her: Night dress. On him: Kinsley jacket and Panos pant from Panos Emporio. COURTESY OF PANOS EMPORIO

Fashion designers have the opportunity to dress their customers for both their careers and their social lives—from their most exciting moments to their very worst days. From the newborn baby on his first day home from the hospital, to a child's first day of preschool, to the teenager attending her senior prom, to the college student walking down the graduation aisle, to the unemployed man who needs to ensure that he lands his only opportunity for a job offer, to the bride-to-be walking nervously but excitedly down the aisle, you will play a fundamental role in supporting and touching people's lives with the fashions you create for them in these vital moments in their lives.

The distinguished Tunisian fashion designer Elie Saab lived this dream, dressing actress Halle Berry for the 74th Annual Academy Awards presentation, when, in 2001, Berry became the first black woman to receive an Academy Award for Best Actress. In her emotional acceptance speech, with tears rolling down her face, she cried, *"This moment is so much bigger than me. This moment is for Dorothy Dandridge, Lena Horne, Dianne Carroll. It's for the women that stand beside me, Jada Pinckett, Angela Bassett, Vivica Fox, and it's for every nameless, faceless woman of color that now has a chance because this door tonight has been opened."* Even though Mr. Saab was not on stage with his client, he played a vital behind-the-scenes role in two very important ways. First, he helped his client to feel confident for her important occasion. Second, he built a certain trust level with Halle Berry that prompted her to select him as her designer of choice for her big moment. The bond that forms between the fashion designer and client often results in a lifelong friendship.

Claudia Schiffer in the Halston Premiere Collection by Randolph Duke. COURTESY OF RANDOLPH DUKE.

It is here, in this fascinating world, that ingenuity comes to life and creative interpretations have limitless bounds. And for the thousands upon thousands of fashion designers around the globe, this feeling, this integral part of who you are and how you express yourself, will become your livelihood. And day in and day out, through the grueling hours and intensely stressful moments, this passion will help drive you to design collection after collection, season after season, year after year.

What Is Fashion Design?

Merriam Webster's dictionary defines a fashion as a prevailing custom or style. Fashion design is the process of applying a creatively envisioned style into wearable clothing and accessories. Clothing (also known as garments, attire, or dress) in its most simplified definition, is a covering for the body, usually made of fabric, and accessories are used to supplement a wardrobe and are either purely decorative (such as jewelry), useful (such as a watch), or necessary for everyday living (such as shoes). The most common fashion accessories include handbags, shoes, gloves, scarves, millinery (hats), belts, gloves, hosiery (including socks, stockings, leg warmers, and tights), jewelry (including earrings; necklaces; wrist, arm, and ankle bracelets; rings; piercings; and watches), sunglasses, pins, neckties, bow ties, and suspenders.

The fashion industry is divided into five main markets according to price point: haute couture, designer, bridge, moderate, and mass. However, there are additional markets that are just as important to be aware of, including one-of-a-kind, bespoke, contemporary, secondary, private label, and discount. The following sections provide a listing and explanation of all of the fashion industry markets, from highest to lowest price point.

ONE-OF-A-KIND

A one-of-a-kind piece or ensemble is the crème de la crème of fashion, and is fully customized, and made-to-order for a specific client according to his or her exact measurements and specifications. One-of-a-kind garments are considered the pinnacle of luxury in the fashion world because only one of its kind is in existence. Custom-made garments are crafted at the haute couture (French for "high fashion" or "high sewing") level, using only the finest fabrics, trims, embroideries, and appliqués. The price point reflects that level, due to the high quality of materials used and the superior extent of detail and workmanship that goes into making each piece.

Custom clothing is often referred to as the pièce de résistance because it is considered a true, irresistible showpiece at every level. It is considered by many to be an art form; finished custom pieces are often displayed in museum exhibits around the world and sell for thousands of dollars at auction. A custom client may request one piece or an entire wardrobe for a series of special events, such as black-tie galas. It is the responsibility of the designer to come up with each of those items according to a specified timeline and perhaps a personal branding theme that the client wishes to be carried out throughout his or her customized ensemble.

Celebrities who are presenters at an awards show, or who have received industry award nominations, will often be seen wearing a custom dress designed especially for the occasion. Other custom clients may include a celebutante (a person who is famous for being famous), a jet setter or socialite who is attending an exclusive event, a debutante who is making her debut into society at the cotillion ball, a high-profile businesswoman who is being honored at a conference, a low-profile client who prefers to remain anonymous after receiving an inheritance, or anyone who has an appreciation for custom clothing.

Angelina Jolie wearing Randolph Duke Couture at the 56th Annual Golden Globe Awards, held at the Beverly Hilton, Beverly Hills, California. GETTY IMAGES, 1999. COURTESY OF RANDOLPH DUKE.

Hilary Swank wearing Randolph Duke Couture to accept her Best Actress Oscar for *Boys Don't Cry*, at the 72nd Annual Academy Awards, held at the Shrine Auditorium and Expo Hall, Los Angeles, California. KABC, 2000. COURTESY OF RANDOLPH DUKE.

AUTHOR'S INSIGHT

Several years ago, I attended a function in New York at which legendary fashion designer Oleg Cassini discussed the custom-made wardrobe he created for First Lady Jacqueline Kennedy during the John F. Kennedy administration. Mr. Cassini was Jacqueline Kennedy's couturier, creating three hundred elegant outfits for her, from her simple A-line dresses to her iconic pillbox hats. Her Inauguration Day ensemble, a pillbox hat and a fawn-colored wool coat with a sable collar over a matching wool dress, dazzled women around the globe, who rushed to find copies so that they could adorn themselves just like Jackie-O. Mr. Cassini spoke about Mrs. Kennedy's innate sense of style and how she knew precisely how she wanted to be portrayed to the citizens of the United States and to the people around the world. Mr. Cassini presented his vision to Mrs. Kennedy, and they collaborated on various looks for all of the presidential events she would attend.

As Mrs. Kennedy was a style icon and a woman who epitomized class and grace, one would imagine that her personal fashion couturier would have dressed her accordingly, and he did, but he also had foresight and took risks. He envisioned a more progressive look for Mrs. Kennedy when he suggested he create a one-shouldered gown for one of her events, a style that was not worn by women at the time. Mrs. Kennedy was open to his idea "as long as the president agreed." President Kennedy obliged, and the world admired the wardrobe statements that Mrs. Kennedy made throughout the years.

Costume designers are fashion designers who design and create customized costumes for film, television, performing arts and stage productions, fashion shows, special events, or other performances for "talent" or show business personalities, actors, models, singers, dancers, and other performers. The process sometimes involves extensive research of a historical component, such as the replication of clothing from a particular era, needs to be reproduced. Once the research is complete, designs are sketched, and fabric is sourced and purchased, then draped on a form (i.e., mannequin) or patterned and then produced. The costumes oftentimes require accessories, such as hats, headdresses, tiaras and other jewelry, hosiery, masks, wigs, and footwear. The process may involve the creation of something unique, like a full-body cat suit for a musical. Costume designer John Napier won a Tony Award in 1983 for Best Costume Designer, for the Broadway musical *Cats*. A singer such as Britney Spears will need a completely customized wardrobe created for her worldwide concert tours, consisting of several head-to-toe outfits for each series of songs, matching each corresponding stage set. So the costume designer will need to carry out a feeling in the costumes and ensembles that will correspond with the overall concert theme. Some costume designers become famous themselves, such as Patricia Field, who created the outfits for the characters Carrie, Miranda, Charlotte, and Samantha for the popular HBO television series *Sex and the City*, as well as the movie and sequel. Singer and actress Madonna had 85 costume changes in the movie *Evita*, which shows how important a role a costume designer plays in the overall production of a movie.

In addition to running his own company, legendary fashion designer Isaac Mizrahi was the costume designer for three Broadway revivals, one operetta, one opera, and a film. Certain unique circumstances come into place for a costume designer that an ordinary fashion designer would not necessarily encounter. For example, costume designers have to pay special attention to the needs of the particular person they are fitting. For a dancer, the fit of his or her clothing is critical in ensuring that movement is not inhibited during performances.

An Interview with Todd Thomas, Costume and Fashion Designer

❭ *Was there a pivotal moment in your childhood, upbringing, or at some point in your life that led you to pursue a career in fashion design?*

I was inspired to design out of necessity, since I was living in a small town at the time and fashionable items were not available to me.

❭ *Please describe any fashion design positions you may have held prior to launching your own collection, Tailor Tinker.*

I started working on Seventh Avenue in New York City and worked for a loungewear manufacturer and learned many important things there. It was not the most artistic or glamorous job; however, it gave me lots of information which has been vital in the way I have approached my career. Along the way, I worked as a fashion tailor on photo shoots for high-end clients. I worked with different photographers and editors who gave me insight into marketing and advertising, and freelanced and consulted for other companies. I've worked on fashion shows, and I've worked with a multitude of entertainers on a personal level and have done some theatrical and movie work.

❭ *What advice would you give an aspiring fashion designer trying to launch his or her own collection?*

Start out with a very concise plan and have an idea of how you want to evolve so you can sustain yourself on many levels, both financially and creatively. It is all about sustaining a lifetime of work.

❭ *What is your design philosophy?*

I have a major reverence for craft and quality, both classic and sartorial. I feel it's important to make

an investment in something that is going to serve you for a while.

❭ *Who inspires you as a fashion designer?*

Geoffrey Beene, who was kind of an iconoclast in that he did his own magnificent thing superbly and was an architect of style and beauty and genius and creativity, and did it in a way that was his own. Another designer and journalist who has moved me deeply is Elizabeth Hawes. She opened her own design house in New York and became a fashion critic and then later became a labor leader. I also love Norma Kamali. She spoke to me at the moments I needed it most in the late 1970s and early 1980s. She was revolutionary then and still is today. I absolutely love Azzedine Alaïa for being consistent, for his aesthetic, vision, and dedication to his work.

❭ *You are the genius fashion and costume designer behind the gorgeous creations for the world-famous Victoria's Secret Fashion Show. Please describe this experience, as well as how far in advance the creative process begins.*

I am now in my ninth season as the collection designer. We work with the design team and try to frame and capsulize what they are thinking and projecting for VS and what their ideas are going to convey, as well as what products will be hitting the stores and what will be featured on their website. We have the luxury of creating something that doesn't necessarily have to translate to sales as much as it is about designing an idea that people want to aspire to emotionally. It is about creating a narrative, something that is going to move people and make a great show. I've had the good fortune of working with the most interesting people, including the House of Lesage who does the embroidery for us, who also does the embroidery for Chanel and all the couture houses. We work with the best shoe designers, corset makers, fabric painters, and jewelry people. We've already begun working on the show this year, so it's nearly a year-round process.

> **How did you first get interested in costume design?**

It's been a multicultural kind of thing. I've always been a visual person, always been inspired by cinema and music; these are all things that have been a driving force in creating image for me. For me, it was many things; it wasn't just the whole fantasy that is the fashion world. For me, inspiration comes on many levels.

> **Describe the ultimate perfect day for you.**

One of those days when things don't go wrong, or if they do, something good comes out of it. You can take the reins off of whatever has been frustrating, and it winds up being an "aha moment." It's that turbulent, cloudy moment that turns into something that ends positively.

HAUTE COUTURE

French for "high sewing," or "high fashion," haute couture (often referred to more informally as "couture"), describes handmade, made-to-measure garments using only the most luxurious fabrics, such as the finest cashmere, fur, suede, leather, and silk, sewn with extreme attention to detail by the most skilled seamstresses, often using hand-executed techniques. It is the fusion of both costume and high fashion and is often seen on the most affluent and famous people.

The Chambre Syndicale de la Haute Couture is an association whose members include those companies that have been designated to operate as an haute couture atelier or house. Haute couture is a legally protected

Bolero detail from the "Elle Gala Dress" worn by Swedish actress Josephine Bornebusch when hosting the Swedish *Elle* Style Awards in January 2010. Couture design by Halewijn Bulckaen for H&M, 2010. COURTESY OF HALEWIJN BULCKAEN.

and controlled label and can only be used by those fashion houses that have been granted this designation by the French Ministry of Industry. This governing body annually reviews its membership base, which must comply with a strict level of regulations and standards in order to maintain membership. The membership list changes annually as a result of its stringent criteria.

The couture house is headed by a fashion couturier who oversees a workroom of skilled workers who practice their hand-made craft as experts in either dressmaking or tailoring. The process may begin with a sketch, an illustration, or a draped and cut muslin or toile, depending on the designer's preference. To finalize a couture piece, fine trim, embroidery, and embellishments are often purchased by outside sources, who are expert practitioners in their respective field and then meticulously sewn into each piece. Exquisite fit is an inherent quality of a

Illustrated by Izak Zenou for Henri Bendel, 2004.
COURTESY OF IZAK ZENOU.

couture piece. The client will endure a series of fittings to determine that exact measurements have been achieved, to ensure not only precise fit but also style and comfort, which are equally essential.

When haute couture collections were first produced, they were presented to the press, buyers, and high-end clientele in a trunk show format in a designated salon. Each model carried a card that indicated a corresponding look number, making it easy for those in attendance to jot down the garments that were to their liking. Once selections were made, the client would sit with the designer, who would then fit the garments to that client's specific measurements and exact preferences, or a buyer would reproduce them for their own store.

Today, the couture collections are seen on the runways during Paris Fashion Week. Pricing typically begins in the high thousands and can reach into the hundreds of thousands for these fine garments. Many companies use the glamour and appeal of their couture collections, which account for a small market share of their overall business, as a catalyst to boost sales for their ready-to-wear, accessories, and fragrance businesses, which represent the bulk of their revenue. Couture collections are often used as a "visual advertisement" to bring excitement to the brand and to elicit sales for the more affordable ready-to-wear collection. Style.com, the online home of *Vogue* magazine is a great resource for previewing the couture runway shows, both in photograph and video format.

Illustrated by Izak Zenou, Personal Collection, 2006.
COURTESY OF IZAK ZENOU.

Some well-known couture labels are Armani Privé, Atelier Versace, Chanel, Christian Dior, Givenchy, Jean Paul Gaultier, and Valentino. The Chambre Syndicale de la Haute Couture accepts "foreign" members; however, there are only a handful of fashion designers outside of Paris who practice the fine technique of couture craftsmanship. Elie Saab, Giorgio Armani, and Paul Smith are examples. The French Ministry allows for outside members in an effort to show their strong belief in the importance of the globalization of the fashion industry. Ralph Rucci, Rick Owens, Adam Kimmel, Zac Posen, and Mainbocher are the only American designers to have achieved haute couture status. They have each been invited by the Ministry to show their collections in Paris and currently are, or have been, members of the Chambre Syndicale de la Haute Couture. Interestingly enough, Thom Browne, a New York–based menswear designer, independently showed his collection in Paris as a nonmember. A complete list of current members can be found at www.modeaparis.com.

BESPOKE

"Bespoke" is a British term used to describe individually crafted and patterned men's clothing. The *Oxford English Dictionary* defines "bespoke" as made-to-order clothing, made to each individual customer's precise measurements and specifications. Although bespoke is not a protected label, like cou-

Gieves & Hawkes bespoke suit. PHOTOGRAPHER: ADRIAN LOURIE.

ture, the Savile Row Bespoke Association (a professional organization consisting of Savile Row tailors) has attempted to set a standard by providing minimum requirements for a garment to be allowed the prestigious use of its name. Savile Row is a very short street in central London, called "the golden mile of tailoring," famous for its bespoke tailors, among them Davies and Son, Gieves & Hawkes, and Norton and Sons. Historical Savile Row clients have included Napoleon III and Winston Churchill.

DESIGNER

Also known as ready-to-wear (oftentimes abbreviated RTW) or "off the rack" and by the French term *prêt-à-porter*, designer clothing is factory made and finished to fit standard sizes. Don't, however, let the phrase "off-the-rack" fool you. Whether mass produced or offered in limited quantities, designer clothing is exclusive and uses the finest imported fabrics and trims. Ready-to-wear collections are generally presented twice a year (Spring/Summer and Autumn/Winter) during fashion weeks around the world, and they appear earlier than the couture collections. The price point can oftentimes exceed $1,000 per garment, but can range in lower price points or skyrocket to high three-figure numbers. Some of the most popular designer labels are Ralph Lauren, Donna Karan, Calvin Klein, Vera Wang, and Catherine Malandrino. Style.com, *Vogue* magazine's online website, offers a seasonal presentation of all designer fashion shows in both video and photo format.

"Quai de la Tournelle" from the Fall/Winter 2011 Catherine Malandrino Collection. The collection follows a girl with a Parisian, edgy spirit, along the promenade of Quai de la Tournelle. COURTESY OF CATHERINE MALANDRINO.

In Paris, the Chambre Syndicale du Prêt-à-Porter des Couturiers et des Créateurs de Mode is an established association, created in 1973, that is made up of all the fashion designers who produce ready-to-wear. The Chambre Syndicale de la Mode Masculine is an association that specifically includes the top menswear designers who produce ready-to-wear collections.

BRIDGE

Bridge garments are in between ready-to-wear and better, and carry a price point generally ranging in price from $300 to $600 per garment. Career wear and separates, along with dresses, are often indicative of a bridge classification. DKNY, CK, and Anne Klein II are examples of bridge labels.

BETTER

Better is one step down from bridge. Sportswear, various coordinates, separates, and dresses may all appear in better collections, and will typically sell for less than $600 per piece, but they primarily fall into a price point range of $150–$300. Some of the most popular better labels are Ellen Tracy, Kenneth Cole, and Anne Klein.

Illustrated by Izak Zenou for John Lobb, 2006. COURTESY OF IZAK ZENOU.

CONTEMPORARY

Contemporary collections offer trendy apparel at a relatively affordable price point aimed at women in their twenties and thirties. Cynthia Steffe, Rebecca Taylor, and BCBGMAXAZRIA are all considered contemporary designers.

SECONDARY

Secondary lines are used by designers who want to offer a lower-priced line aside from their designer collection. The price points differ, but these fashions can generally be found for less than $300 per piece at retail. Marc by Marc Jacobs and Lauren by Ralph Lauren are considered secondary lines.

MODERATE

Moderate fashions are promoted to the average, everyday customer and usually retail for less than $100 apiece. Some of the most popular moderate retailers are Liz Claiborne, Abercrombie & Fitch, Nine West, and the Gap.

PRIVATE LABEL

Merchandise that is manufactured by a store, or in partnership with an apparel manufacturer, is considered private label. Store advantages include greater control over production, cost, pricing, advertising budget, and design. Private label runs a gamut of price points and is generally produced for the bridge to moderate markets. Some of the most successful private label businesses are International Concepts (I.N.C.) for Macy's and Hunt Club for J.C. Penney.

MASS

Mass market or budget caters to the lower end of the apparel continuum, with retail pricing generally under the $50 price point. Product categories generally include casual sportswear such as t-shirts and jeans. Some of the most popular budget retailers are Old Navy, Target, Wal-Mart, Kmart, and Kohl's. Mass market is made in large quantities and is geared toward the general public.

DISCOUNT

Discount merchandise, also referred to as off-price, is excess merchandise that did not sell at its full retail price through its original and intended retailer. These items can be found at varying price points in an array of retail outlets such as Filene's Basement (the inventor of the off-price store concept), Ross Stores, T.J.Maxx, Loehmann's, Marshalls, and Saks Fifth Avenue OFF 5TH. Discount merchandise can also be found in factory outlet stores.

Within these price points, clothing classifications fall into various product categories, including women's, men's, young men's, collegiate, tweens (pre-teen), juniors, children's and layette (newborn) including dresses, casual wear, separates, suits, sportswear, tailored clothing, eveningwear, formalwear, outerwear, intimates, maternity, and swimwear.

An Interview with Nanette Lepore, Fashion Designer

Fashion Designer Nanette Lepore. PHOTOGRAPHER: ELIZABETH LIPPMAN.

Was there a pivotal moment in your childhood, upbringing, or at some point in your life that led you to pursue a career in fashion design?

❯ There were lots of different times in my childhood when I realized I loved making clothing, but it wasn't until I got to college that I knew I could actually be a fashion designer. I used to constantly sew from age 10 up to the beginning of high school. I was sewing every weekend, all weekend, every night. I was up until four in the morning, oftentimes sitting in my room sewing, and my parents had no idea I wasn't sleeping. I loved making clothing! When I got to college, I had a professor who told me about FIT (Fashion Institute of Technology, in New York), and I didn't realize there was a fashion school I could afford until then. I have a bachelor's degree in business, and then I got an associate's in fashion design from FIT. I will always be grateful that my professor took me under his wing and told me to attend FIT.

Please describe any fashion design positions you may have held prior to launching your own collection.

❯ I worked for about 3-4 years before I started my own line, and each job was a very different and unique experience. It was difficult, as fashion design positions are not easy. In my first job, I was sketching in a closet, sitting in between racks of clothing. After that, I went on to a knitwear company whose collection was made in China, and it was a rough crowd (a lot of back stabbing), and my company is not like that at all. I then moved on to a job that taught me so much, which was in a boutique, designing clothing in the basement. I would do collections for her store and do specials for her customers, so I'm really good at doing specials now for people who come in and need something unique. I would travel with her to Europe for her buying trips. She carried Claude Montana, Jean Paul Gaultier, and Moschino in her store, and I got to see the insides of these showrooms, and I went to some fantastic shows in Paris. We shopped tiny lines in London, and it gave me the knowledge that I could do my own line. I learned about all these small factories in the garment center, so I knew I could manufacture in New York, and I didn't even realize they were here the whole time.

Please discuss how you began your line and what your greatest challenge was when first launching your collection.

❭ Originally, I rented a storefront in the East Village in New York that was 500 square feet for $500 a month. I had a partner, and we each borrowed $5,000. We were located between a gas station and a soup kitchen. It was a rough neighborhood. My advice to anyone starting is to be right next to your customer so you can see what's working and what's not working. I quickly went into the wholesale business from retail. We applied to the Coterie and got accepted. Our first season there was unbelievable, as we had $250,000 in sales. Keeping the business afloat without money was our biggest challenge.

What advice would you give an aspiring fashion designer trying to launch his or her own collection?

❭ Think small at first. I think starting out in retail is so much better than wholesale because you don't have all the additional markups. If you are going direct to your customer, you can sell something that cost you $50 for $100. Find a small shop in your area and work at it and learn it before you launch into the bigger world.

What is your design philosophy?

❭ I've always wanted everything of mine to stand out and have some unique look to it, so that on a selling floor in a sea of clothing there was something special about everything I made. So if I made a white shirt, it had to have some special trim or detailing so that it looked different from the rest; it is more about the fineness of the details and also guaranteeing a beautiful fit for my customers so they feel good in the clothing. You learn how important fit is right from the beginning. The first time Neiman Marcus called and said, "You have to take back 200 dresses because

Spring/Summer 2012 Nanette Lepore Collection.
PHOTOGRAPHER: MARIA VALENTINA, 2011.

they don't fit," I made a vow that was never going to happen again. Mistakes still sometimes happen, but they don't happen like they used to when we were smaller and we were just trying to manage it. But you learn to follow the little warning signs that come up so you are better prepared.

How does the design process begin for you? Do you begin with a theme or some form of inspiration, a silhouette or a recently discovered can't-live-without fabric?

❭ It really starts more like a painting and roughing in the prints and the patterns. The boards get put together slowly. It starts with one or two prints, and then we put together a color palette. We ship every month now, so every month is an ordeal of trying to come up with a really special group with unique styling. During the months that coincide with the shows, we really push to explore new silhouettes and work on what really feels new to the customer. I like to push myself into a place that I'm not that comfortable or familiar with, so that I feel like I expand what I love and what I feel my customer wants.

Who has had a major influence on you as a fashion designer?

❯ I have memories of great women who were around me growing up. I was so impressionable as a young person. I remember my mom's style really well. She was really daring and always had great clothes. My Aunt Sandra's mother had a chiffon leopard blouse; I remember she was so beautiful and regal. A woman with great style can make an impact on you as a young kid and stay with you forever.

Spring/Summer 2012 Nanette Lepore Collection.
PHOTOGRAPHER: MARIA VALENTINA, 2011.

You have dressed famous people such as Sharon Stone, Blake Lively, Leighton Meester, Eva Longoria, Scarlett Johansson, Taylor Swift, Miley Cyrus, and many more. Obtaining a celebrity clientele is the highlight of any fashion designer's career. How did this evolve for you?

❯ Jennifer Lopez wore a top from one of our runway shows on an MTV talk show, which happened through a stylist. Sarah Jessica Parker wore our clothes on *Sex and the City*. The press you get from celebrities wearing your clothing really makes a difference in your business. I never wanted it to distract me and allow me to lose focus and productivity because every month I had to come up with a collection, so I never focused on it. But now a lot of it comes naturally. It's fun to balance both of these worlds. I'm lucky to have that opportunity. It's nice when you see a celebrity wearing something in their personal life of yours that you never knew she had. That happens a lot with the actress Kelly Rutherford.

What role does social media play in the promotion of your brand and in staying close to your customer base?

❯ We are all really new to social media and we really just jumped into social media in 2011 in a big way. It moves fast, and people move fast with it. It's a game that you have to play quickly. It's more about sharing ideas and feelings instead of trying to make it about shopping in my stores. The potential for it to grow into something huge is enormous, but you never know where it's going to go. We go through our tweets every day. We'll drop a surprise on somebody that I think is really fun. We have a "Who Wore It Best" contest, and the winner gets a little surprise. I'm not sure if it will actually build clientele from it, but we are having a ton of fun with it.

How do you design garments and accessories that are both true to your design aesthetic and vision and commercially saleable? Is there ever a conflict?

❭ There is a lot of conflict. It's hard because often-times you take a plunge into something that is really different and the customer buys it and loves it. But you always walk the line and question when you should sacrifice a design to become more commercial. It is a question I ask myself at least once a week, if not more. Sometimes your risks take off, sometimes they don't.

Your clothing and accessories can be found in nine of your Nanette Lepore boutiques worldwide, including locations in New York, Los Angeles, Chicago, Las Vegas, Boston, Chevy Chase, London, and Tokyo; in specialty boutiques such as Scoop and Olive and Bette's; and in department stores such as Neiman Marcus, Bergdorf Goodman, Saks Fifth Avenue, and Bloomingdales. What advice would you give to an aspiring fashion designer who is pounding away at the pavement trying to land his or her first retail account?

❭ I had been working in retail before so I knew who to target when I began my collection. You need to make a target list. Look at lines you want to hang with. Don't kid yourself about the cost of things. The lower the price can be, the more of a clientele you are going to pick up. People are not willing to shell out designer prices for an unknown name. It is very rare that someone can be in a designer price point overnight. When I adjusted my pricing to be more in the contemporary world, my business took off because I was hovering between contemporary and designer for a long time, and it wasn't working. Try to listen to the advice of the people around you and from the people you look up to. Barneys is the first account for a lot of designers because they are

open and willing to try new designers. Take many road trips with your clothes in the back of your car, and target the shops you want to be in. Going door-to-door, you will have to be a bit pushy and persistent, but don't be too pushy. You cannot have a feeling that it is beneath you to go in with a suitcase to charm the stores. Be clever about putting your stuff up on a website to try to sell online.

Your website is so inviting and fantastic! Do you play an integral role in its maintenance?

❭ We do meet about it when there is a big change, so when there is anything that they change, they run it past me. I have input over everything that goes up. Although I am not involved in the actual

Spring/Summer 2012 Nanette Lepore Collection.
PHOTOGRAPHER: MARIA VALENTINA, 2011.

logistics of making it happen, I am really involved with the artistic feeling of the website.

Incredibly, 85 percent of your collection is manufactured in New York City, and your design, patternmaking, production, and shipping departments are based in your design studio in New York City's Garment District. How are you able to keep your costs down, since you are not able to directly benefit from the lower labor costs of outsourcing your manufacturing operations overseas?

❯ With a business of my size, Asian factories are really not much cheaper. When we've counter sourced a lot of things, we've come up with very close to the same costs by manufacturing here. By the time you produce it in China and import it here and pay all the import duties and shipping, we are oftentimes at the same cost. I'd rather have the control and be able to maintain it and look at it every day. Manufacturing here, I have better quality, better inventory control, better ability to turn around and restock someone who is selling something well, and I can use higher-quality fabrics. To me, that far outweighs any marginal cost differences that would happen if I was manufacturing in China, or India for that matter. Everything I make overseas, I am disappointed in. I never feel like the fit is as good as the things that we make in New York, and I never feel like the fabric qualities are as nice as the fabric qualities that I am able to use working in New York. When I work in New York, I import all of the Italian fabrics because I am using a lot of the same fabrics that the high-end designers are using. We work with the Italian mills and then import the fabric to New York and cut and sew here. I can't import Italian fabric to China, as it costs me a fortune

to do that because of all the duties they put on it, they make it impossible.

You, along with fashion designer Anna Sui and several other designers, organizations, and companies, spearheaded the "Save the Garment Center" campaign in an effort to save New York City's Garment District. What prompted your involvement with this effort, and what still needs to be done?

❯ I had heard that the Garment District was at risk for being pushed out to move overseas. I couldn't let that happen and knew I had to face it head-on. The small designers are here because the factories are here, and we will lose them all the minute the factories close. The international press and buyers come here because there are so many small American designers here. We need to get the word out. We need more involvement from the entire design community. There is an ethical code here for giving back to the future and keeping the Garment District intact. I want to leave a legacy for my daughter and for the designers coming next.

You run your own fashion design firm and are married with a child. How do you balance it all?

❯ I don't think I balance it all that well. I just try to spend as much quality time with my family as I can. I try to have meals together with my daughter, in which we talk about her day or we play games. I try to be there in the morning to make breakfast for her and help get her out of the door. We take a lot of family trips together with my sister and her kids and my dad. Kids remember those times.

Describe the ultimate perfect day for you.

❯ I would want to wake up in Italy anywhere near water. How about Capri or the Amalfi Coast? I love Italy, I love being on a boat in Italy, I love hiking down the hill in Capri to go to the beach club and then boating and swimming through the emerald grotto, and then getting back out of the boat and having a nice lunch with white wine and fresh fish and pasta, and then hiking back up the hill to burn off the calories and jumping in the swimming pool at the top of the hill, and then taking a little nap to get ready to hike up the hill again for dinner, then taking a little stroll and visiting the shops. That's my perfect life!

An Interview with Reem Acra, Fashion Designer

Reem Acra at work in her design atelier. COURTESY OF REEM ACRA.

Was there a pivotal moment in your childhood, upbringing, or at some point in your life that led you to pursue a career in fashion design?

❯ As a student at the American University in Beirut, Lebanon, I had the opportunity to design and produce a collection for a fashion show there. Two thousand people attended the show. It was when I was on stage that I realized that this would be my career.

What was your major while attending the American University of Beirut?

❯ My major was business administration, which has been very helpful being a business owner of an international fashion company!

While in college, you attended a party wearing an intricately embroidered silk organza gown that you created from your mother's dining room tablecloth. A fashion editor happened to be at the party and took notice. What happened next?

❯ It was this gown that got her attention and inspired her to arrange for me to have a fashion show at the university. It was an amazing and exciting time for me. Everything happened very quickly.

Did you immediately begin working in the fashion industry after completing your studies at both The Fashion Institute of Technology (FIT) in New York and its Paris counterpart, Esmond Ecole de Mode? Also, please describe any internships, apprenticeships, or on-the-job training you had before you launched your own collection.

❯ When I was at FIT in New York it was a very special time for me. I received every award that the school offered its students, such as the Madame Grès and the Woolmark Foundation awards. When I sewed the first dress for my dressmaking class, my professor told the class that the quality of my design should be featured in the windows of the famous New York specialty retailer Bergdorf Goodman. After graduating from school, I worked for a firm as a private-label development designer for several years. It gave me extensive experience in product development and the overall American market. I transitioned into interior designer for a few years after this experience, which I enjoyed, but I always knew I would go back to designing. I started my company not realizing I needed to have a business plan or a strategy, but just out of a love for creating beautiful gowns.

In 1997, you launched the Reem Acra Bridal Collection, which quickly became recognized for its luxurious fabrics, intricate embroidery and beadwork, and elaborate designs. What prompted you to begin designing bridal gowns, and how did this lead to your ready-to-wear collection launch six years later?

❯ It began when a friend of mine asked me to make a dress for her to wear to her wedding at the Hotel Crillion in Paris, and the media loved it both in Paris and New York. That first dress turned into an order for thirty dresses, and so a business was born. I started designing ready-to-wear at the request of Neiman Marcus management, who was looking for a new designer collection for their stores.

In 2003, the same year you launched your ready-to-wear collection, you opened your flagship store in New York. What does it feel like to own a boutique that houses your entire collection in the heart of the luxury retail world?

❯ When I opened my store in 2003, it was the most amazing experience for me. It was a dream-come-true. The opening party was unbelievable, and I was walking on air. I've moved my store from Madison

Spring/Summer 2012 Reem Acra Runway Collection showing strapless beaded gown with side ruching in multicolor embroidery; baby ostrich shrug with beaded embroidery. PHOTOGRAPHERS: DAN AND CORINA LECCA. COURTESY OF DAN AND CORINA LECCA.

Avenue to one of the most prestigious buildings in New York, the Crown Building, located on Fifth Avenue and 57th Street. It's above the Bulgari store on the corner and has a very couture environment.

What is your design philosophy?

❯ I have an insatiable desire for luxurious fabrics, texture, rich color, and anything made by hand. My creations particularly appeal to women who are looking for glamour and sophistication for the most significant moments of their lives. My strong sense of technical acumen, tremendous creativity, and attention to detail are the basis for my philosophy that is driven by my love of fashion and design.

How does the design process begin for you? Do you begin with a theme, an inspiration, a silhouette, or a recently discovered can't-live-without fabric?

❯ I'm inspired by my life—by the places I travel to, the museum shows that I go to, and by my close friends and family. The starting point for me when I'm working on a new collection is often a new silhouette that I am refining or a unique fabric or material.

As a fashion designer, you are renowned for being able to match a look to a woman's personality. Your clientele encompasses celebrities, royal families, socialites, style icons, and all women who have an appreciation for the high level of beauty and workmanship that goes into designing your pieces. Please describe what the process of working with a client is like and what you feel is the most important aspect of this collaboration for a fashion designer.

❯ This is such a hard question, but such an important one because the collaboration between the client and the designer is very exciting to me. When I meet a client for the first time, there is a certain magic that happens when I feel like I can see the essence of the person I am designing for. It's about the client's personality and how she will look in the gown that I design for her. It usually happens for me in just the first few minutes upon meeting her.

Being able to obtain a celebrity clientele is the highlight of any fashion designer's career. Who was your first celebrity client?

❯ The first celebrity to ever wear a gown of mine was Halle Berry, and the dress that she wore reflected her personality and accentuated her beauty. It was a very exciting moment that I will never forget. It took many years to develop the celebrity clientele that I have today and a lot of hard work developing those relationships. Now the celebrities trust me to make them look elegant and beautiful on the red carpet.

The Reem Acra ready-to-wear and bridal collections are sold by 150 of the world's most prominent retailers, such as Bergdorf Goodman, Neiman Marcus, and Saks Fifth Avenue in the United States, as well as Saks Fifth Avenue and Harvey Nichols in the Middle East. Your collection is also available at specialty retailers across the world, in Kuwait, Bahrain, Saudi Arabia, Istanbul, Egypt, Hong Kong, Singapore, Japan, and Korea. What advice would you give to aspiring fashion designers who are pounding away at the pavement trying to land their first retail account?

❯ It's very basic, but very important advice—deliver quality designs on time that the store will be able to sell.

The first wedding dress that Reem Acra designed. COURTESY OF REEM ACRA.

Is there a specific approach you followed that allowed you to reach the level of prominence and success you have achieved in your career that so few designers have been able to attain?

❯ My parents raised me to work hard and never give up. It's a lot of long hours and just plain old perseverance. You have to have a great deal of inner strength and be able to see the big picture.

What advice would you give to an aspiring fashion designer who is trying to launch his or her own collection?

❯ Be true to your own style and aesthetic.

As a fashion designer with a namesake collection, you partner with your executive management team and creative heads to ensure that all the steps of developing and selling a collection—such as design, technical design, merchandising, visual presentation, quality control, fashion show production, public relations, sales, and marketing—are running smoothly. How do you manage this process with your staff?

❯ You have to have the very best staff that you can find to help you be the best designer you can be.

Having great people working with you is an invaluable asset and should never be underestimated. They have to be smart, quick, and ambitious. They have to understand the brand and be able to give you the right kind of support to do what you do best.

Currently, you are designing five different apparel collections, including haute couture wedding and evening gowns, bridal royal and seasonal collections, ready-to-wear seasonal collections, and an accessories line—a huge undertaking for any designer. How do you achieve balance between your career and personal life?

❯ It's not a balance, it's a complete circle. Your career and your personal life become one, and it is your life, not separate parts of your life.

Describe what the ultimate perfect day would be like for you.

❯ My ideal day would be a day to myself to design fabrics, drape, and sketch, while listening to the music of French singer Édith Piaf.

An Interview with Anna Sui, Fashion Designer

Portrait of Anna Sui, 2011. PHOTOGRAPHER: JOSH JORDAN. COURTESY OF ANNA SUI.

Was there a pivotal moment in your childhood, upbringing, or at some point in your life that led you to pursue a career in fashion design?

❯ When I was four years old, I was already talking about becoming a designer (my best friend from kindergarten, Candee, tells me so). I'm not exactly sure where I first got that notion, but it was probably something I saw on television. I always had it in mind that a designer had beautiful fabrics and a big sketchbook and would drape cloth around a mannequin and go out to lunch. It seemed like a very glamorous life. I always went fabric shopping with my mom. I watched her sew and I would take the scraps and make doll clothes. Once I understood how patterns worked, I started making things for myself to wear to school.

Please describe how you landed your first design job.

❯ In my second year at Parsons The New School for Design, in New York, I overheard two seniors talking about a job opportunity at Charlie's Girls, with Erica Elias. I ran up there with my student portfolio, and I got the job. I was in heaven. That was probably the best job I could have ever landed because Erica gave me my very own design room. I had sewing ladies. I had a draper. They had five different divisions, so I could design swimwear, sportswear, and sweaters. I learned how to do everything. She was a very tough boss, but without that experience, I don't think I could ever have had the same opportunities that I later enjoyed. When Charlie's Girls closed, Erica's name still opened doors for me at many of the other big sportswear houses.

In 1981, you were interested in launching your very own collection, but were not completely sure how to proceed. What led you to launch your collection?

❯ I had some friends who made jewelry and were trying to sell it at a big New York trade show. I made five pieces of clothing, and they asked me to share a booth with them. To my delight, I got orders from Macy's and Bloomingdale's (and was featured in an advertisement in *The New York Times*)! At the time, I was working for a company called Glenora. The man who owned the company saw the ad and said: "Isn't this girl on our payroll? Why does she have an ad in the *Times*?" He said if I didn't stop my side business, he would fire me. I had all these orders to fill, so I got fired. That's how I started my business.

Your first fashion show was not until 1991, ten years after you had been in business. Why didn't you decide to show earlier, and what prompted you to stage your first show?

❯ Until then, I never imagined attempting to stage an actual fashion show, as I'm always very pragmatic about business. All my friends at the time worked in fashion, including photographer Steven Meisel, stylist (later fashion editor) Paul Cavaco, hairdresser Garren, and makeup artist Francois Nars, along with the most popular models of the time, Linda Evangelista, Naomi Campbell, and Christy Turlington, all of whom I knew socially. My apartment was like "Clubhouse Central." Everyone would come over and hang out. Birthday parties were always at my house. We all knew each other really well. My friends conspired together to encourage me that it was the right time for me to take the plunge and consider producing a show. This was at the height of 1980s "power-dressing," with companies like Chanel, Lacroix, and Versace at the forefront. Competing against those companies seemed like the scariest thing I had ever done. I felt like I had to find my own voice and present my sensibility in a staging that would stand up next to other big-name fashion houses. Everybody contributed in putting together that first show: the production, the hair, the makeup, the models. It was so touching to me. I was so lucky to have help from all these very talented people.

In addition, the season before I did my first show, I went to Paris with Steven Meisel to see the ready-to-wear collections. We went to the Jean Paul Gaultier show with Madonna. When we got to our seats, Madonna said, "Anna, I have a surprise for you!"

When she opened her coat, she was wearing one of my dresses! I had seen racks and shopping bags in her hotel room from all the biggest, most prestigious houses, and she chose to wear my dress! I was so flattered. I thought if Madonna could pick from the best designers in the world and chose my dress, it gave me a little confidence that I might be able to do a show one day too.

What has enabled the Anna Sui collection to have such a prominent global presence?

❯ That first show was one of the giant breakthroughs of my career. I suddenly started getting a lot of press notice internationally. It was a case of being in the right place at the right time. All the Japanese department stores were coming to New York looking for American designers to develop distribution deals together. I started getting a lot of offers. The company that I finally chose was Isetan. It has been the most amazing partnership as Isetan made my collection so famous in Asia. They opened freestanding Anna Sui boutiques in Japan. I also have 12 licenses, including a cosmetic line. And the German company Wella asked to develop perfume with me (now with Inter Parfums), which is what made me a global brand.

I also give my parents a lot of credit for my success. My father was a structural engineer, and my mother studied painting. They met when they were both students in Paris. I get the business side from my father and the artistic side from my mother. After they married, they traveled throughout Europe for three years and finally settled in the U.S. I was born in Detroit. Growing up and learning about Chinese culture from my parents and hearing them talk about all the different places they had lived prepared me for thinking globally. This perspective took away any fears of being able to function in a foreign country. Their experiences were a gift to me.

Anna Sui and Sofia Coppola backstage after the Spring/Summer 2012 Anna Sui fashion show in New York. COURTESY OF ANNA SUI.

Who has had a major influence on you as a fashion designer?

❯ My favorites from the history of fashion design have always been Paul Poiret, Coco Chanel, Ossie Clark, and Zandra Rhodes. I also am always inspired by what Barbara Hulanicki did with Biba.

What was your greatest challenge when launching your collection?

❯ The biggest problem was always money. Starting with $300 is not a good business plan. I always had to do extra design jobs on the side just to keep my company going for the first ten years. I reinvested every penny I made back into the business. There were times after I paid my employees that I didn't even have enough money for a subway token, and I would have to walk to my office in the Garment Center. In those early years, I was often offered magazine-editing positions, but I had to remain steadfast about being a fashion designer. I wanted my own thing, and I resisted anything that would take me off that path. You have to have an incredible focus. That is one of the big keys to success. There are sacrifices and trade-offs that you have to make along the way. But you have to decide for yourself what's more important.

What is your design philosophy?

❯ People are attracted to my fashions because of all the elements I put into them. There's always a very sweet, feminine, girly aspect: a touch of nostalgia. There's also an aspect of trendiness, the hipness I try to create by adding a dash of rock-and-roll coolness. There's always that ambiguity, the good girl/bad girl thing. All of these facets have to go into my designs or it doesn't look like Anna Sui. Every product I put my name on has to personify the "World of Anna Sui." When a customer buys a tube of lipstick, it should give them the same excitement as buying a dress from my collection. If it doesn't, then I'm not really doing my job.

How does the design process begin for you? Do you begin with a theme or some form of inspiration, a silhouette, or a recently discovered, can't-live-without fabric?

❯ Fabric development and planning for my shoe collection always come first because they take the longest. Of course I have to have a little bit of an idea about the theme, but all the research is done in tandem to other aspects of the preparation. I think I have the perfect job, as everything I'm currently obsessed with can serve as inspiration for my work (films, exhibitions, music, books, travel, flea markets). My personal life is so intricately intertwined with what I do. I love doing research, learning about something new. I always want to share with my customers all the things that I am excited about. I want to take them on that journey with me. I try to get my customer as interested and as inspired as I am.

You are known for being a very realistic fashion designer. How do you design garments and accessories that are both true to your design aesthetic and vision and commercially saleable? Is there ever a conflict?

❯ Yes, I am a very realistic designer. I understand that there's a big difference between a fashion show and the actual product that a consumer buys. In my own store, I see what women want. I hear what they're asking for. On the runway, I'll do crazy styling and crazy accessories (I feel a show has to have a bit of theatrical whimsy), but there's always a beautiful dress or a great shirt underneath.

What role does social media play in the promotion of your brand and in staying close to your customer base?

❯ I understand these venues are increasingly important in the contemporary world. Besides my website, I have a Facebook page that posts up-to-the-minute Anna Sui news.

What advice would you give an aspiring fashion designer trying to launch his or her own fashion collection?

❯ There's only one Calvin Klein and there's only one Tom Ford. You have to figure out your own niche. Competition and circumstances are tough. Be true to yourself, which is the key. Do what you are best at and learn your craft. It is better when you are young to decide for yourself what your main interests are

(couture, ready-to-wear, junior, active sportswear) and only take steps (schools, internships, jobs) that move you in the right direction. My father always told me that if I want to have my own company, I should be in the office every day before the rest of my staff and stay later than anyone else. That philosophy of hard work and dedication has always inspired me.

Throughout your career, you have been recognized with various awards, such as the CFDA's Geoffrey Beene Lifetime Achievement Award, which pays tribute to fashion designers who have contributed to American fashion. You joined the ranks of such legendary fashion designers as Yves St. Laurent, Giorgio Armani, Ralph Lauren, Bill Blass, and Diane von Furstenberg, who were all recipients of this award. Time magazine added you to the list of their top five style icons. What does it mean to you to be recognized by your peers and to receive such high honors?

❯ I am humbled and honored. My motto has always been, "Live your dream," and that's what I am doing. It's a thrill, but a lot of hard work.

You, along with designer Nanette Lepore as well as other designers, helped spearhead the "Save the Garment Center" campaign in an effort to save New York City's Garment District. Why did you get involved with this effort?

❯ All of the Anna Sui Collection is made in New York in sewing shops within five blocks from my office (except a small group of sweaters and some special diffusion projects I work on for department stores). I have a sentimental attachment to New York—it is my home, my identity, and the birthplace of my success. I worked for a lot of big Seventh Avenue junior companies. None of them

Spring/Summer 2012 Anna Sui Runway Look #25. COURTESY OF ANNA SUI.

are around anymore. Seventh Avenue influenced my work ethic. There was no better training. It made me who I am. Today, kids think they'll go straight from school to designing a collection. If they don't succeed, they're finished. The district is not just important for New York, it's important to America. The New York fashion industry was at one time the largest employer in the United

States. New York fashion is of interest to the whole world; everybody wants to show here. What would it mean to me if it dies out? It would break my heart. Also, what is lost is all of the wonderful American-made suppliers of wools, lace trims, pleating, embroidery, buttons, etc. I used to access everything I needed, gorgeous old-world quality workmanship, right in my own neighborhood, and we can't let that slip away.

Your website is so inviting and fantastic! How did the design of the site evolve, and who created and maintains the content?

❯ Our fragrance licensee takes care of all the technical planning aspects. The wonderful illustrator Dean Landry ("Chooch") does all the artwork. I adore his charming cartoon version of my "world."

How do you find balance in the fast-paced world of fashion?

❯ The business part is very difficult and takes up more of my time than you'd think. Figuring out a new collection is a daunting challenge every season. Basically it's simple—I love what I do. Of course I work hard, but I believe that when you are passionate about your work, it's more like a way of life, a true pleasure.

Describe the ultimate perfect day for you.

❯ If I'm not working, I love the flea market. After the market, I love going to lunch with friends and then spending the afternoon at a museum or catching a movie together.

An Interview with Dennis Basso, Fashion Designer

Fashion designer Dennis Basso, 2011.

Was there a pivotal moment in your childhood, upbringing, or at some point in your life that led you to pursue a career in fashion design?

❯ As a child, I actually always wanted to be a designer. I was in kindergarten and very focused about being creative, and I always had a connection to women's things. When everyone was outside playing, I was inside sketching. It was always my desire very early on.

What was your greatest challenge when first launching your collection?

❯ In 1983, I started my company, and my greatest challenge was to develop and be known and have the respect of my peers within the fashion industry. Being a young man, it took a little time, but I was always fortunate because I always received very good reviews from *The New York Times* and *Women's Wear Daily*. It is always a challenge, it never really ends. When you think it's not a chal-

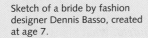
Sketch of a bride by fashion designer Dennis Basso, created at age 7.

lenge is when you are not at your creative fullest. As soon as you become blasé, it completely changes the scenario.

Your collection for QVC is a huge success. Describe what this experience has been like for you.

❭ From day one, I was always involved in the very high-end luxury market. In 2013, I will be celebrating my twentieth year on QVC. I have always had a desire for show business, and when this opportunity came along, to be on television and deal with fashion and reach a huge broad audience, it was just magical for me, and I took so easily to it and I loved being able to dress so many women. It's been a growth process, and it's terribly exciting. To be able to create something that not 20 people are going to wear, but 20,000 people—it changes the chemistry of it a little bit. I love to bring them good fashion. Today, pretty clothing is available at all price points. With good taste and good design structure and vision, you're able to create something great. It's a fun way to communicate. It's like a living, walking, talking catalog.

What is your design philosophy?

❭ Clothing should give you a personal message. Whether it's so comfortable or the fabric is so wonderful or it's just such an amazing design, it should make you feel good. I wake up in the morning very happy for the day, and I like to think that comes through in my collections.

How do you successfully design seasonal collections that are both true to your design aesthetic and vision and commercially saleable? Is there ever a conflict?

❭ This is where the line is crossed: you'll see these spectacular shows in Paris from the haute couture collections, which we all have a fantasy to design, but they are not necessarily saleable. I feel it is im-

Fall/Winter 2012 Dennis Basso Collection illustrated by Dennis Basso.

portant to bring a collection year after year that has some wonderful detail, that sets it apart, and that is wearable. It's my general philosophy to dabble in a few areas, as I like to be able to bring varying things to varying people.

In 2011, you launched a stunningly gorgeous bridal collection for Kleinfeld. What made you decide to branch out into the bridal arena?

❭ Launching bridal was a dream come true for me. The whole concept of bridal and the whole concept of the happy occasion very much appealed to me. It has been so well received, I think it's one of the leading bridal labels at Kleinfeld. To be in that small, elite group has been a wonderful personal award.

Being able to obtain a celebrity clientele is the highlight of any fashion designer's career. Who was the first celebrity you dressed, and how did it evolve?

❱ Over the years, we've dressed some of the great divas of our time, from Diana Ross to Natalie Cole, Liza Minnelli, and Elizabeth Taylor. In the movie *The Devil Wears Prada*, Meryl Streep wears my coat in the opening of the movie; it is the coat you see when she gets out of the car. Jennifer Lopez has worn our things in a music video. Years ago, we

Model is wearing a taupe chinchilla long vest with broadtail trim, along with a cayenne colored embroidered dress. She is holding a cayenne color chinchilla mini-bag. All items are from the Fall/Winter 2012/2013 Dennis Basso Collection. MODEL: COCO ROCHA. STYLIST: LORI GOLDSTEIN. PHOTOGRAPHER: BERNARD HUNT, 2012. COURTESY OF DENNIS BASSO.

did an amazing coat for Barbara Walters. We dress so many different types of celebrities that are reflective of the Dennis Basso brand that appeals to a lot of different women and different looks. Some of the time, stylists approach us, and sometimes it comes from personal relationships I've developed, as I'm very friendly with Natalie Cole, Liza Minnelli, Diana Ross, and Barbara Walters. Other times, it is through great costume designers who have asked to work together. We designed some garments for the movie *Chicago* for Catherine Zeta Jones, and we designed fox-trimmed capes for Renée Zellweger. Sometimes celebrities just pop into the store. It takes on different ways of how they find you.

What advice would you give an aspiring fashion designer trying to launch his or her own fashion collection?

❱ Like any career, you need to have the enthusiasm, talent, and vision to see yourself going in that direction. I think you just have to pursue it, and if you are really focused, you can't give up. If you really want it, granted, it's a little bit of timing and a little bit of luck, and of course, talent, but if you really want it, it's going to be out there.

How do you find balance in the fast-paced world of fashion?

❱ I have found the balance a little better as I have gotten older. When you are younger, you feel the need to be everywhere and everything. As you settle into your career and really know who you are, you are able to participate in what makes you feel good and what is right for you. You have a better vision of where you are going and how important private time is with some of the friends you have made along the way who are in fashion. And when we're together, 20 percent of the time is spent on the design world; the rest is talking about our personal lives.

Describe the ultimate perfect day for you.

❯ The ultimate perfect day is when we are out at our house in Watermill, New York, and we have one or two couples of great friends over for the weekend, and it's an easy-does-it kind of day: lunch by the pool and then a dinner party with other close friends, sort of relaxing, but yet having great food, great wine, great music, and lively conversation. Having great friends around us is a wonderful feeling.

Model is wearing white Russian broadtail and lynx coat and she's holding a white Russian broadtail train case/handbag. Both items are from the Fall Winter 2012/2013 Dennis Basso Collection. MODEL: COCO ROCHA. STYLIST: LORI GOLDSTEIN. PHOTOGRAPHER: BERNARD HUNT, 2012. COURTESY OF DENNIS BASSO.

What Do Fashion Designers Do?

A fashion designer conceptualizes and creates apparel or accessories collections on a seasonal basis, with a target market (end user of product) in mind. Fashion designers can be employed by apparel or accessories manufacturers; couture houses, fashion ateliers, or design studios; department and specialty stores; boutiques and other retailers; in universities, as an educator, professor, fashion historian, dean, administrator, or researcher; and in museums, as a curator.

Fashion design is influenced by cultural norms and is generally dictated by the continuously changing trends in society. Some fashion designers choose to use their own vision as their mechanism for creation and do not follow trends, or follow them minimally, while others follow them on a seasonal basis. While it is often thought that fashion designers only create and sketch concepts for garments, in actuality they are intimately involved with several different aspects of the design process. The apparel designer works closely with a team of workers who play a crucial role in creating a collection on the product development side. They consist of patternmakers who make full-size paper patterns for the manufacture of clothing using their expertise in body proportions and fabric knowledge to interpret the designer's apparel sketches into various pattern pieces, and tailors and sewers who construct and make prototypes and samples. For a more detailed look into the responsibilities of an apparel designer, you may refer to Chapter 3.

Many apparel manufacturers, especially the larger and more established brands, produce more than one product category. Within each product category, there are general subcategories and then successive sub-subcategories. As a fashion designer, you may be responsible for designing one or more product categories, one or more subcategories or one or more of the sub-subcategories, depending on the size and structure of the company. The following is an example of the breakdown of subcategories within a larger product category:

Menswear (Product Category)
>   Tailored Clothing (Subcategory)
>   Suits
>   Sports Coats and Blazers
>   Dress Shirts
>   Trousers
>   Overcoats
>   Formalwear
>   Tuxedos (Sub-subcategory)
>   Cummerbunds
>   Bow ties

There are six different types of designers including, 1) apparel, 2) accessories, 3) footwear, 4) technical, 5) CAD (computer-aided design), and 6) textile. Now we'll take a closer look at the functions of each.

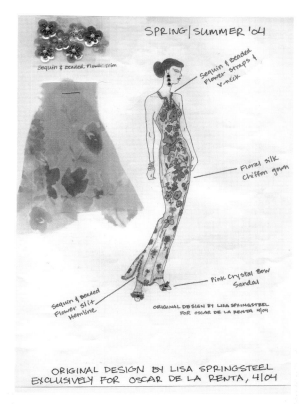

SPRING/SUMMER '04

Sequin & Beaded Flower Trim

Sequin & Beaded Flower Straps & V-neck

Floral silk chiffon gown

Pink Crystal Bow Sandal

Sequin & Beaded Flower Slit Hemline

ORIGINAL DESIGN BY LISA SPRINGSTEEL FOR OSCAR DE LA RENTA 4/04

ORIGINAL DESIGN BY LISA SPRINGSTEEL EXCLUSIVELY FOR OSCAR DE LA RENTA, 4/04

Original design conceived of and illustrated by Lisa Springsteel exclusively for Oscar de la Renta. Floral silk chiffon gown with sequin and beaded floral strap trim detail and floral sequin trim hemline, 2004. COLLECTION OF THE AUTHOR.

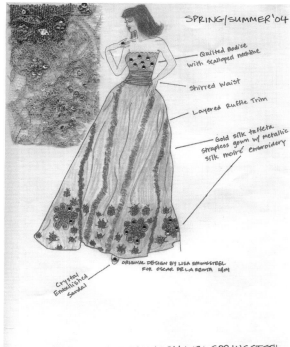

SPRING/SUMMER '04

Quilted Bodice with scalloped neckline

Shirred Waist

Layered Ruffle Trim

Gold silk taffeta strapless gown w/ metallic silk moiré embroidery

Crystal Embellished Sandal

ORIGINAL DESIGN BY LISA SPRINGSTEEL FOR OSCAR DE LA RENTA 4/04

ORIGINAL DESIGN BY LISA SPRINGSTEEL EXCLUSIVELY FOR OSCAR DE LA RENTA, 4/04

Original design conceived of and illustrated by Lisa Springsteel exclusively for Oscar de la Renta. Gold silk taffeta strapless gown with metallic silk moiré embroidery, quilted bodice scalloped neckline with crystal embellishment, shirred waistline, and layered ruffle trim, 2004. COLLECTION OF THE AUTHOR.

APPAREL DESIGNER

An apparel, clothing, or fashion designer creates women's, men's, juniors, children's, and layette apparel, including dresses, casual wear, separates, suits, sportswear, knits, eveningwear, formalwear, outerwear, bridal, intimates, maternity, and swimwear, and usually specializes in one of the aforementioned function areas.

Fall/Winter 2012 Diego Binetti Collection. PHOTOGRAPHER: ADAM WEISS.

An Interview with Randolph Duke, Fashion Designer

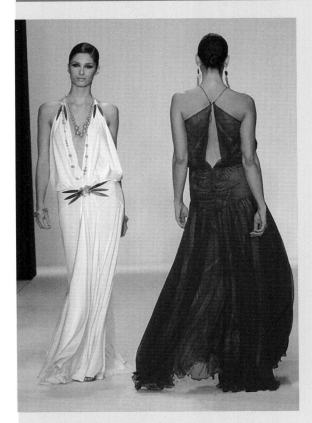

Spring 2008 Randolph Duke Couture, Los Angeles Fashion Week. COURTESY OF RANDOLPH DUKE.

You originally studied classical piano at the University of Nevada, in Las Vegas, before attending the Fashion Institute of Design and Merchandising (FIDM), in Los Angeles, California. What made you decide to pursue a fashion design career?

❯ Piano was not my destiny. I was good, but not great at it. I began painting when I was eight years old and showed promise as an artist. I had a professor who mentored me and guided me to develop a portfolio, which is how it all began.

You began your career designing swimwear for Anne Cole in California and later for Gottex in New York. You then launched your own sportswear line in 1987, complete with a boutique on the Upper West Side of Manhattan. Were you simply over the top with excitement at this time?

❯ I didn't think as much about what I was doing when it was happening, which is the beauty of youth.

What was it like for you to transition from working as a designer for an apparel manufacturer to launching your own eponymous collection?

❯ The progression was natural. When I owned my own store, I produced small quantities. Once I proved myself at retail, I was able to launch my wholesale business.

You are a fashion, shoes, accessories, and home furnishings designer for your Home Shopping Network (HSN) collection called "The Look," a fashion television commentator, an author, previously a consultant, and if that's not enough genius for one person, you've also been a costume designer for various theatrical productions, including ballet. How do you balance it all and still remain sane?

❯ It is the combination of having the right staff in place and being a great multitasker.

Explain the methodology you put in place prior to actually designing the Halston collection that gave you the history and foundation needed to begin the design process. What sort of research did you undertake to understand the heritage of the brand? Did Halston have extensive archives that you were able to dig into?

❯ There was not too much of an archive for me to go through. Instead, I considered the type of modern clothing that I thought Mr. Halston would be making today if he were alive. For example, he wouldn't still be doing Ultrasuede, he'd be into microfibers.

Spring 2008 Randolph Duke Couture, Los Angeles Fashion Week. COURTESY OF RANDOLPH DUKE.

Random House released your book, The Look, in 2006. It helps women of all ages dress most appropriately for their size and shape. Your client Marcia Gay Harden said this about you, "I first met Randolph Duke through my stylist while preparing for the Academy Awards. Randolph studied my body type, he understood a woman's body, and he celebrated hips and busts and elegance and drama and maturity all in one swooping gesture of red. Randolph worked with me and the dress was perfect!" Did the concept for the book stem from your natural ability to transform a woman? If not, how did it come about?

❯ When I moved back to Los Angeles, I did a lot of thinking, and one of the things that kept popping into my mind was that there were so many questions I had about the subject, and what seemed to be a disconnect. It prompted me to get inspired to create a book, a tool that I felt was missing. I started doing some research in terms of what tools there were for women when it came to defining their own personal style and cultivating it and being able to express it on a daily basis. I started this experiment in which I would just look at women in public. And I noticed something universally that stuck out for me in almost every case, and it was a proportion problem. I had something that wasn't on the market—a guide that helped women get dressed almost from the inside out; it was a process. So often people think style can't be learned, but I have the notion that it can be taught to some degree. It was born in the idea that I wanted to create a tool for the customer.

Marcia Gay Harden wearing Randolph Duke Couture to accept the Best Supporting Actress Oscar for *Pollack* at the 73rd Annual Academy Awards, held at the Shrine Auditorium and Expo Center, Los Angeles, California. GETTY IMAGES, 2001. COURTESY OF RANDOLPH DUKE.

So many accomplished designers have developed thriving Home Shopping Network businesses. What prompted your foray into the television retail environment?

❯ I had been on QVC in 1992, and it was a short-lived run. It was very early in the pioneering years of electronic retailing. Then another opportunity came up in 2001 with HSN that seemed like a great prospect, and because I had done it already, it wasn't foreign to me. The formula was good and it made sense, and I wasn't afraid of it at all, and so we began.

Every successful fashion designer who runs his or her own design atelier must put together a talented team who can execute his/her vision. How important do you consider this?

❯ This is an interesting question, as this has always been the biggest challenge for me. There were times in the beginning where you do it all, due to financial restraints. I remember rolling racks to 7th on 6th in New York with dark sunglasses and a hat on so no one would see it was me; you do what you have to do. I've learned over the years that delegating is a wise thing, but it involves a lot of trust. You have to learn how to trust. I've had everything from a skeleton crew to a very fleshed out crew. I do think fashion is a collaborative business, and it relies very much on the fact that you can't do it all yourself. Now I would not have a business without the proper management people in place.

There are so many talented and hopeful fashion designers around the globe. What advice would you give a fashion designer who is struggling to establish that certain je ne sais quoi that enables him or her to stand out among the competition?

❯ I'm not sure there's any one formula to doing that. What I am suggesting for students or people who are considering becoming fashion designers is to stay very aware of what it is that you love, and try not to get too caught in the trap of what you think people will like. One is pandering and a bit manipulative, and one is kind of true. And it doesn't have anything to do with whether you think people will like it or not, because once you go down that road, you've really lost the authenticity. My most successful outings in my shows were when I was completely true to what I liked in every sense, using music that I liked and picking the models I liked. It required the kind of discipline of listening to other people's opinions, but ultimately making your mind up in the end.

What advice can you give to an aspiring fashion designer?

❯ My #1 advice would be to never feel embarrassed to ask for help. In the fashion business, it doesn't seem cool. But it's not the case. I think people want to be a part of your creation. Make friends with as many people in the areas you need to evolve.

The fashion industry has changed so drastically over the years with the proliferation of fashion reality TV shows, such as Project Runway on Bravo. How do you feel about the impact this has had on the fashion industry and on the very heart of what fashion means as an artistic endeavor and an art form?

❯ There are so many designers today who haven't studied fashion in school. It seems a little less defined. I get frustrated because everyone thinks they are a fashion designer. In fashion, it is a little unfortunate because it is underestimated in terms of the ingredients it takes to become that thing. There are so many ways to reach that goal today.

The fashion industry is known as being filled with an abundance of wonderfully creative people with eccentric personalities. At times, the drama can reach operatic proportions. From where do you think this stems?

❯ This is a really interesting question. I think it comes with the territory. It makes it more interesting, more exciting, to be so dramatic. In some ways, it's unique to New York. It's a very New York thing. It's part of becoming a brand. A lot of it has to do with what people expect and want from someone in the fashion industry.

You have been called "Clothing Royalty" and the "King of Red Carpet Glamour." What do you think of these descriptions, and how do you view yourself?

❯ There is a kind of a kismet in how things happen. It's flattering when people think of you in that way and say those things. I was more of a dramatic and serious person in my youth, and now my truer self is coming out a lot more, which is sillier and much less serious.

Describe what the ultimate perfect day would be like for you.

❯ The ultimate perfect day for me would be doing what I love and being completely content and happy where I am. It is when I am completely present in the moment, not thinking about yesterday, not thinking about tomorrow, and at peace.

Spring 2008 Randolph Duke Couture, Los Angeles Fashion Week. COURTESY OF RANDOLPH DUKE.

An Interview with Ralph Rucci, Fashion Designer for Chado Ralph Rucci

Portrait of Ralph Rucci, 2012. PHOTOGRAPHER: RICK GUIDOTTI. COURTESY OF CHADO RALPH RUCCI.

Was there a pivotal moment in your childhood, upbringing, or at some point in your life that led you to pursue a career in fashion design?

❯ I had always been fascinated with the beauty of women and the inner grace that they possess. As a child, I would always go shopping with my mother and was often permitted to choose her clothing from an early age. I remember she had a neighborhood dressmaker, a man of great talent and skill,

and I was allowed to choose Vogue/Butterick patterns of Christian Dior and Balmain. Certain images spring to life immediately. A hot pink slipper satin Dior boxy bodice and straight pegged skirt with a pillbox hat. The hat and the bodice were beaded with small hanging crystals or briolettes. I thought that it was the chicest thing I had ever seen. I also remember that my mother had an emerald-green satin Dior coat which was essentially a half-circle with two flipper short sleeves and a full band collar that extended beyond the décolleté. When she moved in this coat, the flares swooned out in a majestic, regal movement. She had an ivory duchess silk satin Balmain all cut on the bias—a sleeveless narrow sheath, swept to one side and draped to the high waist/low hip, ending with an enormous geisha obi as part of the dress. The obi was doubled so that the fabric remained crisp and stood out so that you could see it from the front. What made this cocktail dress incredibly poignant was that the dress mirrored the social climate of the time. My mother had it made for the opening of a movie she was attending. Imagine this: Women and men wore evening attire to the opening of movies. It was the opening of Elizabeth Taylor in *Cleopatra*. Little did I even dream that I would one day be sitting with Elizabeth on her bed and planning clothes around her mind-boggling jewelry collection. But all of these designs and colors were approved by me with complete calm and a certain unknown authority. Now, you can say that might be the DNA within, but it was years before anything became very clear.

While I was in high school, I discovered fashion magazines and began to approach the study of fashion as an academic. I would discover a designer, and began to find a thread in the work that I was drawn to. It was not until I was in college that a major breakthrough occurred. I was in the stacks researching a paper for my Aesthetics class in philosophy. I was leafing through an issue of *Harper's Bazaar* and was stunned. I discovered a double-page photograph of a bride and her attendant; only both were photographed from the back, and the bride was in white gazaar and the attendant was in black gazaar. Both costumes were trapezoidal, with the bride having a long train. The shots were taken by photographer David Bailey, by the direction of Diana Vreeland. I was speechless. I had never seen anything so pure and so sculptural and so perfect in my entire life. I knew that it was art. I discovered they were conceived of and made by Cristobal Balenciaga. Since I was also painting at the time, I felt liberated. In my mind I related the Balenciaga clothes to American painter Robert Motherwell's piece *Elegy to the Spanish Republic*. Thus, I began my real journey.

You trained under Halston. Please describe how you obtained this incredible opportunity.

❯ I knew from all of my fashion research that I only wanted to work for Halston. I thought he was the greatest designer at the time: the consummate minimalist and revolutionary who created an entirely new fashion after the 1960s. So I devised a plan to get a job interview. If you remember Halston had his cathedral on Sixty-Eighth and Madison Avenue in New York. His made-to-order department (he refused to use the term couture, since we were in America) was on the third floor with his office.

Chado Ralph Rucci Spring/Summer 2012 Ready-to-Wear Collection. White Caviar Beaded Shell and Pant with Satin Apron. PHOTOGRAPHERS: DAN AND CORINA LECCA. COURTESY OF CHADO RALPH RUCCI.

I told my sister that we would go to the made-to-order department and that she would order something from the collection. She thought that I had totally lost my mind. Nevertheless, we went to his office and she ordered a timeless ivory cashmere jumpsuit and matching kimono. This was in 1975 and she still wears it today. While all of this was happening, I asked the vendeuse to arrange an appointment for me to see Halston. She was shocked and amused at my strength and nerve to be so bold. So I enrolled at FIT, took the necessary technical classes, and came back in two years, and she arranged for me to have an interview with Halston. I might have had enormous bravado, but I promise that when I first met Halston my teeth were chattering in front of his mirrored sunglasses. Halston was a genius, period.

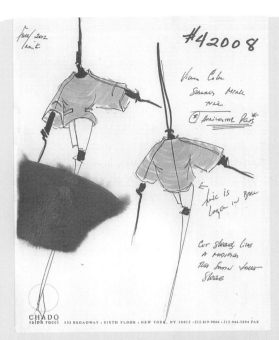

Chado Ralph Rucci Fall 2012 Ready-to-Wear Collection.
SKETCHED BY RALPH RUCCI.

Chado Ralph Rucci Fall/Winter 2012 Ready-to-Wear Collection.
Sage Green Shirred Mink Pullover and White Wool Barathea Pant.
PHOTOGRAPHERS: DAN AND CORINA LECCA. COURTESY OF CHADO
RALPH RUCCI.

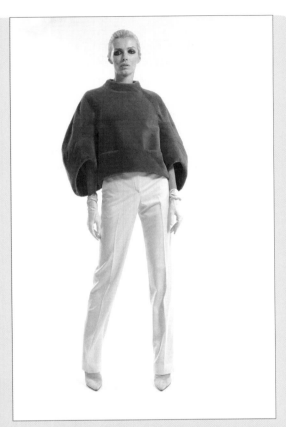

What was your greatest challenge when first launching your collection?

❭ Money. It was in 1981 and I decided it was time. I knew what my life's work was, and I had to get on with it. I was 23 years old, and the important thing to impart is that I already saw myself and knew that I was a fashion designer. I now had to do it and begin my body of work, take all of the influences—Grès, Balenciaga, Halston, Galanos, Norell—and find my own vocabulary. Since I already had relationships with seamstresses, women would come to my one-room studio apartment at night to help me, and I would drape and cut all day. My close friend Vivian Van Natta, whom I met while at FIT, assisted me from then on for the next thirty years, giving me the space to work and think.

What is your design philosophy?

❭ Reduce, simplify, and find the very essence of what you are looking for. Never decorate a woman, but instead, find the elements to enhance and work to erase what is not attractive. Apply the logic of proportion. Add grace to her existence. Honor her. Discover new ways to make clothes and seek the impossible within our métier. Know how to do it right and then discover a new way. Never accept that you have arrived, and always remember that the greatest work comes from a place of humility.

What is the meaning behind the word "Chado" in your brand, "Chado Ralph Rucci"?

❭ Chado is the centuries-old tea ceremony involving 331 steps, each with its own formality, from the greeting of one's guest to the final gesture of offering a cup of tea. In 1987, I chose to use this word to represent all of the steps, significance and participation of other individuals that go into making a collection.

How do you successfully design season after season a collection that is both true to your design aesthetic and vision and commercially saleable? Is there ever a conflict?

❭ You must allow your mind to first find the catalysts that allow you to discover the key themes to a collection, and then through research and sketching and toile development, you begin to find your way. During this process, you begin to see the logic and necessity for more dresses, more raincoats here, more jackets there: the need for the spectacular that pulls the entire picture into crisp clarity. If you go in deep and make sure you not only have clothes for your core audience, but also a newer more youthful audience, and for an international market, as well as what the press needs to seduce them from their daily grind, then you have achieved a small part of your story. But, for me, I must do this within a very particular, controlled environment: office to home, home to office, with only meditation and lifting weights in between. I cannot talk about the collection and feel annoyed if I am questioned, because I am still in limbo. In a way, the collection finds you while in this space.

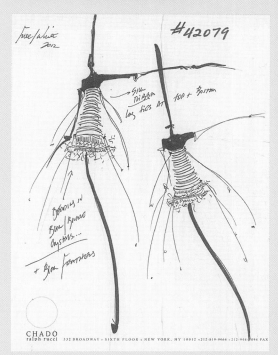

Chado Ralph Rucci Fall 2012 Ready-to-Wear Collection.
SKETCHED BY RALPH RUCCI.

Chado Ralph Rucci Fall/Winter 2012 Ready-to-Wear Collection. Black Silk Ribbon Strapless Dress.
PHOTOGRAPHERS: DAN AND CORINA LECCA. COURTESY OF CHADO RALPH RUCCI.

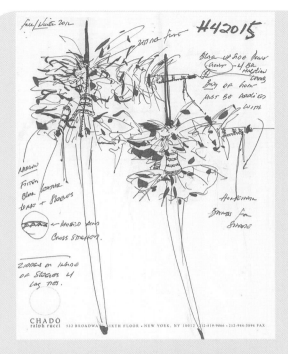

Chado Ralph Rucci Fall 2012 Ready-to-Wear Collection.
SKETCHED BY RALPH RUCCI.

Chado Ralph Rucci Fall/Winter 2012 Ready-to-Wear
Collection. Black Goat and Leather Jacket with Quilted
Embroidery. PHOTOGRAPHERS: DAN AND CORINA LECCA.
COURTESY OF CHADO RALPH RUCCI.

What advice would you give an aspiring fashion designer trying to launch his or her own fashion collection?

❯ Please do not even think about having your own collection until you can do everything. You must be able to design the garment, make the pattern, sew it, fit it, cut or drape it, sell it, produce it, pack it, and follow through. You must know every facet of the business so that you know how and why you want it done a certain way and so that

you may instruct. You must also have the correct money. You must not venture into a fashion business without at least two years' worth of money in the bank, including payroll, taxes, fabrics, overhead, and being able to make it from the first season into the next while waiting to get paid, as you are making your new collection. And don't forget your own salary. Be prepared to have your heart broken many, many times. Be patient because when the time comes, you will know.

In 2002, you were invited by the Chambre Syndicale de la Haute Couture to show your collection in Paris. What was this moment like for you?

❯ After the show, when I came out to take my bow, I knew that my life had changed. You could say that it was a turning point in my life. Dreams met reality and I knew that anything was possible.

The next day in the French press there was an avalanche of positive news. They called me "The American" and questioned how an American knew how to do haute couture. One journalist said my collection was perfection, but questioned who would want perfection in this era. I wanted to prove to myself that my own hands and mind could conceive of apparel, where use meets art.

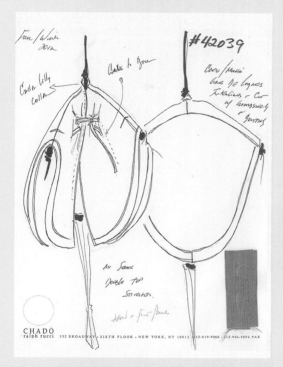

Chado Ralph Rucci Fall 2012 Ready-to-Wear Collection. SKETCHED BY RALPH RUCCI.

Chado Ralph Rucci Fall/Winter 2012 Ready-to-Wear Collection. Beige Silk Cape Coat. PHOTOGRAPHERS: DAN AND CORINA LECCA. COURTESY OF CHADO RALPH RUCCI.

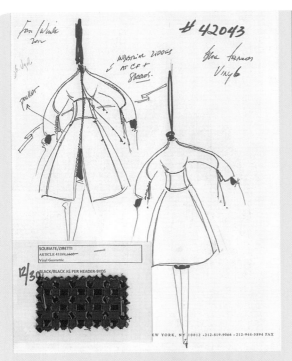

Chado Ralph Rucci Fall 2012 Ready-to-Wear Collection.
SKETCHED BY RALPH RUCCI.

Chado Ralph Rucci Fall/Winter 2012 Ready-to-Wear
Collection. Black Vinyl Raincoat. PHOTOGRAPHERS: DAN AND
CORINA LECCA. COURTESY OF CHADO RALPH RUCCI.

How does being an accomplished painter help you when designing your collections?

❭ The experience of painting moves me into my fashion work with more clarity and inspiration and allows more possibilities. Also, often artwork is screened onto the fabric and then used in the collection.

What can't you live without?

❭ Privacy.

How do you find balance in the fast-paced and ever-changing world of fashion?

❭ Through my friends, family, staff, and the sanctuary of my home, my books, my statuary, and my English Bulldog, Twombly.

Describe the ultimate perfect day for you.

❭ Not speaking, no telephone, and being in the water—the greatest tranquilizer in the world. I am comfortable alone, but it is also quite wonderful spending the day with someone who you love and who loves you back.

ACCESSORIES DESIGNER

An accessory designer creates products such as handbags, belts, scarves, hats, eyewear, and hosiery that will be used to complement clothing.

The "Cassia Weekender" is a multi-purpose carry-all for the office, gym, or a weekend trip by Canopy Verde, 2010.
COURTESY OF CANOPY VERDE.

FOOTWEAR DESIGNER

A footwear designer creates various styles of shoes, including flats, loafers, clogs, moccasins, sling backs, pumps, eveningwear shoes, sandals, wedges, espadrilles, boots, sneakers, and slippers that will be used to complement clothing.

Spring/Summer 2010 Juan Antonio Lopez Collection by Ana Borges.
COURTESY OF ANA BORGES.

Kimi shoe from the 2011 Hetti Rose Collection. Heel type: Plastic covered with kimono fabric. Upper material: Vintage kimono textile fabric/leather. Lining: Leather. Sole: Leather.
COURTESY OF HETTY ROSE.

An Interview with Shoe and Accessories Designer, Stuart Weitzman

STUART WEITZMAN, 2012.

You apprenticed under your father, who owned his own shoe business called "Mr. Seymour," and learned the trade at an early age. However, you graduated from the Wharton School of Business at the University of Pennsylvania, headed for Wall Street. What led to the launch of your own brand?

❯ I originally had planned to conquer Wall Street right out of school, but unexpected circumstances led me to join the family business to help out, and I have never looked back.

You call yourself a "shoe engineer" because you believe footwear must function properly, above anything else. Please elaborate on this point.

❯ A shoe must function, first and foremost, which is why comfort and fit are obligatory elements of a great shoe design. Of course, without beautiful lines, eye-catching appeal, or something fanciful about it that just makes you smile, success will not be the result of just a comfortable shoe.

What is your design philosophy?

❯ I design for the modern woman who wants high fashion, yet doesn't have to sacrifice comfort.

Many people don't realize your shoes are manufactured in Elda, Spain. Please describe why you chose to manufacture in this part of the world.

❯ Ever since a group of shoes made in Elda caught my eye with their exceptional quality and workmanship, it became my home. Our entire team, from sewers to partners, gives their all to the product and treat it as if it's their own. It's quite unlikely that I could have established such camaraderie elsewhere.

You have been recognized for the impact you have made on the Spanish footwear and handbag industry, and as a result, you were named El Hijo Predilecto Adoptivo de Elda, which translates to "Favorite Adopted Son of Elda." This title has only been bestowed upon four people since the end of the Spanish Civil War, and you are the only non-Spaniard to ever receive this recognition. Please explain how you felt when you first learned of this prestigious honor.

❯ I was very proud and humbled to receive such a distinguished honor from the region. It's something I will always treasure deep within my heart.

You have an expansive retail presence with 33 retail stores in the United States and 42 international store locations, with flagship stores in New York, Beverly Hills, Paris, Milan, Moscow, and Beijing. Your collection is also carried in fine specialty and department stores such as Saks, Neiman Marcus, Bergdorf Goodman, and Scoop NYC, and in Harrods in England, Isetan in Japan, Lane Crawford in China, Printemps in Paris, and Harvey Nicols in Dubai. Interestingly enough, you opened your first retail store in Las Vegas. Please describe why you chose this location for your retail debut.

❯ We're a brand who is renowned for its playfully glamorous lifestyle, so Las Vegas seemed very fitting.

STUART WEITZMAN, 2012.

So many women all over the world seem to have such a fascination with shoes. To what do you attribute this shoe obsession?

❯ I have so often been asked, "Why do women love shoes?" and the answer is so obvious. What is the first wonderful story that most little girls read about? Yes, something as simple and accessible as a beautiful shoe, makes her feel like a princess. Who wouldn't want to be Cinderella for a night?

Being able to obtain a celebrity clientele is the highlight of any fashion designer's career. You have provided shoes for the red carpet appearances of celebrities such as Angelina Jolie, Eva Mendes, Jennifer Aniston, Eva Longoria, Katie Holmes, and the list goes on. Who was the first celebrity you dressed, and how did it come about?

❯ A phone call from Barbara Walters herself started my celebrity clientele base.

Your bridal shoe collection has been worn by several celebrities, including singers Pink and Carrie Underwood and socialite and businesswoman Ivanka Trump, for their

respective weddings. Please provide an overview of your bridal collection.

❯ Evening has been synonymous with the brand since its beginning, so a bridal collection was an early product extension of the brand. I do like to create most of my bridal collection in transparent materials, such as vinyl, mesh, and chiffon because they show off a beautiful foot in a sexy way and have the ability to go with anything, from day to night.

Your company offers one of the widest ranges of sizes (4–12), in an unprecedented four widths (slim, narrow, medium, and wide), enabling your brand to capture a large market share. What was your motivation behind this?

❯ Shoes are complicated to construct and are not like clothing, where one size can fit all or can be grouped into small, medium, or large, which is why I added a wide range of sizes and widths. I like to cater to the wants and needs of the customer, which I see as fit and comfort mixed with fashion.

Have you ever considered designing a men's shoe collection? If not, why?

❯ The fun of designing women's shoes is the playful materials you can use, like feathers, crystals, and colorful snakeskins to name a few. Unfortunately, a men's line would not allow me that same creativity that I enjoy so much about the design process!

Is there a new and exciting product launch on the horizon for Stuart Weitzman?

❯ Yes, but everyone will have to wait and see.

What role does social media play in the promotion of your brand and in staying close to your customer base?

❯ Social media allows me to talk directly to my loyal customers to get feedback, especially regarding products, but also all related company initiatives; share exciting company news; as well as offer rewards. It is the ultimate focus group in moving forward toward the future.

What advice would you give an aspiring shoe or handbag designer trying to launch his or her own collection?

❯ If you love what you do, you will never work a day in your life. My job I consider my hobby, so I really enjoy every aspect of it.

I attended a Fashion's Night Out event that you hosted at your Madison Avenue store a couple of years ago. I recall seeing a ping-pong table in your store, which was a unique addition, amongst the other festivities. I understand you hold ping-pong tournaments throughout your showrooms and factories. When did you first acquire an interest in this sport?

❯ It was a favorite pastime of my childhood that I became reacquainted with late in my life. It is the best exercise for the body and mind.

Describe the ultimate perfect day for you.

❯ Playing ping-pong.

TECHNICAL DESIGNER

A technical designer is responsible for establishing and maintaining technical specifications across one or more product categories and for ensuring consistency in fit. A technical designer will attend design and staff meetings, direct and lead fit sessions, and produce technical packages (also known as "tech packs") that communicate the measurements and specifications needed to produce a sample, in WebPDM or some other

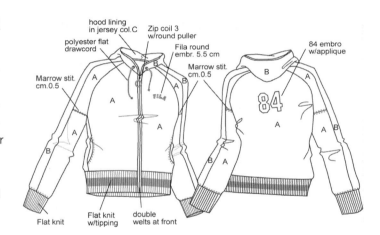

Technical sketch for the technical package specifications for Fila Heritage Collection by Noreen Naz Naroo-Pucci, 2003. COURTESY OF NOREEN NAZ NAROO-PUCCI ON BEHALF OF FILA.

data-tracking software, for each style containing detailed product specifications ("specs"). He or she will also create technical sketches; hand off tech packs to overseas or domestic factories/vendors for sample and bulk production; check accuracy of measurements, fit, and construction of first samples, counter samples, and all pre- and post-production samples; fit garments on fit models or a mannequin/dress form; communicate changes to overseas factories/vendors/sourcing offices; and continue this process until all pre-production and post-production samples are approved. A technical designer will also manage the sample approval process effectively by following a strict production calendar to ensure deadlines are met and the process is kept on track, as well as identify potential production and quality issues and make recommendations to ensure that brand integrity is upheld.

CAD DESIGNER

A computer-aided design (CAD) designer is responsible for creating prints and patterns through original artwork, re-colorations, reworkings, and repeats. One major responsibility is participation in initial brainstorming design meetings, to understand concepts, themes, fabrics, silhouettes, and color stories. Once these items are communicated by the design team, the CAD designer will use a CAD software program to execute flat sketches, prints, look book sheets, detail sheets, and conceptual board and color sheets; create color palettes; and make revisions as needed until all designs have been approved. A CAD designer will also collaborate with internal and external departments, including design, merchandising, fabric research and development, overseas offices, vendors, and print studios to execute the creation of designs and maintain and track all artwork that has been developed.

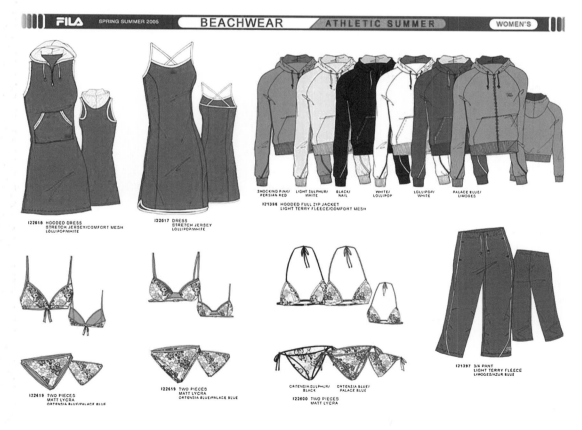

Spring/Summer 2005 Fila Beachwear CAD for Athletic Summer group by Noreen Naz Naroo-Pucci. COURTESY OF NOREEN NAZ NAROO-PUCCI ON BEHALF OF FILA.

TEXTILE DESIGNER

A textile designer uses CAD software to create and execute fabric designs for woven, knit, and printed fabrics, trims, and embroideries used to make apparel. Major responsibilities include researching the latest trends in fabric, silhouettes, and color; attending various fabric trade shows across the country and internationally; reviewing protos (prototypes) and strike-offs; approving final designs; and communicating with overseas mills.

What Do You Do on a Daily Basis?

❯ Every day is different. I like to walk around the different places I visit for research, such as vintage shops, art galleries, and museums, or I spend hours surfing on the Web. Inspiration is everywhere, and I keep a notebook with me so I can sketch everything that comes to mind. I also keep tear sheets from magazines in my notebook.

Marta Buscaroli, Freelance Designer, Emanuel Ungaro, Paris, France

❯ I measure samples, fit samples on a live model with design in attendance, write fit comments that include illustrations and photos of corrections, send the comments overseas, and answer questions from vendors.

Samantha Baxter, Technical Designer, alice + olivia, New York, New York, USA

❯ My job requires me to wear many hats, which include designing women's wovens, knits, shoes, fabrics, trims, beading, and print developments. I start my day by meeting with international mills and selecting fabrics, discussing developments, colors, and lab dips. Later, I work with my director to edit down my selections and discuss trials, beading and print developments and prepare artwork to send out to our agents overseas. Then I start sketching, while keeping in mind our direction for the season, using inspirational research such as pictures, books, archives, and vintage pieces. It's important for me to stay focused and work with a fabric in mind so

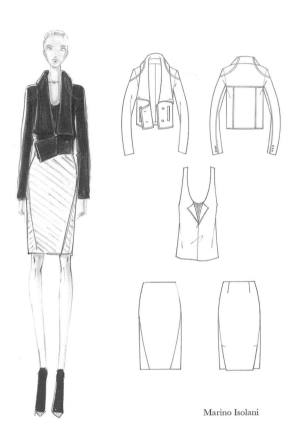

Marino Isolani

Fall 2012 City Hell's Angels sketch by Marino Isolani, 2011. COURTESY OF MARINO ISOLANI.

that I can fully understand how the garment will behave and move. I also work on specs and figure out the proportion and measurements of my designs. I observe the garment with a technical eye and provide as many detailed sketches as possible to properly convey my designs to the patternmaker.

As soon as the first prototype is ready, I review it during fittings and analyze the fit and construction of my design, while making sure that the garment and the body are in perfect harmony. After marking, writing, cutting, and pinning the prototype, I discuss all changes with the patternmaker and move on to the second proto until the design is perfect and ready for the runway.

Marino Isolani, Associate Designer, Bill Blass Women's Collection, New York, New York, USA

❯ As a creative director, it is important to make sure that I have the best team of creative and brand specialists working together to share my vision for the collection and the overall brand image. The world of fashion is forever changing, so I conduct research on future trends, styling, and the arts which I do on a daily basis. I combine this with my passion for color, fabric innovation, and sketching looks. This forms a solid direction for the clothing and accessories collection, so I always have new ideas waiting to be developed when needed.

Eyan Allen, Creative Brand Director, Hugo Boss Womenswear, Stuttgart, Germany

❯ My tasks on a daily basis involve a lot of prep work, pattern and draping, and overseas communication. The work of a technical designer mainly involves the fit of the garment. We fit sewn samples on a live model, adjust the pattern to improve fit, and then communicate the changes and corrections to factories overseas. Our goal is to achieve a consistent fit for all of the garments in our bridge line. We work very closely with our design and merchandising teams to achieve the best look and fit for each garment.

Rebecca Clarizio, Associate Technical Designer, Michael Kors, New York, New York, USA

❯ My day starts with a large hazelnut coffee at Gregory's on 40th Street before heading to my office across the street. I take care of fabric orders from all over the world and oversee samples by communicating with China vendors through e-mail. After that, I stop by our sample room and have a conversation with my patternmakers and sewers about current styles they are working on, to see if the draping or sewing is correct. In the afternoon, I work on sketching, fabrication, print developments, line planning, or costing, depending on collection due dates. Working hours end around 7:00 pm during slow time, and then I go to the gym to work out or meet friends for dinner. However, when our fashion show is close, I stay at work late and contribute to the saying that Fashion Avenue never sleeps!

Christina Kwon, Designer, Mark + James, Badgley Mischka, New York, New York, USA

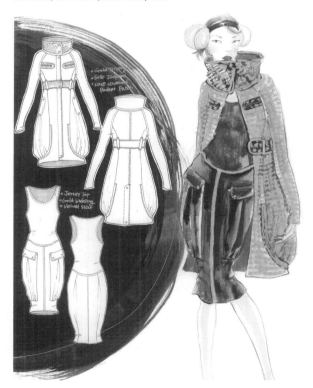

Fall/Winter Collection illustrated by Christina Kwon and inspired by Cremaster, Matthew Barney, 1996. COURTESY OF CHRISTINA KWON.

What Do You Do on a Daily Basis? (Continued)

❯ My work day begins with answering e-mails from overseas agents. Garment construction details, design details, specs, and grading clarifications are a few of the everyday topics of discussion that take place between a technical designer and the factories. Before our customer falls in love with the beautiful clothing items at the store, each style takes a production journey. Technical designers are the builders of the garment. Once designed, every item is developed following technical specifications and construction requests. After receiving a prototype sample from the factory, we measure it, fit it on a fit model, and make necessary corrections in fit and construction. We make sure all design ideas are transformed and interpreted correctly from the flat sketch to the finished garment. We also ensure that the garment is made following the industry's standards for quality.

Andrey Oshlykov, Senior Technical Designer, Anthropologie, New York, New York, USA

❯ The season begins with primary and secondary research collated into mood boards, as well as developing a theme for the season. The previous season must also be taken into account so that there is some cohesion between the two. Above all, the brand's values must be represented and respected. After much discussion, colors for each category are collated, bearing in mind when these colors will hit the store and what will already be on the shop floor, so that two seasons work together in unison. The design process can finally begin, in the form of rough sketches, shapes, and proportions to build a range plan of all categories, which will form the basis of the collection. Designs are worked into, measurements are added, vendors to produce each piece are selected, and the prototyping stages begin. At this time, we will also meet with fabric mills to review their trends and select potential fabrics from their collections that will work for the collection. Prototypes come in, and fittings begin. Once the prototyping stage is over and a final sample is made in the actual fabrics selected from the meetings, the reward comes in photo shoots for the lookbook and the fashion week show. At this point, I'm already back at mood board stage for the next season, so there's no time to stop!

Paul Austin, Menswear Designer, Gieves & Hawkes, London, England, United Kingdom

Spring/Summer 2011 Mr. by Roland Mouret Collection.
SKETCH BY PAUL AUSTIN.
COPYRIGHT 2010.

Fall/Winter 2012
Diego Binetti Collection.
PHOTOGRAPHER: ADAM WEISS.

❯ I see each day as a brand-new opportunity, so I try to make the best of every day by creating adventures, opportunities, and memories. I get up, meditate, give thanks, prepare a fresh cup of coffee, take a shower, turn on my computer, listen to radio news, organize my day, and then embrace the challenges of the day.

Diego Binetti, Creative Director, Binetti, Inc., New York, New York, USA

❯ My day begins with visiting a few online blogs and design resource websites to keep on top of industry news, as well as any emerging trends. Before I begin the design process, the merchandiser and category manager provide a line sheet listing the SKUs (stock keeping units) allocated to each category, including suggested retail cost and channel of distribution. I sketch several versions of a style. After a design is agreed upon, I use a predetermined color palette and print out several options. After the sales force, management, and marketing department approves the design, I create a tech package and send it to the merchandiser. We receive several vendor packages daily, which include protos, lab dips, knit-downs, and fabric approvals. If we receive an accessory proto, I spec it, adjust sizing if needed, cut into it to reshape, or mock up a detail. I then e-mail the comments along with revised tech packages and trim sheets to the merchandiser. When we receive a garment proto, we set up a fit time and discuss pending visual comments and solve any fit issues. I update the sketch and tech pack when necessary. Several times a year we have sales meetings, which require presenting the designs to our national and international sales force. Feedback that we receive is applied to samples, pre-production samples and ultimately in bulk production.

Heidi Honkavuori-Harlor, Senior Handbag Designer, Nixon, Encinitas, California, USA

❯ Contrary to popular belief, a designer does not spend every day sketching new designs. During an entire season, about 10 percent of my time is spent on actually designing. My day-to-day is spent creating tech packs, conducting fittings, having meetings with the merchandising department to strategize, and responding to e-mails from the development team. But I always have time for a foosball break.

Jason Lee, Sport Performance Apparel Designer, eldejo. com

Fresh orange juice, strong Italian coffee, and a croissant start my workday. As soon as I get to the office, I look at my agenda to remind me of the meetings of the day. Almost every day, I have a meeting with my design director to talk about my collections, new ideas, and the development

What Do You Do on a Daily Basis? (Continued)

process, and she gives me priorities for the day. The design process starts with in-depth trends and materials research from magazines, traveling, the Internet, and fashion blogs. We travel every season to the biggest cities around the world (New York, Shanghai, Milan, London, Paris, Hong Kong), shopping, taking pictures, and observing the daily style of the people on the streets. I send the technical sheets to the Chinese factories and then collaborate with the graphic designer on the development of the all-over prints and graphics. Once the prototypes are submitted, we have several meetings and our design team decides which are the best ideas, materials, and concepts to work on, and we discuss target prices and the structure of the collection. Next, we review all the prototypes, colors, and styles and launch the collection, respecting the table time. It's important to keep your mind open to different ideas because often during the seasonal collection you have to change details or add new styles at the last moment, and you have to be ready with a problem-solving spirit. We prepare mood boards and inspirational video clips in Photoshop. Afterwards, we present everything to our agents and distributors all around the world, and at the same time I start to work on the next collection.

Vanessa Marzi, Senior Accessories Designer, Kipling, Antwerp, Belgium

❯ One of the best things about being a handbag designer is that no two days are ever the same. At the start of a season, I mostly spend time researching and sourcing. This involves a lot of time away from the drawing board visiting exhibitions, galleries, flea markets, and any other places of inspiration. I use mood boards to compile this research and present my ideas to the team. Once a basic range concept is established, I attend trade shows and visit leather and fittings suppliers and manufacturers to source key components and materials. I then sketch detailed handbag designs which are then compiled into technical packs. Using Photoshop, I scan my hand-drawn sketches and then render with color and shade and show front, back, base elevations as well as an inside view, measurements, and a half-body pattern. I then add any additional information needed by the factory/sample maker in order for them to make an initial prototype.

Emily O'Rourke, Freelance Handbag Designer, London, England, United Kingdom

❯ On a daily basis, I actually manifest my visions on paper, then I use CAD to bring the designs to a clear visual. Using CAD allows me to easily and effortlessly add colorways, fabric, and textures to perfect the vision. I am also a patternmaker; therefore, I am able to create a pattern based on the CAD, which is my next step. I use a sample sewn out of muslin, or, if available, I will use a

Alexia dress from Panos Emporio. COURTESY OF PANOS EMPORIO.

less expensive fabric similar to the final desired fabric. Once the sample is complete, I have a fit model test the fit and flow according to ease and functional ability. This process is completed for several weeks until a complete seasonal collection is assembled.

Randi Randolph, Apparel Designer, Randi Designs, Los Angeles, California, USA

❭ My daily work routine consists of several tasks, including working on new prints, creating all-over repeats and placement layouts, recoloring existing prints, and creating new colorways. If necessary, I reduce colors for better yardage pricing. Most of my work is done digitally in various CAD design programs, predominantly Illustrator and Photoshop. I present finished artwork to my company's design team. Once approval is received, I assemble a print package to be sent to a factory for production. I communicate on a daily basis both with factories overseas and the local representatives of the factories, to ensure my artwork is being correctly processed from sample yardage to bulk production. After my print package has been sent, I file a copy of it to make it accessible for further development.

Irina Romashevskaya, Textile Designer, Maggy London, New York, New York, USA

❭ My days usually consist of fittings, reviewing patterns, and making appropriate corrections. We have concept and update meetings with production and design to make sure we are all on the same page. There are also seasonal pass-off meetings with design, in which we review design cards to develop new product. Solving production problems and making garments look saleable in a tight economy with increasing costs make the job challenging and fun!

Angela Silletti, Technical Design Management, Men's Wovens, Macy's Merchandising Group, New York, New York, USA

For me it starts with a concept, an idea, a mood which I can find during my travels, going to the museum, watching a film, visiting a tannery, reading an art book or a magazine article. Then different concepts are given from the creative director who follows the development of all the brand's collections and oversees the process, ensuring a common thread that connects everything, while respecting the DNA of the brand. We define lasts and heels, generally following the direction of the merchandising department, which, after a careful market analysis regarding sales and competitors, suggests a skeleton of the collection, indicating occasions of use, heights, and quantities. We then pass all the sketches to the factories, where technicians develop and implement the first maquettes. In the meantime, we draw models, generally divided into thematic groups based on usage or on a detail that is repeated. At this point, we receive a first prototype that will eventually be revised and corrected. After these steps, there is a monitoring meeting, which involves the whole team, including designers, sales, product development, and the shoe technician. During this process, many models will be discarded, and sometimes we will need to add new ones. Then we choose colors and materials before our final presentation.

Lisa Bozzato, Freelance Women's Shoe Designer, Via Spiga, Milan, Italy

❭ On a daily basis, I do about four hours of pure design work, including sketching, writing tech packs, making mood boards, and anything to do with the design process. I Skype clients if I have any questions to ask them, and if I have any upcoming travel, I book that online.

Jessica Good, Freelance Shoe Designer, shoedesign. co.uk, London, England, United Kingdom

❭ Being an independent freelance fashion designer, I have the luxury of choosing my projects. I spend a good part of my day on the Internet gathering

What Do You Do on a Daily Basis? (Continued)

"Step on It" by Dipika Lakshmi, 2010. COURTESY OF DIPIKA LAKSHMI.

materials, conducting research, and discussing the details of the project requirements with my clients. I closely watch the current trends by subscribing to newsletters from fashion magazines and following different brands and blogs. Having my presence on the Internet has helped me connect to my clients and land long-term projects.

Dipika Lakshmi, Freelance Fashion Designer, Coimbatore, India

❯ As a designer, a typical day for me would include attending business meetings with clients, researching global luxury markets and brands on the Internet, sketching, designing, cutting patterns, supervising seamstresses for quality control, traveling to the Irish linen factory to purchase fabrics, responding to e-mails, networking on LinkedIn, carrying out feasibility studies, sales and marketing, checking my e-commerce website to prepare orders to export to international markets and individual clients, and preparing seasonal collections for private showcasing events.

Joan Ghali, Owner, JoanLido, Derry/Londonderry, Northern Ireland

❯ I review programs that are in work with both overseas vendors and with my cross-functional team. We may be working on three to four seasons at a time, which overlap in their particular stage of development. This can involve meetings, market research, quiet design time, creating development packages, and reviewing runway shows.

Diane Mahood, Creative Technical Designer, Sweaters and Knits, White House/Black Market, Ft. Myers, Florida, USA

❯ I spend time researching seasonal trends for men's prints and patterns for the upcoming season. Along with other designers, the directors and I will competitive shop the market, to research any up and coming trends that we should be aware of early in the planning process. Part of my job is to make appointments with various print and textile vendors that specialize in and sell vintage textiles, prints, and original artwork that we may purchase for the season. I will put together trend boards, highlighting what I think are the biggest trends in prints and patterns, and present them to my director and the design team. Based on the items that the team has purchased on various shopping trips throughout the United States and Europe, the directors will start to rig our development room and break down the samples into various trends that they think are relevant for our customer. It is from these rigs that we present to the heads of design and merchandising to get alignment on the upcoming season. Once these ideas have been signed off on and a color palette is in place, we roll this out to the merchandising team ("kick off"), and then design and merchandising collaborate on the big ideas. Merchandising will hand-design a breakdown road map of each product category, representing what is needed for each of their areas, and then design will start designing into it. Once merchandising, design, directors, and senior vice presidents have aligned, I will start sending out artwork to vendors so design can start to receive sample yardage and full garment samples of each print and pattern ready for our next milestone meeting, which is adoption. Sometimes groups are dropped, and sometimes items are added. During adoption and leading up to it, I will be researching the next season, and then the process starts all over again.

Grant Young, Senior CAD Designer, Old Navy, San Francisco, California, USA

❯ Research takes up a large part of my everyday tasks. I'm constantly looking at my favorite websites, blogs, and magazines for inspiration. I try to read about something new each day which might inspire me to create something different.

Rachel Richards, Design Director, Footwear, "B" Brian Atwood, Rachel Rachel Roy, Boutique 9, The Jones Group, New York, New York, USA

❯ We've got four markets a year, spread apart by three months. Each collection starts about four months in advance of each market. I could easily be wrapping up the current market I'm designing for while starting to research the one right after it. The process always starts with researching silhouettes, materials, fashion trends, color, and hardware, as it is key to branding the collection. Internet research, trend forecasting agencies, trend shows, inspirational brand shopping, and working with tanneries are key to idea conception. I work closely and am in contact daily with my product developer and merchandiser. As the day progresses, if there aren't urgent last-minute revisions, which is 50 percent of the time, I research into whatever aspect I am feeling that day. Most of the time, I start off with silhouette. The shape and function of a bag are the most important thing.

Cynthia Chang-Saada, Senior Handbag Designer, The Sak Brand Group, New York, New York, USA

❯ As an accessories designer, I am constantly researching current trends and fashion markets. I visit art galleries, museums, and libraries for inspiration as much as I visit shops and street markets to get a good understanding of current trends and styling. I often find myself checking people out, as it is one of the best inspirations that a fashion designer can get, as you can see everyday people living their lives as they walk on streets, go to clubs, or drink coffee in a sidewalk café. A lot of my research is also done on the Web, where I can check catwalks and research different brands, companies, and fashion blogs. I then translate all the information gathered into my own interpretation of what would match the needs of the brand that I design.

Thomas Halford Ayers, Senior Accessories and Jewelry Designer, Toto Design Studio, London, England, United Kingdom

❯ I currently work as a senior designer for three divisions of a major high-end bridal company in New York City. My primary responsibility is to work directly with the owner of the company in brainstorming, designing, and draping gowns for each collection. However, I am also responsible for overseeing the development of gowns. I am expected to troubleshoot with other teams such as patternmakers, cutters, production managers, directors, and the CEO of the company to make sure that all stages of creating the gowns are running smoothly. In addition I am present at all major design meetings, fittings, castings, styling sessions, photo shoots, major shows, and presentations as needed to ensure that each gown is presented appropriately. Another aspect of my job is to work with patternmakers and cutters to produce garments from previous collections that our clients may order. I also work closely with the director on special orders placed by important clients. Most of my day is spent designing and I start by researching the industry trends with a wide range of resources. From my research, I discuss ideas with the creative director for each collection for which I create mood boards, select fabrics, trims, beading layouts, draping techniques and other embellishments. I then

What Do You Do on a Daily Basis? (Continued)

Sketches for Debut Collection by Paul Hernandez, 2011 COURTESY OF PAUL HERNANDEZ.

drape the dress and work with the pattern maker to create a sample for approval by the creative director. At home and in my leisure time, I like to relax with a cup of iced coffee and a fresh sketchbook and jot down ideas for future use. I invested in my own mannequin and sewing machine at home to experiment with draping techniques and further develop my own skills. Anyone who thinks that being a fashion designer is easy has yet to have worked in the industry, but anyone who says it is not inspiring and fun is most likely not meant to be a fashion designer. It is a tough industry, but it is immensely rewarding.

Michael Cho, Senior Evening and Bridal Designer, New York, New York, USA

❯ I am the head designer at IGO, which is an active wear line for both men and women. Currently we are designing for the United States Army Boxing Team. A typical day can include fitting on models, drafting production patterns, creating new concept sketches, and technical flats.

Paul Hernandez, Head Designer, IGO, San Diego, California, USA

❯ When I wake up in the morning, I do things to ground myself. I usually spend a few minutes meditating before going on my morning run. Feeling great every day by starting off the morning right makes it easier to envision new designs and stay on

task. After exercising, I check my agenda and make an hour-by-hour plan for the day. Because I am an independent design consultant, my days vary. Some days are spent working as a "ghost" designer for one of my clients' brands, and the other days are focused on my eponymous capsule collection. I search for inspiration in untraditional places like vintage art history books, cars, and interior architecture. Design is the ultimate luxury in life, love is the ultimate passion; both are necessities.

Shari Seidlitz-McCandlish, Creative Director/Owner, Geoni Studios, Los Angeles, California, USA

Aramōt Carryall Satchel sketched by Shari Seidlitz-McCandlish for Geoni Studios, 2012. COURTESY OF SHARI SEIDLITZ-MCCANDLISH.

History of Fashion Design: Then and Now

For a fashion designer, it is crucial to have an understanding of how the fashion industry got its start, from both a historical and inspirational perspective. It all began when Louis XIV, the king of France who reigned from 1643 to 1715, ordered life-sized fashion dolls dressed in the latest Parisian fashions to be sent to all of the European courts. Aristocratic women would have their dressmakers copy the clothing on the dolls and grade them to their size. It was Marie-Jeanne Rose Bertin (1747–1813), the French milliner and dressmaker to Marie Antoinette (queen of France from 1774 to 1792), who was credited with being the first French fashion designer who brought fashion to the forefront of popular culture.

CHARLES FREDERICK WORTH

Portrait of Charles Frederick Worth in 1895.
PHOTOGRAPHER: GASPARD-FELIX TOURNACHON.

Charles Frederick Worth (1826–1895) became the first person to emerge as a fashion couturier. He had an established *maison couture*, or fashion house, in Paris; he was a member of the Chambre de la Syndicale and was a registered couturier. Considered the "Father of Couture," he began the tradition of being founder, creative director, and image maker for his own brand and was the first person who decided what his clients should wear. He was English and worked at several drapery shops in London before moving to Paris in 1846. He worked for a Parisian draper and married one of the company's fashion models, who would wear his shawls and bonnets in the store to show his customers. He decided to make a few dresses for his wife to go with the accessories he produced, and as you may have guessed, customers requested copies of the dresses. In 1858, he cut a deal with Otto Bobergh to open Worth and Bobergh. They dressed empresses, countesses, debutantes, and other titled and notable women. He then caught the attention of the rich and famous in New York and Boston, who would travel to Paris to be dressed by him.

He was known for being able to redefine the female shape, by using simple, luxurious fabrics in flattering silhouettes with the perfect fit. This formula proved to be a huge success for Worth, and in a risky move, he strayed from the norm of allowing his customers to dictate their selected designs and instead, four times a year, held what today is known as an informal trunk show. He became so popular that he had to turn away customers, which only heightened his elite status further. He completely revolutionized the dressmaking business by coming up with a concept that

no one else had thought of at the time. Instead of being known as a mere artisan, he was considered a true artiste.

In 1871, Worth had to shut down his business due to the Franco-Prussian War, and when he reopened, he left his original partner behind, now calling his design firm The House of Worth. His sons (one of whom was the founder of the Chambre Syndicale de la Haute Couture) joined the business, and it flourished until Worth's death in 1895. The work of Charles Worth has been commemorated with the Charles Worth Gallery at the Heritage Centre in his birthplace of Bourne, Lincolnshire, in England.

Empress Elisabeth of Austria wearing a Worth Courtly Gala Dress with silver stars, 1865. ARTIST: FRANZ XAVER WINTERHALTER (1805–1873), OIL ON CANVAS.

PAUL POIRET

French fashion designer Paul Poiret (1879–1944) was the second most renowned fashion designer in the late nineteenth and early twentieth centuries. Poiret was ambitious and sold his sketches to couture houses throughout Paris. In 1896, he was hired by fashion designer Jacques Doucet, and they sold 400 red capes made from his very first design. He later joined the House of Worth and designed simple, practical dresses without any fuss. However, his modern take on dressmaking was not well received by Worth's already established and conservative clientele. In fact, Princess Bariatinsky of Russia exclaimed, "What a horror!" upon first sight of a kimono-cut coat designed by Poiret.

Portrait of Paul Poiret circa 1913. COURTESY OF WIKIMEDIA COMMONS.

Poiret decided to establish his own design house at the beginning of the twentieth century. He made a name for himself with his signature kimono coat, the very coat that was initially rejected by his previous clientele, driving the point home that every fashion designer must stay true to his or her brand and vision. Poiret created flamboyant window displays and held legendary parties to market his work; he became known for his innate ability to market and brand himself as no other designer had done at the time. Poiret's house expanded to include furniture, decor, and fragrance. In 1911, he introduced Parfums de Rosine, which was named after his daughter, and he became the first couturier to launch a signature fragrance. For the unveiling of the scent, he hosted a grand costume ball held in his palatial mansion, attended only by the crème de la crème of Parisian society.

During World War I, Poiret served in the military and wound up leaving his fashion house behind. When he returned, his business was on the verge of bankruptcy. In 1929, Poiret's house officially closed. He became a street painter in

Model in Paul Poiret gown in 1914. COURTESY OF GEORGE GRANTHAM BAIN COLLECTION.

Paris and died in 1944, poor and unrecognized for the ingenious ways in which he influenced the fashion industry. His friend Elsa Schiaparelli paid for his burial, which allowed him to regain some recognition.

Prior to Poiret coming onto the scene, women were wearing corsets, and Poiret is best known for liberating women from these tightly fitted garments and using his superior draping skills to create free-flowing, uninhibited dresses (a radical change from the tailored looks that were popular at the time). He invented the hobble skirt (a skirt with a hem at the knees that hinders the wearer's stride) and is also credited with originating harem pantaloons and lampshade tunics. Poiret's inspiration came from antique dresses, and he favored clothing cut along straight lines and constructed of rectangular shapes.

Fashion is the only attempt to realize art in living form.

—PAUL POIRET

JEAN PATOU

In 1912, French fashion designer Jean Patou (1887–1936) opened a rather small dressmaking salon called Maison Parry. An American buyer bought his entire collection in 1914, around the time World War I began. Patou had to temporarily leave his couture house to serve as captain in the French army, and he reopened his business in 1919. At the turn of the twentieth century, the flapper look was all the rage, and he eradicated that look by lengthening the skirt and introducing sportswear for women. He is considered the inventor of knit swimwear, and is credited with creating the tennis skirt. He was also the first designer to popularize the cardigan. His mission was to make clothing comfortable.

Portrait of Jean Patou. PHOTOGRAPH PROVIDED BY BAIN NEWS SERVICE.

He went on to invent the women's designer tie, using dress fabrics. In an unprecedented move, he then created the first suntan oil. When the Great Depression hit, not only did the stock market come tumbling down, but so did Patou's couture business, as customers could no longer afford his clothing. Like any good designer, he reinvented himself and decided to launch a fragrance collection to boost sales. The most recognized perfume he created is "Joy," which remained the most expensive perfume in the world until he invented "1000," based on a rare flowering plant. Before Joy came onto the scene, Patou launched several other perfumes, all based on particular events that were happening at the time. The GWP (gift-with-purchase) was not a common marketing tactic at the time, but Jean Patou came up with the idea of including a silk scarf, printed in the same pattern as the perfume box, with any perfume purchase. Joy remains the world's second-best-selling scent, second to Chanel No. 5. When Patou died in 1936, his sister and brother-in-law continued running his design house as a family business until 2001, when Procter & Gamble acquired the company.

MADELEINE VIONNET

Madeleine Vionnet (1876–1975) was a French fashion designer and was called The Queen of the Bias Cut, because she introduced the bias cut to the fashion world. She was considered an architect of sorts and is best known for her Grecian style dresses. Vionnet did not hide the fact that she was a deeply private individual, taking on a no-nonsense and—as legendary and beloved stylist and fashion editor of 60 years, Polly Mellen, would say—"fussy finished" attitude. Vionnet often articulated a disdain for the fashion world, boldly affirming, "Insofar as one can talk of a Vionnet school, it comes mostly from my having been an enemy of fashion. There is something superficial and volatile about the seasonal and elusive whims of fashion which offends my sense of beauty." Vionnet was not concerned with the glamour of the industry, but rather with her authenticity and her ability to execute her vision of the female form and the beauty of a woman.

> The dress must not hang on the body, but follow its lines. It must accompany its wearer and when a woman smiles, the dress must smile with her.   — MADELEINE VIONNET

MARIANO FORTUNY

Mariano Fortuny (1871–1949) was a Spanish fashion designer, and though trained as a painter, Fortuny was also an accomplished architect, inventor, couturier, and lighting technician. His wife, Henrietta, was an experienced dressmaker and helped construct many of his designs. He lived with his wife in a Venetian palazzo, which he called his "think tank," and he set up separate themed rooms for inspiration. Fortuny drew from the airy Greek styles that followed the natural curves of a woman's shape. He went against the popular styles of the time and created the Delphos dress, a shift made entirely of hand-pleated silk with glass beads.

Fortuny also invented the Knossos Scarf, his first fashion garment, which was made of silk, with a geometric print, and rectangular in shape. He manufactured his own textile dyes and pigments for his fabrics, using methods used in ancient civilizations.

Portrait of Mariano Fortuny. WITH PERMISSION FROM FORTUNY, INC., NEW YORK

Fortuny factory located on Isola Della Giudecca in Venice, Italy, as seen from Zattere. PHOTOGRAPHER: MIKE RIAD, 2009. COURTESY OF FORTUNY, INC. NEW YORK.

Bolts of fabric from the 2012 Colourismo Collection. PHOTOGRAPHER: MIKE RIAD, 2011. COURTESY OF FORTUNY, INC. NEW YORK.

He began to experiment with printed velvets and silks and dyed them using a wooden block press that he invented. His dresses are regarded as art and can be seen in public museums, as well as in his own dedicated space, "Palazzo Fortuny," which is located in Venice, Italy.

JEANNE-MARIE LANVIN

Jeanne-Marie Lanvin (1867–1946) was a French designer and founder of the Lanvin fashion atelier. Her clever use of elaborate trims, fine embroideries and beaded decorations in toned-down floral colorways became her trademark look. Lanvin got her start when the over-the-top clothing that she designed for her daughter caught the attention of wealthy passersby. They requested this clothing be made for their own children, and a business was formed. She naturally evolved to start making dresses for her young clients' mothers, and that led to clientele including the most famous people in European society. She officially became a couturier after joining the Chambre de la Syndicale and opened up a boutique on the Rue du Faubourg Saint-Honoré in Paris.

Illustration from La Gazette du Bon Ton, "Deux modèles de Jeanne Lanvin," 1922. ILLUSTRATOR: PIERRE BRISSAUD.

64

By 1923, the Lanvin conglomerate included a dye factory in the western suburbs of Paris. During this time, she opened additional specialty shops dedicated to specific product categories, such as home décor, lingerie, menswear, and furs. However, her most substantial development was the creation of Lanvin Parfums and the inauguration of her signature fragrance, Arpège. She eventually launched Lanvin-Sport and created another legendary perfume, La Boule. She even created Lanvin-Décoration, an interior design department in her store. She was clearly a forward thinker and was always on the cusp of innovation. She was best known for designing mother-and-daughter outfits and built her legacy around this concept, which was very new at the time.

COCO CHANEL

Portrait of Gabrielle "Coco" Chanel, gelatin silver print by Adolf de Meyer, 1930s. PHOTO CREDIT: ROGERS FUND, 1974.

Gabrielle Bonheur "Coco" Chanel (1883–1971) embodied the true rags-to-riches story. When she was 12 years old, her mother died and her father left the family. She was put into an orphanage where she learned the seamstress trade. She became a licensed hatmaker and opened a boutique in Paris, which she called Chanel Modes. A theater actress wore her hats in a play, and Chanel's company began to thrive. She opened a second boutique called Chanel Biarritz, in Deauville, France, and created casual jersey clothes to sell for this boutique. By 1919, she was inducted into the Chambre de la Syndicale and was then able to establish her couture house in Paris.

In 1924, Chanel established Parfums Chanel and Chanel No. 5 was the first perfume she launched and remains the highest grossing perfume of all time. The French government claims that a bottle of Chanel No. 5 is sold every thirty seconds.

A pivotal moment in Chanel's career came in 1931 when she was introduced to American film producer Samuel Goldwyn (of MGM fame) in Monte Carlo. He presented Chanel with an offer of a lifetime. For one million dollars, he would fly her to Hollywood to design costumes for all the stars of the great films of the time. Of course, she accepted.

At the beginning of World War II, Chanel closed all of her stores, and eventually reestablished her fashion house. She continued to work until the January 10, 1971, when at the age of 87, she died in her sleep, shortly after overseeing the finalization of her spring collection.

Her legend continues today with German fashion designer Karl Lagerfeld at the helm, carrying on her tradition for the house of Chanel. Several films, television shows, a Broadway musical, and many books have been written about her, including the fantastically inspiring children's book entitled *Different Like Coco*, written and illustrated by Elizabeth Matthews. Chanel will go down in history as a woman who lived life in her own way, on her own terms, and in the way she saw fit. Chanel was a pioneering fashion designer and woman whose modernist thought, menswear-inspired fashions, and pursuit of expensive simplistic classics made her a central figure in the world of fashion in the twentieth century. She was the only couturier to be named in the "*Time* 100: The Most Important People of the Century" list.

Fashion fades, only style remains the same.

— COCO CHANEL

ELSA SCHIAPARELLI

Elsa Schiaparelli (1890–1973) was born into a wealthy family, and felt her luxurious upbringing suppressed her creative energy. So she moved to New York and then to Paris to explore her appreciation for both fashion and art. In Paris, she began making her own clothes, and her close friend and confidant, designer Paul Poiret, urged her to start her own business—which she did, with little success. A year later, she launched a new graphic knitwear collection, and with a stable foundation in place, she then launched ski wear, swimsuits, and dresses. She created a divided skirt for a tennis player at Wimbledon. In the early 1930s, she added an eveningwear collection.

In 1940, Schiaparelli moved back to New York and remained there until the end of the war. Upon her return to Paris, her business was never the same, as she could not modify and adjust her collection to the changing times. Her business closed in 1954, and she died in 1973, after writing her autobiography and retiring, with homes in both Paris and Tunisia.

Schiaparelli was known for her creative use of unusually themed prints, and was the first designer to use not only zippers, but dyed-to-match (DTM) zippers. She was highly focused on luxurious and fancy trims in unusual themes, such as bees. She invented culottes, wrapped turbans, embroidered shirts, pompom hats, barbaric belts, wedge shoes, and mix-and-match sportswear separates. Her modern way of thinking extended to her runway shows, in which she tied music into the theme of each of her seasonal collections.

Above anything, Schiaparelli was inspired by modern and contemporary art and surrealism. She collaborated with several artists, including Jean Cocteau, but her collaboration with Salvador Dali produced her most significant designs. They consist of the lobster dress (white silk with crimson waistband and hand-painted large-scale lobster), the tears dress (light blue evening gown with trompe l'oeil tears, paired with a tear cut-out veil, lined in bright pink and magenta), and the skeleton dress (black ribbed crepe with trapunto quilting, producing a raised surface). She launched several perfumes and created the color "shocking pink," based on the 17-carat pink Cartier diamond named Tête de Belier. She designed the wardrobes for actresses such as Mae West, for the movie *Every Day's a Holiday* (1937), using a mannequin created with Ms. West's precise measurements, and Zsa Zsa Gabor for *Moulin Rouge* (1952).

Perhaps Schiaparelli's most significant legacy was that of bringing a sense of playfulness and humor to fashion with her infusion of art and imagination. She loved to experiment with various combinations of fabrics, colors, and textures, and was inspired by new technologies that were coming on the scene at the time. She was the first designer to use synthetic fabrics in a couture line, working with acrylic, cellophane, jersela (a rayon jersey), and a rayon and fildifer (a metallic thread) blend. In 1930, she created the first evening-dress and jacket ensemble, and made the first clothes with visible zippers. This led to her obsession with using eccentric fastenings and buttons, such as a silk-covered cauliflower button on a jacket.

Coco Chanel referred to Schiaparelli as "an artist who designs clothes." She was the first designer who saw the importance of collaborating with other artists of creative genius, and was the first designer who took the seriousness out of couture and brought a rather fun aspect to the process. Her clientele truly appreciated her forward-thinking mentality.

> Fashion is born by small facts, trends or even politics, never by trying to make little pleats and furbelows, by trinkets, by clothes easy to copy, or by the shortening or lengthening of a skirt.
>
> — Elsa Schiaparelli

CRISTÓBAL BALENCIAGA

Cristóbal Balenciaga (1895–1972) was a Spanish fashion designer who ran the fashion house of Balenciaga and who was so highly regarded by his peers that he was referred to by Christian Dior as the "master of us all." Balenciaga got his start by opening a boutique in Spain in the early 1900s. He expanded with two additional boutiques and dressed the Spanish royal family and anyone associated with aristocracy. With the onset of the Spanish Civil War in 1936, he was forced to close his stores and move to Paris.

Balenciaga established his couture house and sent his collection down the

Portrait of Cristobal Balenciaga, 1950. JAYPOFROMVOX/CC BY 2.0.

runway for the first time in the fall of 1937. The press praised him as an avant-garde innovator. This positive press not only popularized him as a fashion designer, but boosted his sales. Carmel Snow, the famous editor-in-chief of *Harper's Bazaar* magazine, became an immediate advocate of his work. His clients would travel to Paris during World War II just to purchase his clothing. His designs were linear, crisp, simplistic, and sleek—a completely different approach from the full skirts Dior was designing.

In an unprecedented move in 1957, Balenciaga presented his runway collection to the fashion press the day before the clothing was to be delivered to retailers, instead of observing the thirty-day standard lead time the industry followed. His purpose in doing this was to try to prevent knockoffs. The press, as you would have guessed, was not so pleased, and he eventually went back to the regular schedule. He had very distinct ways of doing things and rebelled against the Chambre de la Syndicale by never becoming a member. So, technically speaking, Balenciaga's collection could never be considered haute couture.

Cristóbal Balenciaga closed his atelier in 1968 and died three years later, reportedly having never given a single interview to the media. In 1986, Jacques Bogart S.A. acquired the rights to Balenciaga and has gone through several creative designers at the helm, including Nicolas Ghesquière, who has been the head designer since 1997.

Balenciaga is best known for his precise tailoring. The brand is most famous for its motorcycle-themed handbag collection, as well as its structural garments. Diana Vreeland, the legendary columnist and fashion editor for *Harper's Bazaar* and *Vogue*, once said, "In a Balenciaga, you were the only woman in the room." Vintage Balenciaga is a mainstay among celebrities, fashion editors, and fashionistas alike. In March 2011, the M.H. de Young Memorial Museum in San Francisco opened the exhibit *Balenciaga and Spain*, a 120-piece fashion retrospective paying tribute to the legendary fashion career of Cristóbal Balenciaga.

CHRISTIAN DIOR

Christian Dior (1905–1957) was born into a wealthy family and lived in a seaside beach town on the coast of Normandy. Dior's parents insisted he study political science with the hopes that he would one day become a diplomat, but Dior had other plans for himself, as he always had his sights set on the fashion world. He earned a living by selling his fashion sketches on the front stoop of his home and he then began working as an assistant for couturier Robert Piguet. After his deployment from the military, he began working for Lucien Lelong, as head designer alongside Pierre Balmain. Dior firmly believed that women were ready for a new, luxurious postwar look, and, in 1946, after hiring 85 employees, the House of Dior was born and decorated in Dior's favorite white and gray color combination. His first line was shown two years later, and clearly exhibited free-flowing, flowerlike, and billowing skirts with a striking hourglass silhouette.

In order to achieve this hourglass look, Dior lined his fabrics with percale (a plain-weave fabric made of cotton, polyester, or other blend), which made his dresses flare out from the waist,

Portrait of Christian Dior, circa 1950. PHOTOGRAPHER: BELLINI. COURTESY OF CHRISTIAN DIOR, S.A.

Christian Dior with model, Lucky. COURTESY OF CHRISTIAN DIOR, S.A.

giving his models a very curvaceous form. Carmel Snow said to Dior of this collection, "It's quite a revelation, dear Christian, your dresses have such a new look." It was from that moment on that this became known as "The New Look." So the partnership and strong relationship that Dior shared with an editor led him to gain glorious press for his new idea, and in turn helped him gain incredible exposure and success. The Dior client list ranged from legendary film actresses Ava Gardner and Marlene Dietrich to Princess Margaret and the Duchess of Windsor. Dior died while vacationing in Italy in 1957.

Christian Dior was best known for his superior innovations and for creating, for the first time in fashion designer history, a global brand extending across various product categories. Fashion designer Christian Lacroix says of Dior, "He was so famous in France at the time, it seemed as if he wasn't a man, but an institution." Dior himself once related the story of a time when his grandfather took him and his cousins out to dinner, when they were little. His grandfather had asked his young grandson what he intended to be when he grew up, to which he replied, "Christian Dior."

Zest is the secret of all beauty. There is no beauty that is attractive without zest.
— CHRISTIAN DIOR

An Interview with Peter Som, Fashion Designer

Sketch by Peter Som for the Spring 2012 Peter Som Collection. COURTESY OF PETER SOM.

Was there a pivotal moment in your childhood, upbringing, or at some point in your life that led you to pursue a career in fashion design?

❯ I had always loved to sketch clothes and shoes as a kid, but it wasn't until a family trip to Paris when I was ten that I discovered what fashion really was about. My sister bought copies of *Paris Vogue* and *L'Officiel,* and when I opened them, I was awestruck. It was in the early eighties and, seeing Claude Montana and Thierry Mugler all over the pages, I knew at that moment what I wanted to do.

After graduating cum laude (with honors) in art history from Connecticut College, you attended

Parsons The New School for Design in New York. What degree did you obtain?

❯ I received a bachelor of fine arts degree in fashion design.

At Parsons, you were the recipient of the Isaac Mizrahi Gold Thimble Award. Please describe the purpose of this award.

❯ Parsons was known for its designer critic program, where a group of seniors got paired with a designer who would mentor them on their senior fashion show. It was a great honor to receive the Gold Thimble Award, as I greatly admired Isaac and his modern chic take on classic American sportswear.

While at Parsons, you apprenticed with two legendary fashion designers, Calvin Klein and Michael Kors. Please describe how you obtained these incredible opportunities.

❯ The Calvin Klein internship was through Parsons. They needed a group of students for a few weeks to work on a specific project. When the project was done, I asked if I could continue. My internship with Michael Kors came about because I knew that eventually I wanted to start my own company and that interning at a smaller company would be important (at that time, Michael Kors was a small company). I obtained that internship with the help of the Parsons fashion office and lots of persistence! Internships are crucial to gaining on-the-job experience! I did everything from run errands, to dress models for shows, organize fabric, and take notes at meetings.

After graduating, you worked in design for Bill Blass and eventually became creative director of womenswear. Please describe your experience there.

❯ I joined Bill Blass as an assistant designer after graduating from Parsons. It was amazing to be a witness to a world of luxury that his clients lived in and demanded. The fabrics, the embroideries, and this type of workmanship were the closest thing America had to couture. Returning as creative director was a chance to carry on the heritage of the brand into the future.

Who has had a major influence on you as a fashion designer?

❯ There are so many people who have influenced me, as this industry is built on mentorship and passing of information and advice. You need to be open to receiving it, which is the important thing.

What was your greatest challenge when first launching your collection?

❯ Launching my first collection was the easy part, as it is three parts ambition and one part naiveté. There was nowhere to go but up, but it's the challenges of staying in business and building the business that take work!

What is your design philosophy?

❯ Feminine and wearable.

How does the design process begin for you? Do you begin with a theme or some form of inspiration, a silhouette, or a recently discovered, can't-live-without fabric?

❯ I always start with sketching and an idea of a mood or a theme. I usually let the pen and paper lead.

Do you have a separate team that researches, sources, and globally develops your fabrics and trims, or is that the responsibility of you and your design team?

❯ My design team does everything. They are amazing!

How do you successfully design garments and accessories, season after season, that are both true to your design aesthetic and vision and commercially saleable? Is there ever a conflict?

❯ It's all about a balancing act; you need some of each. If I'm going to send a low-cut sheer dress with a train down the runway, I will make sure that I have a version in the showroom that is lined and in a cut that all women can wear, not just the model.

What role does social media play in the promotion of your brand and in staying close to your customer base?

❯ Social media is probably the most important vehicle to get our message and clothes out there. Twitter, Facebook, and Pinterest are how people communicate.

Sketch by Peter Som for the Spring 2012 Peter Som Collection.
COURTESY OF PETER SOM.

What advice would you give an aspiring fashion designer trying to launch his or her own fashion collection?

❯ Have a point of view and believe in it. Let yourself be creative, but also be tough on yourself. Finding a solid business partner is crucial. He or she will allow you to do what you do best—design.

The Peter Som collection can be found in premiere specialty stores such as Bergdorf Goodman, Saks Fifth Avenue, Neiman Marcus, and Nordstrom. What advice would you give to aspiring fashion designers who are pounding away at the pavement trying to land their first retail account?

❯ Never give up. And most importantly, listen to all feedback and adjust accordingly without losing who you are about.

How do you find balance in the fast-paced and ever-changing world of fashion?

❯ Make sure that you make time for friends, family, and loved ones. The pace of fashion is so fast that it is easy to get swept away. It's perfectly okay to miss a party so you can stay home and watch TV and eat take-out!

What three things can't you live without?

❯ Coffee, sleep, and the beach.

What is your favorite quote?

❯ "Tell me the how, why and what."

Look 32 of the Spring 2012 Peter Som Runway Collection.
PHOTOGRAPHER: DAN LECCA. COURTESY OF PETER SOM.

Describe the ultimate perfect day for you.

❯ Morning at the gym, sketching and working on fabric with my team, and then a home-cooked meal with friends!

An Interview with Daymond John, CEO, TV Personality, and Entrepreneur

Portrait of Daymond John. PHOTOGRAPHER: UDO SPREITZENBARTH, 2010. COURTESY OF DAYMOND JOHN.

Along with a few other companies, you helped to pioneer the urban apparel market with the launch of your FUBU ("For Us By Us") collection. Please expand on this.

❯ We were one of about ten who were just starting out in the urban market at the time, but we have been credited with taking our brand to a major global level.

Prior to FUBU becoming an established brand, you and your partners showed the collection in a hotel room in Las Vegas because you could not afford a booth at the MAGIC trade show. You received over $300,000 worth of orders, proving the importance for emerging designers of thinking outside of the box. Were there other examples in which this type of creative thinking played a part in a successful endeavor?

❯ Wow, there have been so many things that I've done. We spent all of our money to get in front of the music producer, Teddy Riley. He was hosting a charity event down in Virginia which we attended with our shirts in tow. We wound up giving the shirts away to all of the artists and important people. One of the local media hosts named Ralph McDaniels wore the shirt often, and people would ask him about it every day, and he, in return, put us on his local cable station, and we gained a lot of publicity from it.

What was your greatest challenge when first launching your collection?

❯ Our biggest challenge was making the goods and being able to broaden the scope of the line.

As the CEO and founder of FUBU, how involved are you in the actual design of the products?

❯ It depends on what brand it is, how much attention it needs, and if it is licensed. Most of my brands are licensed right now, which is not an easy thing to do. But once that partnership is established, my involvement with design comes into play mostly at the beginning, when the licensee is trying to find out the DNA of the brand.

What advice would you give an aspiring fashion designer trying to launch his or her own fashion collection?

❯ Become a local hero first. Sell your product in your local area to family and then to strangers, and get feedback on why your product is working or not working. Then the ambassadors for your brand will start to grow in different territories.

How did you go about landing retail accounts when you launched FUBU?

❯ The first account for me was not the big guys; it usually begins with the specialty stores. It is simpler to work with the specialty stores first. Once I showed sales from the smaller stores, the bigger stores started to look at me.

As one of the "sharks" on the hit ABC television show Shark Tank, ***you have the opportunity to make people's dreams come true by providing funding for their business concepts. When it comes to fashion startups, what are the main factors that prompt you to invest in one?***

❯ First of all, it is always going to be sales. As the saying goes, "You can make up your own opinion, but not your own facts." Sales will prove how great the product is, and I also look at how long someone has been in the business and their total years of experience.

As a CEO, entrepreneur, author, motivational speaker, television personality, and investor, how do you find the elusive work/life balance?

❯ The biggest challenge that I have is time management. Surrounding myself with great people and also understanding that I need to surround myself with great people is key. You will go through a lot of people to find the perfect partners. I don't get discouraged when I fail at finding the right people. Instead, I keep moving on to find that right one. It's like dating.

Describe the ultimate perfect day for you.

❯ Waking up, fishing, and doing some relaxing stuff, making some form of a deal on the phone or in person, and spending time with my kids.

Today, fashion is a global industry and is covered worldwide by the media, which has played a major role in catapulting the fashion industry to the prominence it has today. In addition, two very prominent industries, both music and entertainment, often partner with the fashion industry in various promotional and collaborative ventures and efforts, parlaying the coverage even more extensively. It is important to note how much of an impact the entertainment industry has on the fashion industry. Hollywood has had an ongoing historical connection with fashion, most notably exemplified by our enduring admiration for style icons such as Audrey Hepburn and Grace Kelly. This interest then sparked a curiosity about the costumes these legendary actresses wore in famous movies such as *Roman Holiday* and *Rear Window*, and suddenly costume designers such as Edith Head became a household name. Today, actors and celebrities who walk the red carpet are asked by television hosts to divulge who designed their outfit—with the now ubiquitous question, "*Who are you wearing?*"

Angelina Jolie wearing Randolph Duke Couture at the 56th Annual Golden Globe Awards, held at the Beverly Hilton, Beverly Hills, California. KABC, 1999. COURTESY OF RANDOLPH DUKE.

This media attention and the development of the devoted designer-celebrity relationship catapulted designers to icon status, and they are now touted as celebrities themselves. The societal interest in these fashion designers and the clothes they design has served as a catalyst for the popularization of the career aspect of the fashion industry, propelling the careers of celebrity stylists such as Rachel Zoe, who is now a fashion designer herself, and fashion photographers such as Bruce Weber and Mario Testino into stellar celebrity status.

The media have capitalized on this interest with the onset of numerous fashion-career-based reality television shows, movies, and documentaries, which have become huge successes. (A complete listing of television shows, films, and documentaries with a fashion theme can be found in the Appendix).

Further evidence of the vast coverage of fashion extends to the Internet. With the onset of hundreds of style-related websites that feature media clips, video presentations, and photographs of U.S. and international designers' seasonal collections, never before has fashion been so accessible for so many people around the globe. The dominant crossover of fashion,

Spring 2012 Pamella Roland Advertising Campaign. PHOTOGRAPHER: NIGEL BARKER, 2011.

coupled with the mass media coverage, both online and off-line, demonstrates the sustainability of fashion design as a solid career choice. In the twenty-first century, we are seeing a massive growth rate in the number of famous people who have created their own fashion lines, including Madonna, Victoria Beckham, Jessica Simpson, Mary Kate and Ashley Olsen, and Christy Turlington, to name just a few. Despite all the media coverage and glitterati, at the end of the day, fashion is a business. And what a large business it is! Let's take a look at the fashion industry by the numbers.

Chado Ralph Rucci Spring/Summer 2012 Ready-to-Wear Collection. Python Circular Banded Skirt and White Tucked Chiffon Button Front Blouse. PHOTOGRAPHERS: DAN AND CORINA LECCA. COURTESY OF CHADO RALPH RUCCI.

The Worldwide Fashion Industry by the Numbers

Now let's take a look at the fashion industry by region in sheer volume and numbers. According to the United Nationals Industrial Development Organization (UNIDO), in the year 2006, approximately 26.5 million people worked in the clothing and textiles sector worldwide. In the year 2000, worldwide consumers spent one trillion dollars on clothing.

Over four million people are employed in the fashion industry in the United States, in the areas of design, manufacturing, distribution, marketing, retailing, advertising, communications, publishing, and consulting.

The highest number of fashion designers based in the United States are employed in the states of New York and California. According to the American Apparel and Footwear Association, in 2008, $374 billion was spent on fashion and accessories annually in the United States, making it the fourth largest producing industry for America's economy.

New York City is considered by many to be the fashion capital of the world, serving as the headquarters to more than 900 fashion companies (more than Paris, Milan, and London combined), employing approximately 173,000. It boasts more headquarters of fashion designers and fashion retailers and has more showrooms than any other city in the world. New York City offers the largest amount of retail space in some of the most visible and highly trafficked locations in the world, such as Times Square, Madison Avenue, and Fifth Avenue (40 million visitors annually), and it demands the highest cost per square foot of retail space in the world. It houses the headquarters of the most well-known fashion publications and newspapers (including *Vogue*, *Elle*, *Town & Country*, *GQ*, *W*, and *Women's Wear Daily*). The industry hosts approximately 75 trade show and market week events each year, bringing almost 580,000 out-of-town buyers and other visitors into the city, creating yet another tremendous boost to the NYC economy. The retail market in New York City is the largest in the country and is also growing at an enormous rate, with projected employment by clothing and accessories stores increasing by 17 percent by 2025.

The concentration of fashion jobs in New York City is more than three times greater than the number of fashion jobs across the entire United States. It is the largest manufacturing industry in the city of New York, generating approximately $55 billion a year in revenue, and is expected to contribute a staggering $865 million to the New York City economy during the two weeks of Mercedes Benz New York Fashion Week alone, in 2012.

Look 14 of the Spring 2012 Peter Som Runway Collection. PHOTOGRAPHER: DAN LECCA. COURTESY OF PETER SOM.

A fashion capital (or fashion city) is a city that is classified as a major center for the fashion industry. Activities including the design, production, manufacturing, and selling of fashion goods, as well as regularly hosting major fashion events (such as fashion weeks, award presentations, trade fairs, and career expos) will generate significant revenue for the economy. There are four main global fashion capitals: New York, Paris, Milan, and London. Traditionally held in major fashion markets such as New York and Paris, fashion weeks now take place all over the world, in cities such as Seoul, Tokyo, São Paulo, Buenos Aires, Los Angeles, London, Moscow, Hong Kong, Singapore, and in smaller cities such as Jacksonville (Florida), Charlotte (North Carolina), Charleston (South Carolina) and many more.

Fashion weeks are events lasting approximately one week, in which fashion designers present their seasonal collections to editors, journalists, buyers, and industry heads. Fashion Weeks generally occur twice a year for both women's ready-to-wear and menswear, once in February for the fall season and then again in September for the next year's spring season, each lasting for one week. Spring women's haute couture collections are shown in January, and fall women's haute couture is shown in July of the previous year. Menswear fall collections that are shown in Paris and Milan occur in January, and Spring collections occur in June of the previous year. Pre-fall and resort collections shown in New York generally are presented on a smaller scale in the designer's showroom or another venue, whereas in Paris and Milan, they are usually shown as a regular, full-scale fashion show.

An Interview with Zang Toi, Fashion Designer

Spring 2012 Zang Toi Collection. PHOTOGRAPHER: EKA HALIM.

Growing up, you loved to sketch and draw and dreamed of becoming an interior designer or architect. What led you to pursue a career in fashion design?

❯ I have always been interested in beauty ever since I was young. I would marvel at beautiful things and places and sketch them. When I got the opportunity to further my education at Parsons in New York, I jumped at the chance. I have never looked back since.

Spring 2012 Zang Toi Collection. PHOTOGRAPHER: EKA HALIM.

Please describe your educational background, as well as any internships, apprenticeships, or jobs you held prior to launching your own collection in 1989.

❯ When I was 18, I left Malaysia for New York. Two years later, I began my studies at Parsons The New School for Design. I started working for Mary Jane Marcasiano while I was still in school. I left after five years to start my own atelier.

What is your design philosophy?

❯ Timeless beauty with a touch of movie star glamour

You are known for infusing color into your designs and have produced some of the most stunningly gorgeous and colorful pieces that are truly museum-worthy. Has your Malaysian upbringing influenced your aesthetic? What other factors influence your overall design philosophy?

❯ Malaysia is truly a vibrant country full of different cultures. In terms of aesthetic, Malaysia is so colorful!

When I first started out, I used all the bright colors like fuchsia, orange, chartreuse, and purple because it reminded me a lot of Malaysia. For the past 13 years, my work has been influenced by the beauty of Paris!

At the House of Toi, I understand your design process begins with color. Do all of your initial concepts start from color alone or might you be inspired by a particular silhouette or by a recently discovered fabric?

❯ Color has played an important role in my collection in the past, but in recent years, traveling to different parts of the world has played a much more important influence in creating my collections.

For any aspiring fashion designer, staying true to one's brand is a key component in establishing credibility. What other factors do you feel play a major role in creating a foundation for one's collection?

❯ To me, the single most important factor to success is work ethic; work hard and work smart.

In 1992, you launched your moderately priced bridge collection, Z. Please describe what prompted you to offer a diffusion line.

❯ Z was launched to satisfy the demand from various department stores and is now also available at my boutique in Malaysia.

You've dressed such famous women as Sharon Stone, Eva Longoria, and singer Fergie from the Black Eyed Peas. Obtaining a celebrity clientele is the highlight of any fashion designer's career. How did you acquire your first celebrity client?

❯ Through word of mouth, as I have never had a publicist since I established my atelier in 1989.

What advice would you give an aspiring fashion designer who is trying to launch his or her own collection?

❯ Hard work and always stay true to yourself.

Actress Kirstie Alley closing the Spring 2012 Zang Toi Fashion Show. PHOTOGRAPHER: EKA HALIM.

Actress Sharon Stone wearing Zang Toi. PHOTOGRAPH PROVIDED BY WIRE IMAGE.

You were quoted as saying, "There are so many young designers who are eager to be stars right away. But ego can be the worst killer to any young designer. You can't let the press and the hype go to your head. If the work doesn't meet the demand and the quality, it doesn't mean anything." Please describe how you were able to keep your ego in check as your career progressed and you became more successful and famous.

❭ I was born and raised in a small village in Malaysia, and I had to work extremely hard to get to where I am today. I feel most successful when the ladies pay full retail for my designs. I work hard at designing and creating beautiful clothes in the best possible quality that earn the trust and admiration of my ladies.

You are the recipient of many prestigious awards and recognitions, including knighthood by the Sultan of Kelantan from your hometown in Malaysia. Can you describe what it is feels like to be given such high honors?

❭ I feel incredibly privileged to be awarded such high honors. I didn't expect any of these recognitions and awards, but I'm definitely very thankful for all of them.

How have you dealt with the press and fashion critics over the years, especially at the beginning of your career when you were still trying to establish a name for yourself?

❭ I'm grateful for the praise I've received from fashion critics and press over the years. I feel encouraged to work harder to deliver my best efforts. I also appreciate the constructive criticism that I've received because these comments help me reevaluate my work so I can see things from different perspectives. From both good and bad press, I've definitely improved myself as a designer.

Spring 2012 Zang Toi Collection. PHOTOGRAPHER: EKA HALIM.

How do you sustain balance between your personal life and your work life?

❭ I am very busy every day, but I love being productive, so it has never been an issue for me. I am very close to my family and a small circle of loyal friends, so I try to make time for them. I keep in constant touch with them, and I visit my family in Malaysia whenever I can, and they visit me here in New York as well. I also like throwing intimate dinner parties to host my friends. It's something I enjoy doing to show my appreciation for their beautiful friendship.

Describe what the ultimate perfect day would be like for you.

❭ I would start the morning with a run around the Central Park reservoir, then head to the office and get some work done for my collection with my amazing House of Toi angels, followed by hosting an intimate home-cooked dinner for my family and friends in my home. Productivity and being surrounded by family and friends, now that's perfect.

An Interview with Kay Unger, Fashion Designer

Kay Unger, 2007. PHOTOGRAPHY BY STYLE*EXPO*.

Was there a pivotal moment in your childhood, growing up in Chicago, or at some point in your life that led you to pursue a career in fashion design?

❯ There was not necessarily a pivotal point, but I got a sewing machine when I was eight years old, and I taught myself how to sew using the instructions; it was very inspiring. When my parents went to sleep, I took the quilted bedspreads off the bed and cut them up and made skirts. I was lucky enough to grow up in a family of very fashionable women. My grandmother was a milliner in Chicago. She was head of the millinery department at Saks Fifth Avenue and eventually opened up her own milli-

nery store in Chicago. She was a very elegant woman, and my first real inspiration and indirect mentor. She was so spectacular. My parents would go to the best events at the White House and they were part of the Rat Pack, and my mom wore the most outrageous, incredible clothing by Norman Norrell, James Galanos, and Charles James. I would literally sit on the floor of her dressing room and watch her get dressed, and to this day, I remember every one of those dresses. All of this affected me. And because I was so exposed, I thought how in the world could I become a fashion designer? It seemed like they were such geniuses, and I thought there was no space for someone new. I always pursued the art side of my career because I didn't know until later in life that this kind of career was available to me.

You studied painting at Washington University in St. Louis, Missouri, before switching to the fashion design program at Parsons The New School for Design in New York. What led you to pursue a fashion design career?

❯ I have always been a very independent person and always wanted to pay my own way and take care of myself. I never thought I could make a living out of being a painter, and I wanted to keep it more of a hobby. Washington University had a fashion design department, and I decided during my second year to try it and see how I did. I actually did very well, and I decided to try Parsons. I wanted to try for the most prestigious school, and that's basically how I went about it.

Upon graduation, you apprenticed with the legendary fashion designer Geoffrey Beene. Please describe what this experience was like.

❯ It was spectacular! I was his assistant, and Issey Miyake was also his assistant at the same time. I was the only female assistant that Geoffrey Beene ever had. What I learned from Geoffrey because we were lucky enough to sit in the same room was how not to ever give up. I was taught to work very hard on each garment to try everything to make it the best it can be. The other really interesting thing that I have taught everybody for all the years I have been in business is the way of charting a collection that I learned at Geoffrey Beene. There were little sketches of everything he was working on and it was pinned on a bulletin board by product category for every month of each delivery for each season, and it has been my formula that I have used ever since I've been in business.

Please describe any internships and design jobs you had prior to launching your own line.

❯ One of the first places I worked was Gayle Kirkpatrick. I worked on the fashion shows, I worked with the drapers and helped them pick the fabrics, and I did all the sketching. My first real design job was with Traina-Norell. I did formal fashion shows, my clothing was on the cover of *Harper's Bazaar* and *Vogue*. From there, was when I went out on my own. Back in those days, internships did not exist. You could not intern unless you already had a job.

Under your company, Phoebe Company, LLC, you oversee the design for four separate labels, including Kay Unger New York, Phoebe Couture, Unger by Kay Unger, and Kay J's by Kay Unger. Please provide an overview for each of these collections.

❯ Kay Unger New York is daytime clothing, evening suits, eveningwear, and evening separates for a sophisticated customer who is very fashionable, but not a fashion victim. We are very well known for our gorgeous prints, which comes from my painting background, and we develop most of

our fabrications. Phoebe Couture is what we call "Younger Unger." Phoebe is the name of my partner's daughter. Whereas Kay Unger is the first dress that a mom buys her daughter, Phoebe is a little bit less expensive than Kay. Color drives this collection. The customer is from age 13 to 60. We also make women's sizes to 14–24 in both Kay Unger and Phoebe Couture. Unger by Kay Unger was initiated in 2001 after September 11th. So many women were looking for jobs, and I wanted to make clothing that women could wear to interviews. For the first year, the collection was completely made in New York to support the city during that difficult time. It is conservative with flair. Kay J's is on a temporary hiatus. It began when Neiman Marcus came to us and said we love your prints and fabrics, and we want you to make pajamas for us. We also did robes. Everyone loved it. It's been a lot of fun. Often a store will come to us with a niche for a certain product, and a specific program will be developed.

What is your design philosophy?

❯ Fit and femininity. I always challenge my customer and myself to evolve and to try new things. Wearing my collections, a woman will always feel fashionable and appropriate.

How does the design process begin for you? Do you begin with a theme or some form of inspiration, a silhouette, or a recently discovered can't-live-without fabric?

❯ For me, it is a variety of things. The times I've done themes have been the most unsuccessful, because it seems forced. I like the collection to be cohesive. There is always real data that we look at. I'll look at what did well last year and the year before that: what colors sold, what things were too early. And then I look at what I feel is changing. I look at vintage and my own personal vintage by shopping my own closet. And then I revamp and rework them. I do a tremendous amount of fabric research, but I have to work on silhouette and fabric at the same time. A lot has to do with what the fabric market is offering now. We also listen to our stores' needs.

What advice would you give to an aspiring fashion designer who is trying to launch his or her own collection?

❭ Having done it two or three times, one of the really important things is you must know how to make a garment, how to construct it, drape it, sew it, and everything about it. There are so many great vehicles for getting advice. As an aspiring designer, you can go to the CFDA and speak to so many organizations to gain mentorship. You must have a good lawyer and a good accountant before you begin. Don't try to be everything to everyone. If you look at a Michael Kors garment, you know it's Michael Kors; the same holds true with Marc Jacobs and Donna Karan. It has to make a statement. Nobody is going to buy your clothes and promote them if you don't stand for something. It has to have a look. Having a great logo is quite useful as time goes on. For Phoebe Couture, people fell in love with our label before they fell in love with the clothes. Start with online selling before you go to the department stores, because they buy small quantities and your clothes get automatic exposure, and you don't get markdowns. It is a fabulous way to sell.

As a fashion designer with a namesake collection, you partner with your executive management team and creative heads to ensure that all the steps of developing and selling a collection—such as design, technical design, merchandising, visual presentation, quality control, public relations, sales, and marketing— are successfully implemented. How do you manage this process with your staff?

Resort 2012 Kay Unger Floral Printed Gown. PHOTOGRAPHY BY *STYLEEXPO*, 2012.

❭ This is the biggest challenge. Designers are never taught how to run a business, how to be a boss, how to run a team, unless they've gone to business school. Business coaching is extremely important. I have a head of each design team, each reporting in to me. The hardest thing is to keep in touch with everyone, and delegating and letting people make their own mistakes once I've guided them. That's part of my philosophy. It's not easy because I travel a lot. You have to communicate and talk to each other all the time.

You spend a large percentage of your time interacting with your customers through in-store appearances. Please describe what role you play with them.

❭ I go into the dressing room with my customers 90 percent of the time so I see exactly what's going on.

I have an incredible relationship with my customers. I respect them, I am designing for them, so if I don't connect with them, I can't design what they want.

What role does social media play in the promotion of your brand and in staying close to your customer base?

❯ It plays a huge part, and it is hugely successful. We don't have a public relations department, we do it ourselves. The customers love it when we post photos of what we're doing and tips we offer. It is an easy vehicle for showing things quickly, rather than having to update an entire website. I wish I could write a blog. You can see an instant response from your customers—it's really great.

Among your many recognitions, in 1999, you were inducted into the prestigious organization Leading Women Entrepreneurs of the World. Ten years later, in 2009, you were recognized by the City of Hope National Medical Center (a cancer treatment facility) as Woman of the Year for your contributions to your profession, community, and various charitable causes. What did it feel like to receive such high honors?

❯ Honors are always wonderful. It acknowledges the hard work you've done and recognizes you. The best part is that it has allowed me to move forward with my philanthropic endeavors. You can help people immediately, and I love being able to do that.

In 2007, you began opening Kay Unger and Phoebe Couture boutiques in China through a licensing agreement with the JT Group of Hong Kong. Asia has become such an emerging and prominent retail market for the apparel industry. Are there plans for continued expansion throughout Asia?

❯ Yes. Within this year, we opened two stores in Seoul, Korea, which has been hugely successful. It is an easier market than China. We have a franchise model that works really well. It looks like we will be expanding to Toronto next.

In 2008, Kay Unger New York Eyewear and Phoebe Couture Eyewear were launched. Please explain why you decided to expand into the eyewear category.

❯ Licensing is interesting. Sometimes it is successful and sometimes it is not. It all depends on the company with which you are working. The purpose of licensing is to get your name out there and to add to your brand a product that you think your customer would like. We do not sell in department stores, but rather in doctors' offices all over the world and in stores like Sam's and Costco. We make glasses for all nationalities. Each nationality has a differently shaped face, so it gets very interesting. We do teen wear as well; it's fascinating.

Kay Unger New York and the Phoebe collections are sold in more than 20 countries, including the U.K., Turkey, Brazil, Australia, and Canada. The Kay Unger New York line is sold at fine specialty retailers, including Neiman Marcus, Saks Fifth Avenue, Nordstrom, Bloomingdale's, and Lord & Taylor. What advice would you give to an aspiring fashion designer who is pounding away at the pavement trying to land his or her first retail account?

❯ There are many stores that will help young designers, for example, Opening Ceremony. Make sure you get paid up front once you deliver the product; otherwise, you won't ever get paid. Look for stores and websites that sell your look. They are all looking for new merchandise, and they all love the idea of somebody new, providing you can show them you can deliver.

You have dressed several celebrities, among them Oprah Winfrey, Vanessa Williams, Tyra Banks, Angela Bassett, and Marcia Cross.

Spring 2012 Kay Unger 3/4 Sleeve Lace Sheaths. PHOTOGRAPHY BY STYLE*EXPO*, 2012.

Being able to obtain a celebrity clientele is the highlight of any fashion designer's career. What are some of the ways in which you get connected to celebrities in order to dress them?

❯ A stylist will call, or we will start to notice that everyone is wearing our clothing on television. So we'll pick up the phone and call their stylists and discuss ways in which we can offer our clothing for them to borrow to wear to different events, and now we dress everyone on the *Today* show. I am on the Democratic National Committee and have had some introductions that way. I was really excited when I dressed Tipper Gore for the gala the night before the presidential election. Tipper's assistant called and asked to come to the showroom with her and their entourage, including the secret service. We wound up doing the inaugural gown, as well, and her mother-of-the-bride dress for her daughter Karenna's wedding. I've also dressed Hillary

Clinton. Oprah's stylist called me up for one of our red velvet embroidered pants for the cover of her *O, the Oprah* magazine, holiday issue.

In addition, your designs have been featured on the actresses starring in television programs including **Gossip Girl, The Sopranos, Ugly Betty, Pushing Daisies, 30 Rock, Two and a Half Men, Today, Sex and the City, Tim Gunn's Guide to Style,** *and* **Dancing with the Stars.** *Do you have established relationships with stylists who personally request your clothing for TV show placement?*

❯ Yes. We get calls from the stylists who request clothing for the television shows they work for, and we loan out pieces from our collection. We are not vigilant about it and can certainly grow that aspect of our business.

Fall 2012 Kay Unger Sequin Shift Dresses. PHOTOGRAPHY BY STYLE*EXPO*, 2012.

What did it mean to you to be inducted into the Council of Fashion Designers of America (CFDA)?

❭ There was an organization called Designers of America that Stan Herman, Liz Claiborne, Art Ortenberg, a few other designers and I started that eventually grew into the CFDA. It's a real honor to be a member, as it's a great organization. They do things that mean something, and they really help a lot of people in becoming a fashion designer.

You serve on the board of directors of your alma mater, Parsons The New School for Design. You have been a longstanding member of the Boys & Girls Clubs of America, of which you also served as the first woman board member. Your passion for women's causes led to you becoming a board and founding member of The Committee of 200, an organization that advances women's leadership in business, and the Women's Campaign Forum (WCF), an organization dedicated to advancing the political participation and leadership of women who support reproductive health choices for all. Please describe what led you to pursue philanthropic efforts for these organizations.

❭ My family taught me when I was young. For some reason, I have always liked helping and got a tremendous amount of pleasure out of running fund-raisers. I think a lot of it comes from your upbringing.

How do you achieve balance between your career and personal life?

❭ It's hard. The hardest part is doing this and trying to have a personal relationship. You need a partner who feels great about themselves, and they must be passionate about what they do in their life. If he doesn't respect the passion I have, then it doesn't work. You do not want a needy partner.

Do you have a favorite quote?

❭ "Friendship with oneself is all important because without it, one cannot be friends with anyone else in the world." — Eleanor Roosevelt.

Describe the ultimate perfect day for you.

❭ A perfect workday for me is a day when it is not daylight savings time and it stays light longer, and when I've managed to get to bed early enough the night before that I can wake up early, like 5:00 or 5:30 am. I do Pilates with a trainer in my home in Soho and make myself breakfast or meet someone for a quick breakfast. I am happiest when I am able to come to work fully prepared for whatever it is that I want to do, and things are more on schedule. I happen to love a day working with buyers, and I love the days when I am doing a personal appearance. I love when I can leave at a decent hour and then meet friends or family for a fun, late dinner or show or movie screening. My perfect weekend day is getting up early and walking around the city. I love going to Noho and the West Village and, if I do go uptown, Central Park, the museums, and Madison Avenue. I also like entertaining a lot.

Embracing the World of Fashion

Karl Lagerfeld once said, "Fashion is ephemeral, dangerous and unfair." It takes a certain personality to be able to survive and thrive in the fashion industry. The most accomplished people who work in fashion adapt to change, are politically savvy, work hard, dress the part, possess a passion for what they do, and, as Sir Winston Churchill once said, "Never never never give up." While some things can be learned, you'll be on the right track if these traits are already a part of your persona. If they aren't integral to how you operate, quickly jump on the bandwagon to incorporate them into your everyday work ethic, because they are the key to helping you excel and rise to the top of your fashion game. You can spend your days wishing the industry functioned differently or wondering why the people aren't a little more tame or sane, but at the end of the day, this is quite simply the way the industry ticks. The following are techniques that will help you fit into the inner workings of the world of fashion:

Chado Ralph Rucci Fall/Winter 2012 Ready-to-Wear Collection. Barguzine Sable Coat, Black Leather Shell and Black Cashmere Skirt. PHOTOGRAPHERS: DAN AND CORINA LECCA. COURTESY OF CHADO RALPH RUCCI.

Thrive in a fast-paced environment. Just as quickly as styles go in and out of fashion, so does the tempo of everyday work life. It's fast and furious, and you have to roll with the punches to keep up. Things get done at supersonic speed, especially during crunch times, such as market or fashion week. Some people get thrown by the pace, but you will be expected to work effectively under these conditions. This means time managing like there's no tomorrow, taking initiative, and making quick decisions without much contemplation, question asking, or hand holding. You'll need to multitask under strict deadlines, troubleshoot hard-to-solve issues, and tap into resources without delay, all on a moment's notice. Your tenacity will be tested over and over again, which may become overwhelming. However, this will likely wind up becoming a confidence booster, setting a foundation for your future success.

Always pitch in, with a wink and a smile. Enough emphasis cannot be placed on the importance of doing whatever it takes to get the job done. Nike's tag line, "*Just do it,*" fits perfectly into this scenario. I know that being a team player sounds cliché, but it has and always will be highly regarded and expected. If everyone is under the gun prepping for the fashion show, and your manager asks you to make 100 color copies of a look, jump right in and help out. When company-wide lay-offs are happening en masse, you may just be spared a termination if you continuously pitched in, with a "can-do," positive attitude.

Autumn/Winter 2012 New Choicez Collection.
PRODUCTION: MERLIN PENGEL AT BLACK PEPPER,
AMSTERDAM. HAIR AND MAKE-UP: BARBRA OLIEMANS.
MODEL: NATASHA ROGER FROM D&A MODEL
MANAGEMENT. PHOTOGRAPHER: GIOVANNI MARTINS.

Acclimate to the corporate culture. Work cultures vary from company to company and job to job. Equally important to fulfilling your job responsibilities is the notion of fitting into the corporate work environment. Patrick Montana and Bruce Charnov define corporate culture in their book, *Management*, as "the character of an organization since it embodies the vision of the company's founders. It is the total sum of the values, customs, traditions and meanings that make a company unique." The corporate culture is usually dictated by company history, brand heritage, and senior management, with the expectation that employees will follow certain standards of behavior and organizational norms. It includes aspects of work life such as how meetings are conducted, how coworkers communicate with each other, and the expectations of employees (e.g., volunteering). An easy way to adapt to the corporate culture is to look around and observe how people function in various circumstances, and mimic their behavior. Do most people leave at 6:00 pm, or do they stay later? You can also pick up on the sense of the work culture from reading the employee manual (if available), perusing the company website, studying the tone of marketing materials, and asking the advice of your colleagues.

Remain curious. Being inquisitive about virtually everything enables you to learn more, which can help you progress faster in your career. When you're curious, you tend to encounter new experiences that stimulate your mind and keep you motivated. Curiosity feeds one's inner creativity, a crucial trait in fashion design positions. It drives you to dig deeper and stretch your mind.

Have *Bon Chic, Bon Genre*. Literally translated, it means "good style, good attitude," and it is a French phrase used primarily on the streets of Paris. Style, to me, is not just how you look and how you dress, but how you live. Style defines your own, unique lifestyle, and when you incorporate an all-encompassing sense of style into your attitude—how you work, how you live and how you treat others—you create a positive aura around you, which can be wonderfully invigorating.

Bottom-line it. When it comes to communicating with your colleagues, higher-ups, and executive management, it is best to be concise and to the point, unless an explicitly detailed explanation is required or specifically requested. This is true when it comes to both verbal and written communications. Get your point across as quickly as possible when giving design presentations and compiling spreadsheets, documents, and e-mails. Think through how you want to articulate your talking points (the main points of what you are communicating). Given the quick pace of this

Epic editorial for Master's of Art degree at the London College of Fashion. STYLIST: JASON PATRICK CARVALHO. MODEL: IGNAS JUKSEVICIUS FOR M+P MODELS. PHOTOGRAPHER: GIOVANNI MARTINS.

industry, you'll find people are more concerned with the bottom line (the "what") and less interested in the precise details (the "how").

Possess grace under pressure. Do you have a tendency to have a meltdown every time the going gets tough? Pressure comes in many forms, from finalizing the collection to dressing a celebrity for an awards show with very little lead time. It's how you handle it that makes all the difference. When those stress-inducing, anxiety-filled moments creep up on you, just breathe! If you are not naturally good at reacting in this way, it is worth your time to practice so it becomes habitual. The key is to try to avoid what I call "crisis overload." Additionally, in a world where short deadlines are king, preparation and speedy decision making without much contemplation are the secrets to maintaining resiliency. You'll especially find this helpful during the 11th hour of trying to finalize a project, when papers are flying, people are running around frantically, and everyone is under the gun.

Communicate your point of view. You will often be asked your opinion about a certain silhouette, color-way, look, fabric, advertisement, or design. If you are unsure or other-wise ambiguous and answer with a neither-here-nor-there, "I don't know" or "I'm not sure," it will not allow your supervisor and colleagues to develop a trust in your competence, understanding of the brand image, and most importantly, your personal aesthetic. Confidently expressing your perspective on things is a truly good thing in the fashion world.

Illustrated by Izak Zenou for Henri Bendel. COURTESY OF IZAK ZENOU.

AUTHOR'S INSIGHT

While working for a runway designer in New York, part of my job was to fulfill special client orders. One particularly hectic day, our celebrity relations manager came rushing into my office, and shouted, "We need to select her fabric for the awards show and we only have one day to get the dress made!" He was in such a frenzy that he forgot to mention the important details: who the dress was for and why it was needed. An immediate calm came over me, and I serenely asked, "For whom and for what?" Within 10 minutes, I had selected a super-gorgeous deep sapphire blue silk crinkle chiffon fabric for Terri Hatcher's gown for the Emmy Awards. Various discussions ensued and he came back into my office, now slightly calmer, and indicated that the fabric was perfect, but that the color needed to be sky blue. With my innate sense of color intact, I insisted that it remain sapphire blue. The media praised Ms. Hatcher's gown choice that evening, and I remained true to my personal aesthetic.

Autumn/Winter 2012 Emma Griffiths Collection. STYLIST: RACHEL ANTHONY GREEN. HAIR AND MAKE-UP: NEIL GOGOI. MODEL: SKYE VICTORIA. PHOTOGRAPHER: GIOVANNI MARTINS.

Lead. In every field and industry today, leadership continues to be one of the most sought-after qualities of an employee. By taking charge, recommending solutions to challenges your department faces, and implementing new procedures that improve work-flow efficiency, you'll come out the front-runner and will impress those around you, allowing people to see they can count on you to produce at an above-and-beyond level.

Rely on your sense of humor. If you can laugh when things get insane, you'll be far better off than your catastrophe-seeking counterparts. Scientific studies have shown that laughter has many health benefits, including lowering our blood pressure and boosting our immune system, which leads to an ability to think more clearly. Being able to laugh under a high degree of stress allows you to focus on the big picture with a more lighthearted approach and, in turn, to problem-solve better.

Be a self-promoter. Don't be afraid to let others know just how fabulous you are, but do so in carefully measured doses. After all, who really wants to be around people who are constantly boasting about how well-received their fashion illustration was or how elated they were that their design concept was implemented? However, in any competitive environment, it is imperative to make your accomplishments known to the people who can make a difference in your career progression.

Don't take things personally. Take an assortment of people, with an array of personalities, com-ing from a variety of backgrounds, and put them all together in a high-pressure environment, and

Chado Ralph Rucci Fall/Winter 2012 Ready-to-Wear Collection. Black Silk Velvet Leopard and Leather Coat. PHOTOGRAPHERS: DAN AND CORINA LECCA. COURTESY OF CHADO RALPH RUCCI.

you have the recipe for potentially bad behavior. Unless it becomes a habit, try to let it go and take it for what it is worth, which is basically a misdirected lash-out.

Live, breathe, eat, sleep and think fashion relentlessly. Through the thick and the thin and the ups and the downs, the people who choose to let fashion encompass their everyday mode of thinking tend to be the most successful. It is crucial to stay current with industry trends by reading fashion magazines, books, newspapers, and fashion-related websites. You should also watch award shows, paying close attention to what and who the celebrities are wearing, especially if your company dressed one of the presenters, nominees, or attendees. Be cognizant of what is going on around you. Look at the visual displays of store windows to stay aware of up-and-coming fashion designers and trends.

Many specialty stores such as New York–based Barneys, Bergdorf Goodman, Henri Bendel, and Saks Fifth Avenue; Dallas, Texas–based Neiman Marcus; London-based Harrods and Selfridges; Paris-based Galeries Lafayette; Galleria Department Store in Seoul, Korea; and Siam Paragon in Bangkok, Thailand, are known for their on-trend store displays and merchandise. Research their online websites and visit the actual stores if you are near any of these epicenters. Subscribe to international trend reports, read about the latest trends in trade publications, and review the various runway reports. Be aware of current events and various economic and political events across the world, as they have an influence on fashion trends. Attend fashion trade shows showing the latest in fabric trends and designs. It is important to possess explicit insight into the fashion world, on both a domestic and global scale. See the Appendix for a complete list of fashion resources.

Figure things out autonomously. Overall, there is a *"baptism by fire"* approach in the

Illustrated by Izak Zenou, Personal Collection, 2011. COURTESY OF IZAK ZENOU.

fashion industry. Working in fashion design, usually entails very little orientation or training, with an inherent expectation that you will complete your tasks on your own, ask few questions, and teach yourself the tricks of the trade. And yes, that does mean through trial-and-error. Some companies, however, do provide on-the-job training and/or orientation sessions, especially if you are working for a large corporation (such as Ralph Lauren Corporation or Limited Brands, most famous for its Victoria's Secret brand) or for a retailer in an executive training program (e.g., a buyer, planner, or merchandiser at Macy's). However, as a general rule, there is an expectation that you will tap into the proper resources and do your best to get your tasks done on your own.

Shift gears on a dime. The fashion industry naturally breeds a constantly changing environment, and it is important to be amenable to these changes. Very often, you will be asked to drop everything in order to help out on a task that takes precedence. Don't think twice about it; the ability to switch gears is just a natural part of the design process. People like to work with people who are flexible, people who say, "Sure—no problem" when asked to do a task.

An Interview with Pamella Roland, Fashion Designer

Fashion designer Pamella DeVos of Pamella Roland.
PHOTOGRAPHER: NIGEL BARKER, 2011.

Was there a pivotal moment in your childhood, upbringing, or at some point in your life that led you to pursue a career in fashion design?

❯ I wouldn't say when I was young I knew I wanted to be a fashion designer, but fashion was always an interest of mine. I was voted "Best Dressed" in high school. I would love to sit and watch my mother get ready. My mother always had great taste and beautiful clothes and she had the most gorgeous swing coats in the 1960s. I started working at a clothing store during high school and throughout my college years. During college, I was in an art program, but my father had pushed me to study business, which I did. When I reached my forties, I always thought I was missing something by not being in fashion. It was something I always wanted to do, and I knew I needed to make the jump, which I did.

Prior to launching your collection, you worked in marketing and public relations. Had you gained any fashion design experience prior to launching your label?

❯ I started in public relations and marketing for my family's business, which gave me the confidence and guts to launch my own collection. However, I did not have any fashion design experience prior to launching my own label.

Spring 2012 Pamella Roland Runway Collection.
PHOTOGRAPHER: NIGEL BARKER, 2011.

Fashion designer Pamella DeVos of Pamella Roland.
PHOTOGRAPHER: NIGEL BARKER, 2011.

In just your second year of operation, you received the 2003 Gold Coast Award, and in 2010, you were inducted into the Council of Fashion Designers of America (CFDA). Most fashion designers are unable to rise to this level of success in such a short period of time. What was it like to receive these honors?

❯ I will never forget when we won the Gold Coast Award. I screamed so loudly when I found out. The same holds true with the CFDA award. It meant a lot to me to be inducted. I was so thrilled and so excited to be a part of this group because you know you've made it with your peers once you are inducted.

How does the design process begin for you? Do you begin with a theme or some form of inspiration, a silhouette, or a recently discovered can't-live-without fabric?

❯ Most of the time, it starts with fabric (what we are known for), and I really love the fabric selection process. And then I work from there.

Being able to obtain a celebrity clientele is the highlight of any fashion designer's career. How did this come about?

❯ Actress Megan Mullally wore one of our black lace dresses when she was starring in the hit television show *Will and Grace* (her stylist requested it). Actress Kim Cattrall was up for an Emmy and we just had a fashion show the day before, when her stylist, (who was in attendance at our show) requested it. The Emmys were the very next day. You never know if the actress is actually going to wear the dress, and I started screaming when I saw Kim walking the red carpet wearing my dress. She

Fashion Designer Pamella DeVos of Pamella Roland.
PHOTOGRAPHER: NIGEL BARKER, 2011.

really worked that dress, and the next day it was in magazines all around the world. It was incredible publicity for us.

What role does social media play in the promotion of your brand and in staying close to your customer base?

❯ It plays a big part. I was urged by my daughters to get involved. I am getting better at Twitter, and we know it is very important and it is getting even more important. In fact, I was not aware that Carrie Ann Inaba, the judge on the ABC television show *Dancing with the Stars* was wearing one of my dresses on the show until she tweeted it to me. It was so incredible to have found out that way. We also have a Facebook page. My good friend, fashion photographer Nigel Barker got me started on creating a blog and pushed me into various social media outlets as well.

What advice would you give an aspiring fashion designer trying to launch his or her own collection?

❯ You have to really love it passionately and live it and breathe it. You have to go into it because it is something that you love. Don't go into it because you want to be famous, because that is really difficult. Sometimes the younger designers come in and think they can be famous overnight; it's very unrealistic. You better love it and you better know that it can be 24/7. You get zero sleep during fashion week. You work during the night, and you are on the phone with media even when you are at home. If you are going for the glamour of it, you are not going to make it.

Spring 2012 Pamella Roland Advertising Campaign.
PHOTOGRAPHER: NIGEL BARKER, 2011.

You are known for playing a major role in every facet of your business, from design to final approvals to hiring staff to public relations. How do you manage this process with such limited time on your hands?

❯ I need to learn to let go a little bit. I am kind of a control freak—after all, my name is on the door. But I am getting better. It's hard to have that trust, which is why I have a hand in everything. I fire quicker than I used to, if I know someone is just not working.

You run your own fashion design firm and are married with three children—certainly an inspiration to people everywhere. How do you balance it all?

❯ In the very beginning, it was not easy. I was constantly working. But my husband and I have an agreement that when he is traveling, I stay home, and vice versa, so either one of us is always with our children. But now our kids are 25, 21, and 15, so it's much easier.

Describe the ultimate perfect day for you.

❯ We have a summer home in Northern Michigan and I love it up there. There is nothing better than a beautiful summer day on Lake Michigan. We have a boat, and we love to have friends and family around. It is absolutely one of the most beautiful places in the world. It was recently voted #1 spot in the world by *Good Morning America*.

An Interview with Deborah Lloyd, Chief Creative Officer and President of Kate Spade New York

Deborah Lloyd, chief creative officer and president of Kate Spade New York. PHOTOGRAPHER: ANDERS OVERGAARD. COURTESY OF KATE SPADE NEW YORK.

Was there a pivotal moment in your childhood, upbringing, or at some point in your life that led you to pursue a career in fashion design?

❯ I was always intrigued by clothes and national costume, and it really crystallized when I was sixteen years old during high school.

What university did you attend for your fashion design program?

❯ In order to qualify in the United Kingdom, you have to do a foundation course. I did my foundation course at Plymouth College of Art and Design in Plymouth, England, which was a year's study in everything from design to graphics, sculpture, and photography, so that you could really decide what path to take. Even though I knew it was fashion, I still had to go through it. I then earned a bachelor's degree in fashion design from the Ravensbourne College of Art and Design. Then I earned a two years' master's degree in fashion design at the Royal College of Art in London, in which I graduated with distinction.

Please describe some of the positions you held leading up to your current role as chief creative officer and president of Kate Spade New York.

❭ My first job out of college was with Byblos, which was the hottest brand at the time. I was invited to be the assistant to the designer in Italy. My second job was with Daniel Hester in Paris, and my third job was with Kenzo in Paris. After that, I went to Aquascutum, the British brand, and then I had my big break at Burberry in London. After Burberry, I moved to America and became the creative director at Banana Republic.

Since your arrival at Kate Spade New York, the transition has been seamless. How did you prepare for your current position?

❭ All of the past brands I've worked on have had a very strong brand message. I cut my teeth at Burberry and always went to brands where I thought something big was going to happen. In preparation for this role, I pooled together my experiences from Burberry where I learned about brand building and brand message, and from Banana Republic, where I learned how to lead a team to get everyone on the same page. The amount of work needed to make it a seamless transition was a huge undertaking.

What is your design philosophy?

❭ Do what you love. This has always worked for me.

Fall 2012 Kate Spade New York collection illustrated by Deborah Lloyd. COURTESY OF KATE SPADE NEW YORK.

How does the design process begin for you? Do you begin with a theme or some form of inspiration, a silhouette, or a recently discovered can't-live-without fabric?

❭ Each season can be slightly different. It can be a color I keep seeing, a silhouette I have seen or the most gorgeous pair of leather gloves I picked up at a flea market. So many things can spark off inspiration: a story, a film, a book. It's important to have an open mind, and these things come to you. It's hard to pinpoint how it happens, as it's more organic rather than structured, but you then have to put the structure into it. The ideas can come from anywhere.

Being able to obtain a celebrity clientele is the highlight of any fashion designer's career. How did this generally come about for the company?

❯ As we launched apparel, it became much more obvious to people what our brand was about. From Beyoncé to Eva Longoria and Anne Hathaway, we've been fortunate to dress a lot of celebrities. Our first celebrity face for our campaign was Bryce Dallas Howard (Ron Howard's daughter). She was an amazing brand fan. The day we contacted her she had just received a shipment of Kate Spade china for her home. Usually it comes about when stylists approach us. They like what they see in our collections, and they find the perfect things for their clients.

What role does social media play in the promotion of the Kate Spade New York brand and in staying close to your customer base?

❯ It's been huge and we've received so many accolades this year in terms of social media. I work with an amazing team that are of a certain age, and it is so natural for them and they love it. We have an amazing dialogue with our customer base, which allows us to keep really close to them. I went on a trip to Sonoma and we got so many comments about my trip, all in the Kate Spade spirit. They love the interaction and they certainly tell us what they think about things.

What advice would you give an aspiring fashion designer trying to launch his or her own collection?

❯ Stay true to yourself and own your own look and stay constant. That is what I've learned by building brands. You have to figure out how you can cut through and be different from everyone else and stick to it.

Holiday 2011 Kate Spade New York Bow Bridge Little Kennedy Bag. COURTESY OF KATE SPADE NEW YORK.

Your company blog, "Behind the Curtain" is fantastic! It really enables people to get a behind-the-scenes feel for what you do every day and gives the public a true sense of what inspires you. Describe how it came into being and what prompted you to implement it.

❯ It started with a section on our blog which was about the things we love. People would come back to us with comments regarding the things they loved, and a dialogue began. We began posting about things going on in the office, whether it was about somebody's birthday or a trip I was taking to Rwanda. It gives them the inside scoop and people love it. We get a huge reaction when we share what we are doing.

What is your favorite quote?

❯ "Live colorfully." I love color. I love wearing color. I love living in color.

Describe the ultimate perfect day for you.

❯ I love when I have a blank canvas right at the beginning of the collection. When I'm traveling abroad and going to places I have never been, these things will inspire a brand-new collection. My perfect day would have something to do with travel and inspiration.

What Advice Would You Give to an Aspiring Fashion Designer?

❯ Go for it! Be bold in your choices and with your decisions. All of the people that I really admire in this business have boldly pursued their chosen direction. Stay optimistic. The key thing to understand in fashion is that sometimes you will be required to fail numerous times in order to succeed. More pragmatic advice is to choose the right environment in which to study and work.

Kinga Malisz, Womenswear Designer, Prêt-à-porter, Nina Ricci, Paris, France

❯ Experience is essential. Internships teach you many aspects of the process from the basics of how a design office works, to the practicalities and realities of production. It is essential that you make the most of these experiences and be as pro-active as possible (there is nothing that reflects worse on an intern than if they shrug off tasks they are asked to take care of, even if they are menial and feel be-

Spring/Summer 2012 sketch by Ben Stubbington. COURTESY OF BEN STUBBINGTON.

low you). The better the impression you make, the quicker you can jump-start your career. For instance, I have had great interns that I haven't had a position for to hire full-time, but have managed to get them placed in positions in which they are now thriving. Remember, the fashion industry is a very small world and everyone knows everyone or someone that knows someone. You have to show you understand the aesthetic and soul of a brand and designer.

Ben Stubbington, Design Director, Theory, New York, New York, USA

❯ To become a fashion designer, one should be humble and patient. Our profession is based on talent, but foremost on experience. One should have the ability to articulate and express their vision. One must understand the evolution of trends, the nature of fabrics and proportions, bestsellers and key items. Be open to learning new techniques, while learning from mistakes. Accept leadership, direction, and learn key fundamental skills from an experienced designer and follow their guidance. I often compare a fashion designer's growth to a young actor who gets feedback from the director and learns their profession on the stage, judged immediately by the audience. This experience forms character. Be open to a different perspective, always try to push yourself to the next level, be your own motivator, and believe in yourself. Don't allow boundaries or fear to limit your ability to comprehend and aesthetically be able to conceptualize trends and fashion needs.

Bernd Kroeber, Design Director, BCBG Max Azria Group, Los Angeles, California, USA

❯ Knowledge is the most powerful tool, and then comes a willingness to learn. It is important to be curious—watch movies, read books, observe people on the streets. It is so crucial to really love what you do because it is a tough business, especially at the beginning of your career. It is important that you

Sketch entitled, "Romantic Rhythm" by fashion designer Emily Tischler. This collection captures the romance and rhythm of downtown New York City. COURTESY OF EMILY TISCHLER.

have confidence in your abilities, but at the same time, you should be humble and receptive so you can learn from any situation.

Pamela Costantini, Junior Footwear Designer, Roberto Cavalli, Bologna, Italy

❯ The most important advice I could pass on to an aspiring fashion designer is to shoot for the stars when starting out in your career by going to the most high-end company you can. Do not settle at the start of your career for the position that pays the most. Instead, strive for the job that is going to teach you and push you the most. Study abroad. Seeing the world gives you richer inspiration to pull from and trains your mind to be open to new ideas. Tell everyone your goals and ambitions. Stay away from people that don't believe in you. Be inspired by authentic ideas, not other people's work. Always

stay hands-on with your product. Continue to go back to school even after graduating. Never stop improving your skills.

Emily Tischler, Designer, Catherine Malandrino, New York, New York, USA

❯ The first piece of advice I would give is to be humble. You will have a lot to learn. Work overtime. Do things nobody wants to do. Smile and try to learn something from everyone in the office. Looking for a job is a job in itself! Create a résumé that makes you stand out from the crowd. Put your best sketches in your portfolio; an image is worth a thousand words. Learn how to use LinkedIn to get in touch personally with people you wouldn't have the chance to know in other ways.

Arianna Mereu, Freelance Fashion Designer, Max Mara Fashion Group, Reggio Emilia, Italy

What Advice Would You Give to an Aspiring Fashion Designer? (Continued)

❯ When launching your own collection, be careful what you spend and partner with a smart business person. Developing your social skills, friendships, and relationships with key editors and store executives are essential for making it in the business. It is helpful if you can figure out an underserved part of the marketplace. Build your brand on one set idea and slowly expand from there, never losing sight of your own original voice.

Kym Canter, Creative Director, L-atitude, LLC, New York, New York, USA

❯ Don't be snobby about a particular position, just get in and start working. Impress people and build your network. Like anything, you have to put in the years before you can begin designing a collection. Do anything that is asked of you the best you can do it. Take pride in each task.

Ryan Clements, Design Consultant, Belstaff, New York, New York, USA

❯ Never forget why you decided to pursue a fashion design career. You need to have at least two skills in hand to support your career. For example, you need to understand the basic fashion business theories to support your design skills and run your fashion business, and you need to take a communications course to know how to sell your brand. Purely studying fashion design is not enough in today's market!

Jessica Chuan, Fashion Designer, Ghim Li Global, Singapore

❯ The fashion industry is not a 9–5 business and many think it's purely glamorous, but it involves more hard work than you can imagine. Never give up!

Reem Alasadi, Designer/Director, The House of Reem, London, England, United Kingdom and Tokyo, Japan.

❯ The most important thing is to have passion and a love for what you do. Do not waste your time with a job and a team who cannot teach you with

passion. Traveling is very important. Always keep your eyes open and look around your environment and observe. Remember to learn more languages because the fashion field is full of people from different parts of the world and it is important to be able to communicate with them on their level and to learn different cultures and traditions.

Annalisa Caricato, Freelance Accessories Designer, Guess Europe, Neuchatel, Switzerland

"Twisted Oliver" from the Reem Alasadi 2012 Collection shown during Japan Fashion Week, 2011. Dress: Silk with acid drips. Leather gillet with knit sleeves. Hat: Oliver tweed. PHOTOGRAPHER: YOSHIKAZU ENOMOTO.

Autumn/Winter 2012 Tina Lobondi Collection. Designer: Tina Lobondi. MAKE-UP ARTIST: TAMARA TOTT. MODEL: VIKTORIA PRICOVA. PHOTOGRAPHER: MARIAH DO VALE.

❭ Be ready to lose sleep and work hard! A business plan will take you a long way when launching your own collection. You will need it for sponsorship or for a bank that might be able to give you financial support. When times are hard, surround yourself with people that will push you forward, boost your mood, and make you laugh. Good energy is more important than we think.

Tina Lobondi, Founder/CEO, Tina Lobondi Collection, London, England, United Kingdom

❭ Start developing your aesthetic early. Begin with one design at a time and do not let yourself get overwhelmed with the idea of developing an entire collection.

Shari Seidlitz-McCandlish, Creative Director/Owner, Geoni Studios, Los Angeles, California, USA

❭ The advice I would give to an aspiring fashion designer is to persevere. Have your vision and stick with it. It is very easy to get sidetracked in this business. There are so many options, inspirations, and avenues out in the world that sometimes you begin to question your own ideas and creations. It is very important to choose your road and maintain your vision. Trust your gut. There will be endless amounts of decisions to make throughout your journey. There will be a lot of people giving you their opinions. You will make mistakes, and you will learn. Stay on course, and you will eventually achieve your vision.

Laura Dotolo, Principal, clutchbags.com, New York, New York, USA

❭ Take risks, have passion in everything you do, have creative curiosity, and be prepared to work hard to achieve your vision. Don't ever give up, but do, however, learn to take feedback—good, bad, or indifferent. Learn to process the feedback into a learning that leads to success.

Noreen Naz Naroo-Pucci, Senior Creative Director of Apparel, Under Armour, Baltimore, Maryland, USA

❭ Before even thinking about a career in fashion design, it is important to understand that good old-fashioned hard work makes up around 90 percent of the work week. Days are long, and without ambition and a thirst for seeing a product develop from 2D to 3D, the world of design is best left alone. Understanding yourself and what you can offer to a brand is key, as is behaving with integrity and wanting to learn and develop so that you can grow and work to the best of your ability. Professional behavior and keeping a smile on your face, even during difficult times, will benefit you in the long run. Above all, remain true to yourself and trust your instincts, because fashion design is ever-changing.

Paul Austin, Menswear Designer, Gieves & Hawkes, London, England, United Kingdom

What Advice Would You Give to an Aspiring Fashion Designer? (Continued)

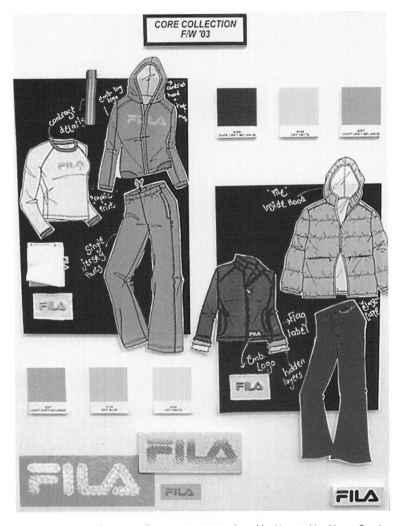

Fall/Winter 2003 Fila Core Collection presentation board by Noreen Naz Naroo-Pucci.
COURTESY OF NOREEN NAZ NAROO-PUCCI ON BEHALF OF FILA.

❯ I would tell an aspiring designer to intern in the area of design where they think they'd like to work. The fashion industry has so many different areas and positions to explore, and the responsibilities can vary greatly from one company to the next. It can be quite eye opening to get a taste of what you *think* you want to do. You may be surprised to find yourself working in a niche of fashion that you may not have even been aware of. Also, don't forget that this is still a business and you need to sell the product in order to be successful.

Nicolette Dennis, Sweater Designer, Minnie Rose, New York, New York, USA

❭ I was sketching glamorous models well before I learned how to write an essay. I always say it's in my blood, part of my DNA, but it takes more than that to become a fashion designer. To know how to analyze and understand your market, to learn how raw materials are made, how to treat and manipulate them in order to create something not only unique, but also practical and cost efficient. The fashion industry is one of the most competitive industries out there, and designers must be aggressive and passionate in order to make a difference. They should be able to access many different resources in order to keep their creativity fresh and on target. Make life their inspirational playground, finding the next "it" item while playing with technology or enjoying a movie, a ballet, or a concert and then be able to interpret their vision into something wearable. One of the most important tools to be successful in any business is to believe in yourself, to believe in your dreams and fight for them. I can recall during my last year of design school how many people told me I was not going to find a job in such a competitive industry. I got tired of getting so much negative feedback about my career choice, and

I told my friends and family, "Tomorrow I will be working for my dream designer, Oscar de la Renta," and they laughed. But I called Oscar de la Renta's showroom and the next day I started the internship there that changed my life.

Betsy Carlo, Design Director, Girls, Squeeze Jeans, New York, New York, USA

❭ Being successful in the fashion industry means finding the right opportunity, and sometimes that means having to be patient. As glamorous as it sounds, it is an extremely hard profession filled with many obstacles and challenges. It is a career as well as a business, and in any business, one needs to develop a thick skin to survive. Many doors will open and many will close, but always remember to be true to yourself, your design aesthetic, and your love of this art. I would tell an aspiring fashion designer to never give up on their dreams no matter what anyone tells you. Aspire to be the greatest at your craft. Being successful will ultimately be determined by you; your diligence, willingness, and motivation will carry you far.

Emileny Gonzalez, Technical Designer, Imports International, Allendale, New Jersey, USA

Back to School 2010 Photo Shoot, Squeeze Jeans. PHOTOGRAPHER: LENNART KNAB. COURTESY OF SQUEEZE JEANS.

What Advice Would You Give to an Aspiring Fashion Designer? (Continued)

❭ Fashion is a business. Art and creativity are key elements to fashion, but so is understanding that these products get manufactured at certain costs and sold at certain prices. Every successful designer has to work with production, sales, and merchandising; it is not just about creating. If a designer understands the industry of production and retail, it can shape and change the manner in which they design and develop in order to create very real, relevant, and saleable work. Another very important piece of advice is to change with the times. For example, a designer who sketches by hand, but has not yet been introduced to CAD, will become outdated with time, so it is important to keep up with the ever-changing technologies.

Alicia Fazio, Managing Partner, fourthFLOOR Fashion, New York, New York, USA

❭ On your rise to conquer fashion stardom, far beyond amazing talent and drive, you must acquire your own unique design work philosophy and ethic and use it as a compass throughout your career to guide you. My design philosophy trifecta consists of faith, excellence, and giving 200 percent effort. As an aspiring fashion designer, you have to look at what you've done today, this week, this month, and this year to set you on your path. For me, in high school, action meant booking the job to design and make the cheerleading uniforms my senior year and sewing every day after school so I could sell my clothes to my classmates. In college, action meant jumping on a train to Soho and selling my designs to boutiques. After college, action meant designing mini-collections each season and motivating my photographer, makeup artist, and hair stylist friends to produce awe-inspiring test shoots, and throwing renegade fashion shows on the steps of Bryant Park in New York. My line appeared in magazines, and soon stylists were using my designs for album covers and shoots for their celebrity artists, which, along with a great deal of faith and many answered prayers,

is how I landed my dream career in Hollywood. There are so many avenues today for aspiring designers to gain experience, exposure, and success; use them all, have faith, take action, and when the doors of the fashion world open, you'll be ready to walk right through. Design everything with excellence and integrity. Whether it's a job that will gain you huge exposure or a job that will end in obscurity, every job deserves to be entered into with the same excitement, enthusiasm, hustle, and inspired forethought. As you navigate through your design path, create solid business relationships with everyone

Red Dalilah "2056 Collection" from the Kara Saun 2006 runway presentation. COURTESY OF KARA SAUN.

who crosses your path. If you give at this level, it will take your fashion career to greater heights.

Kara Saun, Fashion/Costume Designer, Kara Saun, Los Angeles, California, USA

❯ Be strategic. Know who you are as a designer and determine your career path before you apply for your first internship. Identify potential employers and their competitors. Create a strategic plan of companies you will apply to, and tailor your cover letter, résumé, and portfolio to the company's aesthetic. Utilize your existing network to leverage new contacts in a desired place of employment. Build and maintain relationships with fellow students, coworkers, and managers. Always be willing to help anyone in your network who asks, and expect nothing in return. Complete at least one internship and maximize your experience. Learn everything you can, and make as many connections as possible. The most sought-after and successful designers are those who don't complain, work well with others, and focus on doing the work. Don't change jobs every year. Learn to stay in one place for a minimum of three to five years. This will make you more desirable in the long run and provide you with more options when you are ready to make a change. Be humble. No matter how talented you are, remain teachable and listen to others. Express gratitude to those around you.

Dione Katelhut, Executive Director, The Fit, Portland, Oregon, USA

❯ Have patience, be humble, and take criticism well. There's always room for improvement, and you're going to be learning something new when you are open to receiving feedback.

April Oh, Design Director, Line & Dot, Vernon, California, USA

❯ Fashion designing demands creativity, hard work, and an innate ability to define and identify yourself through your work. A passion for fashion trends, both old and new, coupled with a strong theoretical and practical understanding of clothing is essential. Every designer, whether working for their own label or for a brand, needs to be a self-starter. As a designer, always keep a few tools handy—pencils, markers, sketch pens, erasers, scissors, a sketch pad for quick fashion illustrations, a research journal for collecting anything and everything that inspires you, and a good digital camera. Having a pictorial interpretation of your goals in front of you helps you to stay focused and motivated. The struggle is monumental, but the satisfaction you derive when a design comes out just the way you envisioned it is ample reward. Above all, work hard, follow your passion, and keep your eye on the goal at all times. Dream big and start each day with a healthy dose of inspiration.

Supriya Ghurye, Fashion Designer, Fuel4Fashion, Bangalore, India

❯ Be patient, have perseverance, take in what happens in the culture of everyday life, have a critical and constructive mind in order to improve yourself and your work, keep an archive of everything you like, be concise, direct, and as precise as possible when you transmit a thought or an idea, and create an emotion and a philosophy in everything that you design.

Nuncia Ammirata, Freelance Fashion Designer, Florence, Italy

❯ Whether you work for a company or have your own line, you need to know who you are appealing to, and you have to position yourself in the right marketplace. Be a goal-setter and learn from your own mistakes. Be progressive and always remind yourself why you are doing this and stick to your vision. Work with other people if possible to bounce off ideas among the group.

Aram Lee, Creative Director, Kooba, New York, New York, USA

What Advice Would You Give to an Aspiring Fashion Designer? (Continued)

Study of Formation #1, Fall 2011, by Aram Lee. COURTESY
OF ARAM LEE.

❯ As an aspiring fashion designer, you really need
to know the strength of your brand. I always encourage the designer to focus on the quality of the
pieces rather than the quantity of the collection.
I recommend a designer to use a certain element
repeatedly in the collection. It can be a pattern, a
small detail, or a specific color combination. This
way, not only will the audience see a cohesive collection, but this may also help you to develop the
gimmick of your brand (think about the red plastic tag of the Prada *Linea Rossa* line). Also, you
have to know your target market. If you target the
wrong market, you will not be able to create a fan
base. Finally, make sure you have wearable pieces

in your collection. You can have some statement
pieces to show your craftsmanship, but if you have
no wearable pieces to back up your collection, you
may lose a lot of money, and chances are you may
not be able to create your next collection.

*Marcus Kan, Fashion Director, Ukamaku, Toronto,
Canada*

❯ When starting out, you may have a limited budget for everything, but you still have to maximize
opportunities for publicity at fashion events and
to show your product to the press, as well as collaborating with fashion stylists who dress the
celebrities. Don't forget you are designing for your
customer, not for yourself. Marketing is as important as your product. Try to participate in fashion
competitions, as it forces you to design with an aim
in mind. You will not only need creativity, but resil-
ience and an entrepreneurial drive.

*Zuzana Kralova, Creative Director, Kralova Design,
Madrid, Spain, and Prague, Czech Republic*

❯ Capitalize on your ability to be a designer who
understands the commercial aspect of fashion,
while keeping true to your creative self. The
most extravagant and conceptual design may be
beautiful in presentation, but may not generate
the volume needed to be successful in the sales
reports. Become an expert in your area. Research,
practice, ask questions, and remain curious. The
more you know, the more people will recognize
your potential and trust your point of view. Never
stop growing, have fun, and keep an open mind.

*Raquel Caruso, Design Director, Steve Madden, New York,
New York, USA*

❯ Observation, patience, and good research is the
key to the design process. Don't be obsessed with
fashion; instead, get inspired by other things such as
art, music, film, and books. Designing can be done
alone, but finalizing is a collaborative effort. Educate
yourself by listening to others, and be a team player

Spring 2010 watercolor handbag painting by Raquel Caruso. COURTESY OF RAQUEL CARUSO.

if you want to grow in your career. Enjoy what you create. Keep yourself updated with new techniques. Visit fabric fairs and shops. The most important thing is to trust and love your work.

Tugce Ozocak, Designer, Beymen, Istanbul, Turkey

❯ Learn the business side of your industry, as it is important to understand how the business operates from a product development, sourcing, and costing perspective. Learn how to make your designs commercial. Understand your target consumer and their product expectations. How is your product positioned in the market, including price point? Who is your competition? Learn to sketch with accuracy and speed. Know your target distribution and what they expect from supply partners.

Michael Beckwith, Founder, Encore Jobz, Blufton, South Carolina, USA

❯ The best advice I received was from an influential college professor during a project critique. She told

the class to always be ready to defend your designs. This still applies to me every day. As a designer you will have to present and explain your concepts and designs to numerous people to make them believe and be part of your vision. You must be ready to answer any questions and make others understand your point of view and aesthetic. A fashion designer must be able to clearly communicate ideas to various people, including the design team so they can execute the designs, the production team who will make them into real garments, the sales team who will sell the product, and the customers who will buy it.

Connie Byun, Women's Outerwear Designer, Outerwear Company, New York, New York, USA

❯ Stay true to your vision, but also stay informed of the trends, economy, and pop culture. Work in the industry for three to four years with another company before launching your own collection (learn before it's your money on the line). Be prepared for how costly a fashion business is to start. Get a plan of action in mind, but don't be afraid to go off the beaten path. Fashion is about change, and there's no reason your process needs to be formulaic. Get a foothold in the marketplace and grow from there. Start small, think big.

Rachel Rose, Owner/Designer, Rachel Rose Designs, Brooklyn, New York, USA

❯ Be open-minded with a humble attitude, and show desire and willingness to learn in every situation. For example, your boss may send you to pick up samples or ask you to make copies. While not glamorous, it's important to learn about every part of the process. Do your best not to take criticism personally. Criticism is always a part of the job, and it doesn't mean other people don't like you. At the same time, you need to have your own point of view when doing your job. Present yourself with confidence when your boss gives you an assignment, and ask for guidance when you are unsure of next steps.

Mina Cha, Accessory Design Manager, Milly, New York, New York, USA

What Advice Would You Give to an Aspiring Fashion Designer? (Continued)

90 degree silk top from the "Square Collection" by Rachel Rose. PHOTOGRAPHER: CLAIRE BENOIST, 2011.

❯ Go to fashion school and get industry experience. Intern or work in the fashion business as much as possible during college. Hands-on experience and making personal connections is invaluable. Try to experience working for companies with different business models, as you may find that you enjoy working for a small, emerging designer label or prefer a fast-paced corporate environment. The more you know about sales, marketing, and the entire business, the better. Get inspired! Travel as much as you can, and don't forget about cultivating your own sense of style.

Sue Stemp, Designer/Owner, Sue Stemp, Los Angeles, California, USA

❯ Everything starts by having a dream, a passion, and a goal. Talent is a good ingredient, but it takes more than just talent to make it as a designer. You have to stand for your dreams, no matter what people say or think about you, your work, or your vision. The challenge is to find ways to integrate your own signature into the work opportunities you get.

Remember to stay humble. Don't focus too much on the superficial side, the prestige, what others say or do. Take every opportunity to develop your skills, to learn about the world and about yourself. And mostly, live for your passion!

Halewijn Bulckaen, Print Designer, H&M, Stockholm, Sweden

❯ Shoes and bags are accessories and therefore must be utilitarian, as well as compelling. No matter what your point of view on fashion, the product must be well made for the asking price, and you, as a designer, must understand the manufacturing process used to make your product. You should be knowledgeable about materials and components. You should be able to write all the specifications for your product and give all the measurements. Drawing skills are a plus, but today, computers can achieve a more neutral form of sketch and can be a better way to begin the process. All your designs should fit today's lifestyle and be relevant in today's context. You are designing for life, not a film.

Jamie Lawenda, Vice President of Design, 2568 Shoes/ Sendra Boots, New York, New York, USA

❯ Brace yourself for high stress and late nights. You may find your work will consume 80 percent of your life. Make it work for you and find a good support system.

Jenny Lew, Freelance Handbags/Accessories Designer, New York, New York, USA

❯ Be patient, persistent, and stay humble. It is also very important to observe and absorb information from designers that surround you and, in turn, develop your own skills based on their successes or by avoiding their mistakes.

Stella Vakirli, Vice President of Men's Outerwear, Weatherproof, New York, New York, USA

❯ Be true to who you are as a designer and always be open to learning.

Leila Tadros, Freelance Design Director, various companies, New York, New York, and San Francisco, California, USA

❯ As a designer, you must learn to deliver your creativity and aesthetics into a successful product that fits your target market and your business model. The product should always be aligned with the values of the company.

Monet Lugo, Senior Fashion Designer, Guess, Los Angeles, California, USA

❯ You will need all your strengths and passion to succeed. Be ready to compromise. It is a very personal path you are taking. It is essential to have a network, as you never know who will give you your next job. It is important for a fashion designer to communicate well and to succeed in expressing designs in a clear and simple way. Learn to be patient.

Amélia Teniere Buchot, Head Designer, Inditex, Barcelona, Spain

Finding Balance

The demands of working in the fashion industry can take a toll on even the most unflustered designer. Since the fashion industry is especially high-pressure, being able to find a sense of calm in the rush-rush pace can sometimes be tricky. Being able to maintain balance in your daily routine makes all the difference in the world to help you keep your creative energy flowing, keep your stress level in check, and keep you positive and happy. Whether that means taking an early morning yoga class, strolling through the park after work, reading a book while drinking your favorite iced-coffee, or setting aside time to quiet your mind, it's a good idea to find a plan that works for you, specifically one that can easily become a part of your everyday routine.

When you live your life in balance, I believe you can succeed at anything you set your mind to, whether it means becoming a creative director for your favorite couture label or taking the plunge to launch your own eponymous collection.

Illustrated by Izak Zenou for Henri Bendel.
COURTESY OF IZAK ZENOU.

"The Fashionista Girls" illustrated by
Izak Zenou for Henri Bendel, 2009.
COURTESY OF IZAK ZENOU.

2 The Education for a Fashion Design Career

I don't design clothes, I design dreams.

—Ralph Lauren

Choosing a Collegiate Educational Program

Fashion design is more than just glamorous runway shows and celebrity dressing. It requires an in-depth understanding of design construction, technique, form, and proportion, as well as knowledge of business operations and consumer behavior. Some of the most famous and successful fashion designers did not obtain a formal fashion design education and instead started their collection because they had an innovative idea or could not find a particular product in the market. However, they represent the exception, and it is still of utmost importance to obtain an education because a fashion designer is, by and large, required to hold an undergraduate degree in fashion design to be considered for a job opportunity. Most employers seek individuals who hold a minimum of a four-year fashion design degree. By earning a degree, you will not only make yourself more marketable to hiring managers, but will learn the ins and outs of the craft that will prepare you for your future job as a fashion designer.

Those who plan to one day launch their own collection can benefit from earning a combined degree in fashion design and fashion marketing or a business major, such as business management. Since business knowledge is such an integral part of being a successful fashion designer, it is a good idea to supplement your fashion design studies with business-centered courses such as business principles, fashion marketing, and merchandising.

In determining which school to attend, there are both accredited and nonaccredited schools from which to choose. The National Association of Schools of Art and Design (NASAD) serves as the national accrediting agency for over 300 design and art schools across the United States. A listing of these schools, as well as the degree programs offered can be found on their website. Additionally, the Accrediting Council for Independent Colleges and Schools (ACICS) is recognized by both the U.S. Department of Education and the Council for Higher Education Accreditation for institutions offering degrees from the associate level through to a master's degree. Colleges, universities, and schools accredited by the ACICS are required to maintain high standards in terms of faculty credentials and student placement and retention. For a list of accredited schools, go to www.acics.org.

Undergraduate Education

A fashion design program trains students in the fundamentals of fashion design and teaches students to create fashions using a global point of view. Choosing an educational program for your college education is a personal process involving a variety of factors, including location, program ranking, accreditation status, internship program, well-known designer alumni, and job placement percentages.

There are two main undergraduate degrees that are available for fashion design programs: the associate of applied science (AAS) degree and the bachelor of fine arts (BFA) degree. The associate of applied science degree program in fashion design lasts two years and trains students in the fundamentals of design techniques and technical design skills, such as tailoring and sewing. With an AAS degree, students can acquire broad insight, knowledge, and awareness of the fashion design and construction process from concept inception to finalized product completion. Typical courses will include fashion design fundamentals, textiles, clothing construction techniques, sketching, draping, pattern grading, and history of fashion. Some universities and fashion schools offer study abroad associate programs, with one out of the two years of the program taking place in Paris, Milan, or a similar fashion epicenter.

The application process for an AAS degree requires the completion of an application (which is usually accessible online), a small fee, an official high school transcript, an essay, and a creative assignment which varies by school. International students wishing to enroll in a school or university located in the United States typically would need to have their transcript reviewed by World

Illustrated by Izak Zenou for Henri Bendel. COURTESY OF IZAK ZENOU.

Education Services (WES). WES reviews international transcripts and prepares an evaluation report to send to the institution to which the student is applying. This report makes it easier for the U.S.-based school to interpret the student's transcript, to ensure that proper credentials are met. Students may also have to take the TOEFL, or Test of English as a Foreign Language, if English is not their native language.

Whether you have already completed an AAS degree program and have an interest in furthering your studies, or you would like to earn a bachelor level degree, a BFA degree program in fashion design will prepare you to be in the running for the top fashion design jobs in the industry. A BFA program lasts for four years and offers more extensive fashion courses along with the liberal arts (or basic education) courses, such as English and math. Classes can include fashion drawing, color theory, computer-aided design (CAD), portfolio presentation, fashion technology, apparel development, fashion as a business, portfolio presentation, and advanced fashion sketching. The environment tends to be more challenging, which allows for further refinement in color, technique, and process.

Students from Lasell College learning from Olivier Roux, a French fashion consultant, about the luxury segment of the fashion industry, at the Paris American Academy in France, 2009. COURTESY OF MARY RUPPERT-STROESCU.

The difference in the admissions process versus most other college-level programs is that fashion design students will need to submit a portfolio. Most schools will provide the criteria for proper portfolio submission. No matter which program you decide to take, you may want to look into the scholarship offerings and financial aid requirements. Policies, procedures, and the application process vary, so contact the school directly for additional information. You can also choose to attend classes on campus, online, or a combination of both.

How Did You Decide Which University to Attend to Obtain Your Education as a Fashion Designer?

I got a scholarship to the school I attended. It wasn't a top choice for me, but it also meant I had no student loans.

Samantha Baxter, Technical Designer, alice + olivia, New York, New York, USA

❯ Choose your school well! When I graduated from high school, I knew I wanted to study fashion, but I had no friends or connections in that field who could suggest a good school. Now, I can say I wish I had received more information from someone in the know. I believe I chose the wrong path for myself, which was an ordinary university program in Florence, Italy, where I live. Everything was very theoretical, and we had no labs for patternmaking. I graduated with the highest grades, but when I started sending résumés to fashion companies, nobody knew about my program, and I had to work twice as hard to get an internship. I graduated not even knowing what a mood board was, and it was really difficult for me at the beginning of my career. The only thing I would change if I could do it again is the choice of a reputable school with solid connections to fashion companies.

Arianna Mereu, Freelance Fashion Designer, Max Mara Fashion Group, Reggio Emilia, Italy

❯ During my senior year of high school, I had already been accepted into Kent State University's fashion design program and was waiting to hear back from the University of Cincinnati's design program. I had never heard of Savannah College of Art and Design until a family friend had told me about it. I had done some research and their fashion program was ranked one of the highest. Over my spring break, I visited the school and fell in love with it and the city. I knew right then and there I was meant to attend this school. I applied on a whim just a few weeks before my visit, and only a few days after I got back, I received a phone call that I had been accepted. I never thought I had a chance to get accepted, especially after the University of Cincinnati fell through, but it goes to show that one door is not shut without another one being opened, and I have never looked back since.

Kendra Barnes, Fashion Design Student at Savannah College of Art and Design (SCAD), Savannah, Georgia, USA and intern at Michael Kors, New York, New York, USA

❯ I received my bachelor's degree in industrial design at Politecnico of Milan. When I chose my field of study, I was not sure of my exact career direction. The fashion world, and footwear in particular, have always been my passions, but it was only during the last year of my degree that I decided to dedicate myself strictly to fashion, especially to accessories. I believe that Politecnico has given me the foundation for my professional growth.

Lisa Bozzato, Freelance Women's Shoe Designer, Via Spiga, Milan, Italy

❯ When deciding which university to attend, a few major factors came into play. Does this university have a strong fashion design program? Is this a diverse university where I can meet people from all walks of life? Will I be challenged at this school, both in the design world and the academic world? I researched and toured many schools, both design schools and liberal arts schools with fashion design programs. I needed to take classes honing my other interests besides studio arts classes and fashion requisites. I ended up choosing Syracuse University because of its strong academic program, as well as its attention to the arts.

Rebecca Clarizio, Associate Technical Designer, Michael Kors, New York, New York, USA

❯ I am from South Korea, and when I decided to study fashion, I immediately knew I wanted to pursue my studies in New York. When I began my research, I learned that Parson's BFA program offered intensive courses on concept development, and also found out that the notable alumni from Parsons were the designers of my dreams. I decided to follow the same path. I enrolled at Parsons and found it to be very competitive, which enabled me to learn a lot from both my professors and classmates. However, I have no complaints about how competitive my school was because it prepared me for the real world.

Christina Kwon, Designer, Mark + James, Badgley Mischka, New York, New York, USA

Spring/Summer 1997 Collection illustrated by Christina Kwon and inspired by Lee Bontecou. COURTESY OF CHRISTINA KWON.

How Did You Decide Which University to Attend to Obtain Your Education as a Fashion Designer? (Continued)

❭ Deciding which university to attend is a fastidious process. I went with my gut feeling. It was important to me to be in the heart of the fashion industry, and I knew that my final destination was going to be New York, Paris, Milan, or London. Since I was already in London and I had just finished my apprenticeship in tailoring on Savile Row, I decided to move and explore a different environment. I was unsure about moving to the USA, but after hours of research, I would somehow always end up at the website of Parsons The New School for Design and realized it was a sign, and I applied. A few months later, I received my letter of admission and the journey began.

Marino Isolani, Associate Designer, Bill Blass Women's Collection, New York, New York, USA

❭ As there was only one university in the United Kingdom offering a footwear design degree at the time, it was a no-brainer. There are now two. The important thing for me was how many graduates would gain employment. There was an excellent employment rate for my program, and I had two job offers before graduation.

Jessica Good, Freelance Shoe Designer, shoedesigner. com.uk, London, England, United Kingdom

❭ The reason I selected the American College in London for my fashion design course was twofold. First it was located right in the middle of the West End, close to the rag trade and designer shops, in a fashion capital showcasing London Fashion Week. Secondly, the flexible American system allowed me to pick the courses I wished to study. This was especially important as, at the time, they were one of the few colleges that offered fashion business practices and merchandising classes. I picked several of these courses to supplement my BA degree design program. Considering that Calvin Klein and Ralph Lauren were franchising the market at the time, it was important to learn how the Americans were expanding their designer brand businesses.

Wambui Njogu, Designer/Director, Moo Cow Kenya, Nairobi, Kenya

2011 Moo Cow Bougainvillea Collection. PHOTOGRAPHER: JOSEPH HUNWICK. ART DIRECTOR: LARA UBAGO. JEWELRY: LE COLLANE DI BETTA. MAKE-UP: SAIMA RASHID. HAIR: RANDOLPH GRAY OF REVLON PROFESSIONAL. MODEL: GERTRUDE OGADA. LOCATION: SAROVA SHABA, SHABA GAME PARK, KENYA.

❭ I decided which university to attend based on the school's reputation and environment. Then I researched what kind of fashion design program they offered. Lastly, I considered the lecturers' experience and which companies they offered for internships, as well as the types of job opportunities available after my studies concluded.

Jessica Chuan, Fashion Designer, Ghim Li Global, Singapore

❯ From the time I was very young, I had been seeing posters and ads in magazines about Fashion Institute of Technology (FIT) in New York. I had only dreamed about being accepted into their design program and, once accepted, I never gave another school a thought. To me, they were the "gold standard." Widely recognized all over the world, I knew it would be a selling feature on my résumé.

Diane Mahood, Creative Technical Designer, Sweaters and Knits, White House/Black Market, Ft. Myers, Florida, USA

❯ After I finished high school in the UK, I went on to study for a General National Vocational Qualification (GNVQ) in art and design at West Herts College in Watford, UK. This was a two-year program that during the first year covered all aspects of art and design. We then had to specialize in one of these areas for our final year. I was torn between fine art and fashion and, after discussing it further with my tutors, I received much encouragement from them and decided to take the fashion route. They had spoken highly of University College Northampton so I decided to check them out once I was at the point of looking for another university to attend. I decided to go there as it was a creative program which taught garment construction as well as life drawing, fashion illustration, fashion photography, fashion marketing, and fashion history. It was a three-year program, and, while seeing out my first year, I saw the very first graduates show at London graduate fashion week. While there, I won portfolio of the year, was one of ten national finalists in a design competition sponsored by Daks, and was part of a design team who won a design competition sponsored by Mercedes Benz.

Grant Young, Senior CAD Designer, Old Navy, San Francisco, California, USA

❯ I went to the University of Cincinnati for a bachelor's in science in industrial design. I wasn't sure what I wanted to do in the beginning, but I loved fashion and I wanted a more technical education.

I think industrial design is a great focus to help blend technical product design with fashion. This is where I found my love for footwear design, which brought me to where I am now.

Rachel Richards, Design Director, Footwear, "B" Brian Atwood, Rachel Rachel Roy, Boutique 9, The Jones Group, New York, New York, USA

❯ I've always had a passion for creating, and throughout my high school years, I had always been fascinated with New York City. And with a tiny bit of soul searching, I found that the Fashion Institute of Technology (FIT) in New York was the right place for me to grow that passion.

Cynthia Chang-Saada, Senior Handbag Designer, The Sak Brand Group, New York, New York, USA

❯ I chose to attend Goldsmith University in London, as their bachelor of arts design program has an approach to a multitude of design disciplines other than just fashion. The program gave me the necessary skills to tackle any design brief and promotes an intellectual approach to design, highlighting the fact that a great designer has to be a great thinker. It offered me the opportunity to experiment with different media and materials as much as to really engage in the creative process. I also chose this program as it requires work placement within the industry and gives good insight into the technical aspect of design.

Thomas Halford Ayers, Senior Accessories and Jewelry Designer, Toto Design Studio, London, England

❯ A major requirement for me was that the university was located in one of the major fashion centers of the world. After all, if you want the best fashion education, it is ideal to be surrounded by the best. Having lived in New York City for most of my life, Parsons The New School for Design was an obvious and early choice, along with The Fashion Institute of Technology (FIT). In addition, I had a strong desire to apply to Central St. Martins in London because many of my favorite designers graduated from there. I actually ended up applying and entering Otis College of Art and

How Did You Decide Which University to Attend to Obtain Your Education as a Fashion Designer? (Continued)

Design in California due to strong suggestions by my instructors in high school and because I received a full scholarship. However, I did not stay long in California as my heart remained in New York City, and I was unable to find myself inspired by my experience there. As a result, I went home to New York City and ended up accepting admission to Parsons. Becoming a successful designer in the industry requires more than just an education at a reputable institution. Over time, I have come to notice that those who survive the intense fashion industry are the ones who not only acquired good skill sets from their school, but also are willing to work hard, are open to learning, and have great creative talents.

Michael Cho, Bridal Designer, New York, New York, USA

❯ After high school, I chose to go to The Traphagen School of Fashion. It was the oldest fashion school in New York City and eventually merged with the Wood-Tobé Coburn School long after I graduated. You didn't have to take a liberal arts program, as they were dedicated to helping you fully understand the art and trade. Every day, all day long, you draped or were making patterns from scratch and designing. One or two days a week was dedicated to each. Geoffrey Beene, Anne Klein, and James Galanos all attended Traphagen. I was originally in the design program, but two and a half years after I graduated, I saw that every company wanted to see a degree, so that's when I decided to go to FIT for patternmaking.

Marina Spezakis, Senior Technical Designer, dress company, New York, New York, USA

Sketched by Michael Cho, 2011. COURTESY OF MICHAEL CHO.

"Big Blue" red carpet gown illustration for the FIDM DEBUT Designer Exhibition. COURTESY OF PAUL HERNANDEZ.

❯ After high school graduation, I knew I would be going into fashion. I decided to attend San Diego State University and while I was working on my general education, I realized that no matter what assignment I was given in my classes, I always found a way to incorporate fashion into the project. It was then that I realized I had to follow my dreams. I had looked into attending the Fashion Institute of Design and Merchandising (FIDM) and decided that it was the right fit for me. The main reasons I chose FIDM was because of the great connections they have to the industry and because it is in the heart of the fashion industry in Los Angeles. I went on to be one of ten designers chosen to present a women's collection at their annual DEBUT fashion show, and I am very happy to be part of the FIDM family.

Paul Hernandez, Head Designer, IGO, San Diego, California, USA

❯ My mom and I decided to take a trip to visit all the schools I had interest in, but it wasn't until I stepped foot on the Pratt Institute campus that I fell in love. The green grass, and gated campus located in the middle of Fort Greene, Brooklyn, was like finding a diamond in the rough. At the time, Pratt was run down and had not yet been remodeled, but I could still see its beauty. Something about the edgy elegance of the dusty cracked red brick with the metal sculptures coming up out of the ground appealed to me. I was drawn to the history of New York City and knew I needed to attend school there.

Shari Seidlitz-McCandlish, Designer, Geoni Studios, Los Angeles, California, USA

❯ One thing I was sure of while selecting my fashion program was that I wanted to be close to London's West End, but not necessarily in the heart of it. Harrow School of Art and Design, now absorbed by the University of Westminster, had an excellent reputation, with some of the best faculty. I was involved in a project and critiqued by the famous fashion designer, John Galliano. I loved the fact it was a subway ride away from the heart of London, yet was located in a backdrop rich in English history. The first year was very broad, with a focus on true life drawing, learning the basics in fabrics and fibers, as well as initial construction techniques. The second year progressed to focus on color theory, draping print techniques, knitwear, and all gender design, as well as pattern cutting. During the summer of my second year, we had to do a three-month internship. The final year was largely focused on developing individual aesthetic and vision. Part of the final requirements was a 1000-word dissertation, along with a final collection of 6–8 outfits, fully designed, pattern cut, and constructed. It was an incredible experience!

Noreen Naz Naroo-Pucci, Senior Creative Director of Apparel, Under Armour, Baltimore, Maryland, USA

How Did You Decide Which University to Attend to Obtain Your Education as a Fashion Designer? (Continued)

❯ I chose the industrial design school instead of fashion school because I thought that having industrial skills could you give you the capability of designing everything, from a stove to an airplane! I chose to design accessories and specialty handbags because the bags are functional and you can play with the design around them by making different shapes, using different materials, and designing hardware to make the bag more comfortable to carry. Many top couturiers were also architects, for example Gianni Versace and Gianfranco Ferrè, so I am very happy that I am educated with both an industrial and fashion design background.

Annalisa Caricato, Freelance Accessories Designer, Guess Europe, Neuchatel, Switzerland

❯ I knew I wanted to attend a four-year university and live on campus while studying fashion, which narrowed down my choices. My high school actually specialized in fashion design and the arts, so recruiters from Syracuse University came to our school to interview students for their design program. It seemed to be a very easy choice for me once I got in because I knew I would have the big university college experience I had dreamed of, which would offer me a wide array of classes outside of fashion to enrich my education.

Nicolette Dennis, Sweater Designer, Minnie Rose, New York, New York, USA

❯ I always knew I was going to do something in fashion. While I was attending high school, my art teacher recommended that I look into Parsons

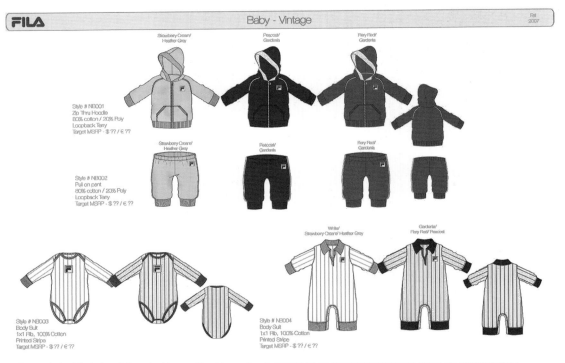

Concepts for Fila baby vintage by Noreen Naz Naroo-Pucci. COURTESY OF NOREEN NAZ NAROO-PUCCI ON BEHALF OF FILA.

The New School for Design in New York and take their summer intensive program. I did, and it gave me a taste of what would be expected at the college level. We had live model drawing classes, illustration classes, draping and patternmaking classes. After taking this program, I knew I wanted to continue my studies at Parsons to earn my BFA in fashion design. I recommend looking into the colleges that interest you and seeing if they offer pre-college classes. It really helped me get a feel for what was to be expected in the next four years of education.

Christina Caruso, Creative Director/Founder, Christina Caruso, New York, New York, USA

Photograph of Christina Caruso, 2011. COURTESY OF LIFETIME.

❯ I went to a vocational high school in New York City, which specialized in the fashion industry. During my senior year, I looked at different colleges and universities. I was interested in Parsons The New School for Design, F.I.T, and the Art Institute of Philadelphia. I was also interested in out-of-state schools like Kent State University, which had a design program. I knew I wanted to be a designer and I knew I needed to be in the heart of the fashion district. I visited the F.I.T., toured the school, and attended a seminar for prospective students. The school was as impressive in curriculum as it was in names of famous alumni that had attended. Sitting in the seminar and listening to the presentation, I knew then and there what my decision would be. The school catered to all the areas I needed to know about and would give me all the tools I needed to be successful in my career. Many years later, I can now say that I absolutely made the right decision.

Emileny Gonzalez, Technical Designer, Imports International, Allendale, New Jersey, USA

❯ I was financially unable to attend a private design school, and Oklahoma State University had an impressive reputation as a state school with an apparel design program. I visited a fashion show put on by the current students and was won over immediately.

Emily Ferrell, Fashion Design Student at Oklahoma State University, Stillwater, Oklahoma, USA

❯ There was really only one choice for me and that was Parsons The New School for Design, which was well before the success of the television show *Project Runway*. The focus was on art and design, and I applied and was accepted! I knew the name carried a lot of clout in the industry, which was important to me. I thought it would be a great place to get my start. Later, I attended Fashion Institute of Technology (F.I.T.) to hone my patternmaking skills, so I'd like to believe I had the best of both worlds!

Angela Silletti, Technical Design Management, Men's Wovens, Macy's Merchandising Group, New York, New York, USA

How Did You Decide Which University to Attend to Obtain Your Education as a Fashion Designer? (Continued)

❯ I decided to study at the European Institute of Design (IED) in Milan because of its contemporary program for fashion design and reputation for excellent instructors. Additionally, I knew I would benefit enormously by studying in a fashion metropolis. At IED, you have to be disciplined and motivated; you have to put everything into it to get the most out of it.

Paula Coelho Izzo, Fashion Designer and Design Director, Twelve Twenty, Lucerne, Switzerland

❯ Central Saint Martins School of Art and Design, University of the Arts London is unique because of how much freedom the students are given. It is an inspirational place where famous alumni such as John Galliano, Stella McCartney, and Hussein Chalayan started out. The school has given me the freedom and support to discover who I am as a designer.

Scarlett Tull, Fashion Design Student, Central Saint Martins, London, England, United Kingdom

An Interview with Mary Ruppert-Stroescu, Assistant Professor, Apparel Design and Textile Science, Oklahoma State University

Students from Lasell College in Paris, dressing models for the Songzio menswear show, 2010. COURTESY OF MARY RUPPERT-STROESCU.

What are some of the basic courses that are required for an undergraduate fashion design degree?

❯ An undergraduate fashion design degree in the United States requires that a student gain skills and knowledge in the following three areas: (1) the global scope of the business of fashion, including marketing, retailing, and merchandising, (2) technical skills for fashion design, both manual and computer-aided, including sketching, technical drawing, visual presentation, and prototype generation (sewing, pattern drafting, and draping), in addition to understanding different types of production practices, and (3) personal development, including attention to internal characteristics such as critical thinking and analysis, organization, problem solving, and communication skills, as well as developing a sensibility for understanding and practicing ethical behavior and cultivating lifelong intellectual and cultural awareness.

Do you feel creativity can be taught, or have you found it to be an innate trait in your fashion design students?

❯ Creativity includes such a vast scope of behaviors; I am a firm believer that each individual is creative. The manner by which students express creativity depends on the type of creativity most prevalent in the individual (the left brain/right brain theory). Too often people associate artistic ability with creativity, and while natural artistic talent makes expressing ideas easier most of the time, drawing beautiful illustrations is not a prerequisite for making incredibly directional fashion. Some of the most revolutionary designers throughout history barely could sketch (Paul Poiret, Madeline Vionnet, and Gabrielle Chanel, for example) but had a vision and creative sensibility that changed the course of history. Such designers demonstrate leadership creativity; they create trends, focusing on the product, putting a high value on research and development, drawing inspiration from ephemeral, abstract, non-clothing sources, and are content with producing few pieces at very high prices. Designers who put more emphasis on the process—searching for the least expensive way of producing fashion that follows trends, satisfies the target market, and can be produced at high quantities for low prices—give more attention to the process than the product. The product itself is often an adaptation of an existing contemporary garment.

In the fashion industry, creative work can focus on the product or the process; there is a place for everyone in this vast pipeline. One trait that everyone in this industry needs is the desire to succeed and the willingness to work hard. Possessing creativity isn't enough—students have to show their work to others.

What can students do to stand out amongst their classmates and excel in a fashion design program?

❯ Excelling in a fashion design program requires careful time management, being your own best critic, doing more than just the work required, and meeting deadlines sooner than everyone else. If your professor asks for 10 sketches, come to class with 20. If the deadline is Tuesday at 4:00 pm, show the finished product to the professor the Friday before for critique, digest the recommendations, critique the work yourself and take appropriate action, then turn it in on Monday; pulling an all-nighter before the due date is almost never pretty. Don't just design for class. Make sketching, patterning, and sewing part of your lifestyle. A successful designer never turns off; fashion is a synthesis of everything around us, from art and culture to politics to sports. Absorb it all. Dress the part. You are designing fashion; show some style!

Do you think it is imperative for students to spend at least a semester in a study abroad program?

❯ I love this question and would love to see our world one in which every fashion design student could spend a semester abroad! Personal exposure to another culture is an enriching experience like no other. Reality, though, doesn't always allow time for a full semester. Any time abroad helps; even short-term programs open students' eyes to different customs and habits. In the U.S. we are so ethnocentric. A major characteristic of a good designer is the ability to have empathy for "the other," and travel/study is one of the best ways to discover different ways to live, love, work, and consume. Travel doesn't only have to be abroad, though. We have some of the most exciting fashion centers in the world right here on U.S. soil! Students should experience New York and/or L.A. as well. Internships are an excellent way to get a taste of the city while working in the fashion industry.

What are some qualities and skills that are important for fashion designers to possess?

❯ Really successful fashion designers understand how to instill desire and need for their work into the hearts, souls, and wallets of their customers. They understand how to build and cultivate relationships between their brand/products and each consumer. Of course, it is essential to have an impeccable sense of style, rigorous quality standards, an unfailing work ethic, and determination.

What advice would you give to an aspiring fashion designer?

❯ Don't wait—take action now! If you want to be a fashion designer, you must make it a part of your lifestyle. Learn the basics: elements and principles of design, life drawing, fashion drawing, draping, patternmaking, and sewing, and practice these skills as part of your daily routine. Be a sponge. Absorb everything in the world around you and translate it in your own unique way. Document your work; keep a design journal and make friends with a good photographer. Create a digital portfolio. Get a job in retail. Many companies look for designers who understand the environment where the product will meet the consumer. Go for your dream. No matter whom you want to work for, learn everything about the company and the design aesthetic. Design a line for the company as if you were already an employee; it will be a real plus in your interview portfolio when you go for a job. If you want to start your own line, define your closest competitor and research that company to the bone. Be different and better. Create a distinct brand image for your line, and be sure to be realistic about costs and production abilities. Partner with someone who is good at money and business management, and marketing.

Beyond academics, what role should a university play in preparing students for their first job?

❯ In addition to possessing the skills and knowledge required for being a fashion designer, graduates should be prepared to communicate well, to learn quickly, and to adapt to the ever-changing world. Graduates should understand the importance of the global picture and, ideally, a university education would include cultivating a desire to contribute positively to the community and to integrate sustainable practices into all aspects of their lives.

An Interview with Kendra Barnes, Fashion Design Student at Savannah College of Art and Design (SCAD)

How did you become interested in studying fashion?

❯ Growing up, I was always artistic. I loved to work on different projects and make things sparkle, and over the years, it never changed. I was always the one who designed the class t-shirts and hoodies for the soccer team and even school banners. I not only loved to do these things, but I was good at it. However, working as a bridal consultant made me fall in love with fashion and want to pursue it as a career.

What are some of the courses you are currently taking?

❯ As a senior, most of our classes revolve around the development of our six-look senior collection. I just completed "Senior I," which is all about sketching, and I am about to take "Senior II" and "Senior III," which consists of actually developing the pieces. I am also taking a decorative surfaces class, which is about fabric manipulations and how to take ordinary fabrics and transform them into couture pieces.

What has been your favorite class so far, and why?

❯ My favorite class has been my fashion portfolio class. It entails what should be included in your portfolio to help you stand out, show off your skills, and display a sense of how well rounded you are as a designer.

What do you get inspired by when creating your design concepts?

❯ Anything and everything, but it is something that can't be forced, it has to just come to you. When I am stuck trying to find inspiration for a project or whatever I may be working on, I like to look at photography. Looking at a picture, whether it is a person, place, or thing, can affect the way you feel on so many different levels, and when I find a photo I'm in

love with, my inspiration comes from how it makes me feel and my interpretation of that feeling.

Are you planning to study abroad, or have you already enrolled in a study abroad program?

❯ Unfortunately, no. The times available for fashion majors to study abroad never worked out in regards to my class schedule.

What advice would you give to a person who is planning to enroll in a fashion design program?

❯ My best advice to give is to be prepared to work. Fashion is not easy and not always glamorous like you see on television. You have to have a passion for it because if you lack passion and drive, you will have no motivation to get you through those many sleepless nights. In addition, develop a thick skin. You will be critiqued and judged with every step you make and every breath you take. People aren't always going to like what you do, but you just have to remember they are pushing you to be the best designer out there.

What are your career goals once you graduate?

❯ My plans are to get a job soon after graduation, hopefully in a big city, such as Chicago or New York. I want to work for a big company for a while, to meet people and to grasp an idea of how to run and maintain a successful business. Bridal design is my passion, and one day I plan to open a bridal salon featuring my own designs.

Who is your favorite fashion designer?

❯ My favorite fashion designer is Elie Saab because his designs take my breath away and give me goose bumps whenever I see them on the runway. His designs are the epitome of elegance and grace and capture the essence of a woman's femininity.

An Interview with Emily Ferrell, Fashion Design Student at Oklahoma State University

How did you become interested in studying fashion design?

❯ Fashion is a compulsion for me; I have always been obsessed with it. My mother tells me that as a two year old, I was perpetually putting outfits together, much to her consternation leaving a trail of options behind me! While I was in high school, I enrolled in a cooperative technical school for apparel design. I fell in love with it instantly and had an unquestionable knowledge that I would not be happy doing anything else.

What are some of the courses that you are currently taking?

❯ I am currently taking Mass Production, Advanced Apparel Design, Textiles, Apparel, Interiors and Related Products in the International Economy, and Environmental Sustainability Issues for Designers.

What has been your favorite class so far and why?

❯ Advanced Apparel Design has been my favorite class so far because we are able to take the concepts that we have learned in all of our previous classes and begin to work on our own collections. I love this class because we are able to design with creative freedom.

What do you get inspired by when creating your design concepts?

❯ Everything around me inspires me endlessly. I enjoy getting lost and truly paying attention to my surroundings. I am inspired by music, cities, feelings, nature, photographs, and so much more.

Paris-themed mood board created by Emily Ferrell, 2011. COURTESY OF EMILY FERRELL.

Are you planning to study abroad, or have you already enrolled in a study abroad program?

❭ I spent six weeks in Paris studying the history of haute couture, and it changed my life! It is amazing to see where so many incredible designers began and to think that we've been inspired by the same sparkling sights, eaten at the same sidewalk cafes, and spent moments dreaming and hoping in the same streets. There is also something to be said for taking yourself out of your comfort zone and having to use your creativity in practical ways; it opens you up to so many new experiences. I hope to return and study for a longer period of time in the future.

What advice would you give to a student who is about to enroll in a fashion design program?

❭ Don't give up and don't get discouraged. Do some soul searching and be sure that fashion design is really what you want to study. It is not going to be all glitz and glamour, but rather a lot of hard work and sleepless nights!

What are your career goals once you graduate?

❭ I dream of working in Paris for an haute couture designer, before starting my own line.

Who are your favorite fashion designers?

❭ Elie Saab, Oscar de la Renta, and John Galliano.

"Brigitte" Coquette, illustrated by Emily Ferrell for senior collection, 2011. COURTESY OF EMILY FERRELL.

"Aurélie" Coquette, illustrated by Emily Ferrell for senior collection, 2011. COURTESY OF EMILY FERRELL.

The Value of Internships

Fashion design internships are among the most highly desired internships in the world. A college internship is a formal program that lasts for a set period of time, allowing students practical work experience in the field of their choice. It gives a student the opportunity to receive on-the-job training and direct work experience, while still attending school, thereby enhancing the classroom learning experience. An internship program allows students to use their fashion design knowledge from the classroom in a real-world format, under the watchful eye of a design team, learning from and being recognized by the most talented designers in the world. In most industries, but especially in fashion, name recognition, essentially "who-you-know," is highly regarded and goes a long way.

Year after year, the competition in the job market increases, so the need for job applicants to be more experienced than their counterparts becomes even more critical. Completing an internship allows you to become better qualified. In addition to providing great experience, internships allow you to build both your portfolio and résumé, which will be very helpful in the job search process. Internships give students the chance to make valuable industry contacts, which can greatly improve their chances of landing a full-time job after college graduation, offering individuals a foot-in-the-door opportunity for potential job offers in the future.

When you enter the work force, your internship will count as direct experience in the field, which is highly sought out and of utmost importance to human resources executives, hiring managers, fashion recruiters, and potential employers, all of whom are measuring your criteria for a potential hire. While fashion internship programs vary, most are offered only to undergraduate or

Oklahoma State University fashion design student Emily Ferrell at her internship at Red Engine Jeans in Los Angeles, California, Summer 2011. COURTESY OF RED ENGINE JEANS.

graduate students who are enrolled in an accredited college or university. Students will generally receive college credit in exchange for their work, as most internships are unpaid, although some companies offer minimal compensation in the form of an hourly or project rate or weekly stipend. Some universities require that a student complete an internship in order to graduate.

The length of time for internships varies by company, but most take place during the fall, spring, and summer semesters and last for a period of 8–10 weeks and can be part-time or full-time. The application process generally begins two months prior to the start of the internship. General qualifications include being a full-time junior- or senior-year college student with an overall minimal 3.3 GPA, currently enrolled in a fashion design major, and able to show proof of eligibility to work in the United States.

Some companies have very detailed programs with a set agenda, including various projects and activities, culminating with a design presentation to senior design management. In other cases, the internship program will be less structured, but the student will gain in-depth knowledge and responsibility for viable tasks that are important to the overall work flow of the design team. No matter what you do, there is value to all types of experience.

Typical fashion design internship tasks include researching key design trends, creating look books and storyboards/mood boards, presenting concepts to design, assisting in the global research and sourcing of fabric and trim, placing sample fabric and trim purchase orders, creating mock-up designs, evaluating lab dips, creating sketches by hand, using CAD or Illustrator, assisting in getting approval for samples, prototypes, and strike-offs, communicating with overseas vendors and factories, reviewing color palettes, creating "tech packs" (technical packages), and performing various administrative functions, such as making copies of looks or assigning seats at the fashion show. While it may not always be the case, prepare to work long hours, oftentimes in a high-pressure environment, especially during typically busy times, such as right before a product presentation or launch, market week, or a trunk or fashion show. Some companies offer a major perk by giving their interns a clothing allowance and/or access to the designer's seasonal sample sales.

The internship coordinator at a university manages the internship placement process and has relationships with various apparel manufacturers and design houses. In most cases, the internship will take place out of state, and housing will be provided for a fee, or the student will be responsible for making his or her own housing arrangements. Each school or university offers a different internship program, with varying regulations and procedures. Prior to placement, some companies will expect you to interview for the internship spot, while others work with the internship coordinator for direct placement. It is important to be prepared either way. A fully detailed explanation of interviewing techniques is given in Chapter 3.

It is important to communicate and discuss your career ambitions with your internship coordinator before your placement is decided. All internships expose you to the work culture and functionalities of different companies within the fashion industry, but it is ideal to get placement in an internship that most closely relates to your direct career goals so that you can get the most value out of the experience.

An Interview with Katie Fong, Studio Design Intern, Oscar de la Renta

White gouache, watercolor and color pencil sketch by Katie Fong for senior portfolio, 2011. COURTESY OF KATIE FONG.

How did you land your internship?

❭ I have been posting my artwork in my father's dry cleaning business, Thomas Cleaners in my hometown of Greenwich, Connecticut, ever since I was five. In 2009, when I was a sophomore at the Fashion Institute of Technology in New York, a customer of his asked if I would like to interview at Oscar de la Renta for an internship. I was interviewed by a couple of the designers, and soon after landed my position there as a studio design intern.

What are your main responsibilities as a fashion design intern?

❭ On a normal day, I assist mainly the design director and first assistant designer with first clothing samples, which can vary from patternmaking and draping to embroidery layouts and fabric manipulations. During look book photo shoots, I get the opportunity to help style the looks. I also work with various local sample-making houses and assist the designers in presentations to Mr. de la Renta. As fashion week approaches, I assist the designers with model fittings as I am responsible for a certain amount of looks that go down the runway.

What is the most challenging aspect of being an intern?

❭ The most challenging aspect of being an intern is being able to balance my internship with schoolwork.

What advice would you give someone beginning an internship?

❭ Be quick, yet accurate, and always keep your eyes and ears open to what a designer might need (whether it is help with pinning, getting a copy from the photocopier, etc.). Always be available and/or on standby, yet invisible to those in a higher position. It can be overwhelming to a designer who already has a lot of stress to be surrounded by a lot of people. In addition to this, I'd say to always keep busy. If there isn't a specific project, you can always organize or bring a sketchbook and sketch. Do not make personal calls on your cell phone in the office. Be friendly to everyone around you, but speak only when spoken to with those who are working, as you would not want to disrupt their concentration. Most of all, be positive and take up any challenge, because you never know what may come of it.

What has been the best part of your internship?

❭ The best part of my internship is being able to work so closely with the designers of such a well-respected company. Seeing Mr. de la Renta working every day and showing such passion in his work is extremely motivating. I couldn't be happier as an intern with this company.

What is your favorite fashion quote?

❭ "When you rest, you rust."—Oscar de la Renta

An Interview with Rita Valkovskaya, Fashion Design Intern at Derek Lam

How did you land your internship?

❭ I found my internship on the Parson's Career Board through the Student Central program.

What are your main responsibilities as a fashion design intern?

❭ The main job of the intern is to be helpful in any way possible. I have done internships where interns are responsible for cutting production and sample fabrics, tracing patterns, working out embroidery and embellishment layouts, as well as finishing garments (including sewing on embellishments like beads, sequins, etc.). At other more corporate companies, interns maintain the filing system of fabric cards and color standards, run errands to

the Garment District where production is done, and draw or render flat sketches to be put into tech packs.

What is the most challenging aspect of being a fashion design intern?

❭ The most challenging aspect of being a fashion design intern is keeping perspective about your worth as an employee in an environment where you are not being paid for your labor. It can at first be easy to forget that the contribution of interns not only saves the designer's time, but at times is actually vital to keeping the company going. Having respect for yourself and the work you do and continuing to maintain professionalism and sustain your work ethic is very important because your performance is not forgotten, even if you are just making photocopies. It is often not the task that matters, but the speed and lack of fuss with which you complete it. Designers often remember their most helpful interns and bring them on as freelance or full-time designers or provide recommendations to their colleagues in the industry.

What advice would you give someone beginning an internship?

❯ My advice is first to choose the right company with which to invest your time. Think of the long-term goals, even if they are a year or two away. Do you want to be working for this designer in the future? Is the design team one who can promote you and one day mention you to other designers with whom you would like to work? There are only so many internships one can do, and it is important to invest your time in the right place. That being said, sometimes it is worthwhile to intern with smaller, lesser-known brands to learn the job and get experience, so that when you move on to your dream brand, you are prepared to do the job immaculately. The second piece of advice is to come every day to the internship and act as if this is an extended job interview. Always be prompt, helpful, and complete tasks quickly and thoroughly. The top priority should always be to be noticed by and impress the people in the company who make hiring decisions in the long run.

What has been the best part of your internship?

❯ The best part of the internship is having the privilege to be in an environment where you participate in creating beautiful garments and working with people who share your passion. Going through the season from concept development to the end presentation of the collection is exciting. It is inspiring to be able to continue your own work in a more professional way, thinking about fashion as a real-life business aimed at a customer base, instead of just an artistic creation.

What is your favorite fashion quote?

❯ "Interns should be seen and not heard."

An Interview with Joseph Singh, Fashion Design Intern at Donna Karan International

Spring/Summer 2012 Joseph Singh Collection, New York Underground. COURTESY OF JOSEPH SINGH.

How did you land your internship?

❯ I landed my internship by chance, through networking. While attending Parsons The New School for Design in New York, I had a part-time job working in cosmetics. My coworker's best friend works for Donna Karan International, and he had recommended that I apply for the internship, knowing I was getting my degree in fashion design. At the time, I was only a sophomore and was not allowed to intern until my junior year. I was introduced to the head of creative direction and fabric development and received the internship my Fall 2011 semester of my junior year. I'm actually staying on board another semester. However, there are many ways to land internships. Check with your school's career center or even look online. I know many people who have landed internships from just searching the Web.

What are your main responsibilities as a fashion design intern?

❯ Working in creative direction and fabric development, we are the center of nearly everything that happens at Donna Karan International. In this department, we are responsible for sourcing, in-house dyeing, developing treatments, and assisting in creating the color story for the current seasons (my boss has an amazing eye for color, which I am currently being trained for). We are also responsible for production, and we constantly run to the sample room making sure all the correct fabrics for the season have been delivered.

What is the most challenging aspect of being an intern?

❯ There isn't only one challenging aspect of being an intern, as everything is challenging. You are always learning the business in the beginning. There are deadlines to be met, and I can tell you from experience that deadlines are probably the most important and challenging aspect. Since you are always sourcing from overseas and always shipping things back and forth, trying to get multiple things done at once and getting things done on time is the hardest part.

What advice would you give someone beginning an internship?

❭ My advice to someone just starting out as an intern is to give 200 percent while you are there, be prepared, and be confident. Whatever they want you to do, do it. I've seen a lot of interns who come in and are scared and nervous. When I first walked in, I had the impression that it would be like the movie *The Devil Wears Prada*; little didn't I know, it wasn't. My first couple of weeks, I was so stiff, so scared, but Donna Karan International is such a friendly environment. I would always get nervous when I was around the creative director and other designers, but as I got to know them, they were very welcoming. Ask questions! You are there to learn; if you have questions, ask, but ask at an appropriate time. Also, keep a notebook with you at all times and write down all contact information of everyone you work with because, in this industry, you will always be networking. If you are running an errand for someone, grab a business card and file it, because you will never know when you will need that information.

What has been the best part of your internship?

❭ Everything! I love everything about this company. Just being in this creative environment is amazing. Watching a collection come to life is breathtaking. When I am here, I feel like nothing else in the world matters but that collection, what's in front of me. I get so involved that sometimes I forget I'm there, it feels like I'm dreaming when I'm running around the place. The people here have made me feel that I have become a part of their team; it feels like a second home.

What is your favorite fashion quote?

❭ I have a couple of favorite fashion quotes I have posted on my wall.

"I think there is beauty in everything. What 'normal' people would perceive as ugly, I can usually see something of beauty in it."—Alexander McQueen

"In order to be irreplaceable, one must always be different."—Coco Chanel

HOW TO TURN AN INTERNSHIP INTO A FULL-TIME POSITION

Your internship experience has the potential to land you a full-time job, if you make a great impression. The first thing employers look for during the hiring process is relevant work experience. Internships not only give you that experience, but offer you the opportunity to gain important skills that you can take with you wherever you go. Internships also afford you the chance to find out which product categories you prefer designing. Over half of employers say that they hire interns as permanent employees, so you've got a solid chance of scoring a full-time job upon completion. Following these guidelines will significantly increase your chances of landing a full-time job:

Partner with your supervisor. Your number-one mission as an intern is to collaborate with your supervisor to make his or her daily work grind easier. Think ahead to what your supervisor may need to accomplish a task, and find ways to help him or her complete these tasks more efficiently. Find out from colleagues what makes your supervisor tick, and lend a hand in that area.

Wow them from the get-go. Treat your internship just as seriously as you would a full-time job by arriving on time on a consistent basis, deliver compelling work, taking on additional tasks, and working whatever hours are necessary to get the job done.

Over-deliver. Arrive early. Leave late. If you have a question, try to answer it yourself before asking anyone else. If you are not given a deadline, ask your supervisor when he or she expects the task to be completed. Make sure you understand what is expected of you at all times so you can become a person whom the design team depends on and goes to first for an assignment.

Build your network. Networking is an important first step in developing your contacts, so meet as many people as possible when you begin your internship. Your supervisor or point person will usually give you a tour of the office on your first day and introduce you to several different people in various departments. Really take the time to remember their names and get to know them so that you can begin building relationships. Ask for a few minutes of their time to better understand what they do and what role they play in the entire design process.

Take initiative. Interns who take initiative to help out on a project, take on additional tasks, or show a desire to learn the ropes and develop more competencies become a stand-out member of the team. Your efforts will not go unnoticed.

Don't gossip. You should avoid participating in office gossip at all costs. Not only will gossip not help you get ahead, but it may deter you.

Be enthusiastic. Enthusiasm is contagious, and it makes your colleagues happy to be around you. It also shows your boss that you are motivated and excited to be there, and that, in turn, will give you added bonus points.

Stay positive. It is important to find healthy ways to relieve your stress so that you can stay positive on the job. Nothing is more appreciated than a person who can maintain positivity when the going gets tough.

Be willing to do any task. As an intern, you will be expected to eagerly jump right into your role and help out with whatever task needs to get done. When your superior asks you to do something, it is always appreciated if you maintain a "sure, no problem" mind-set. These tiny touches go a long way. When you finish the task, you should ask if there is anything else that is needed of you before going back to your regular work routine or leaving for the day.

Pay close attention to detail. Being detail-oriented is a highly desirable and fundamental trait to have as it is often the tiniest details that, when overlooked, can prove to be disastrous. So it is up to you to notice these things and make sure they are carried out correctly. Your coworkers and supervisors will truly appreciate your efforts.

Leave a lasting impression. Being professional at all times, meeting deadlines, being positive, and going above and beyond will all lead to making an enduring impact on your coworkers, boss, and company management, which should help you to get a full-time offer.

Studying Abroad

Imagine yourself taking in the chic style of the locals roaming the streets of the Rue du Faubourg Saint-Honoré in the Paris fashion district or researching design trends at the famous upscale boutiques on Bond Street in London. Most students who have completed study abroad programs describe them as life-changing. This experience not only can enhance your educational experience, but also your social life, with the opportunity to make lifelong friends.

In the global business setting we face today, gaining international experience is crucial in staying one step ahead of the competition. By studying abroad, a student can gain working knowledge of a foreign language, an increased knowledge of how business is conducted internationally, and an understanding of cultural differences. Study abroad programs exist throughout the world with a concentration in the United States, England, France, Italy, Hong Kong, Mexico, Australia, and Canada and provide students with a hands-on learning experiences and opportunities that will give them direct experience and knowledge in the field of international fashion design. There is a wide range of specialized programs offered by various colleges and universities, whether you are thinking about spending a summer, semester, or an entire year abroad. Most universities and schools have an international program, study abroad, exchange, or consortium office or department that is available to students for planning the study abroad experience. They will coordinate all international programs and provide all logistical information necessary to apply for, start, and complete your program.

The Institute for the International Education of Students (IES Abroad) conducted the first large-scale survey to understand the impact that study abroad programs had on the personal and academic aspects of students' lives. The findings show that the majority of respondents felt their study abroad experience positively influenced their career path and increased their confidence level. Study abroad programs help students to become empowered, open-minded, and ready to take on the world.

Panorama of Paris, featuring the Pont des Arts and, behind, the Pont Neuf and the Île de la Cité. The Institut de France stands on the right, at the end of the Pont des Arts. The towers of Notre-Dame de Paris Cathedral can also be seen in the distance, 2010. PHOTOGRAPHER: BENH LIEU SONG.

Postgraduate Education

Most fashion design positions do not require a postgraduate degree, such as a master's or PhD, however these degrees often set the stage for a career as a fashion design educator. Graduate programs in fashion design focus on the theoretical study of fashion design and philosophy, rather than the fundamentals, and prepare students for advanced fashion design or teaching positions. Classroom teaching is usually supplemented by guest lecturers, tours of apparel and accessories companies, and design house and museum visits. A graduate student will be exposed to advanced development of technical skills, in-depth research, case studies, and experimental applications in the classroom. Graduate courses typically consist of a combination of functional hands-on, self-directed, and hypothetical studies. Graduate students are able to explore their specialty areas in an advanced capacity.

When receiving a master's degree, a student will be required to develop, create, and present a thesis. A thesis is a document that presents the student's research and findings on a particular subject. When the student is earning a PhD, the equivalent is called a dissertation. The student will have to present his or her thesis or dissertation to a committee, who will then thoroughly review it, make suggestions, and decide whether to accept or reject it. A dissertation is much more extensive than a thesis; it reports on a particular research project or provides an extended analysis of the subject matter. An oral examination is usually a requirement of receiving a master's degree or PhD and occurs after the thesis or dissertation is finished, but before it is submitted to the university. The student presents it to a committee or board and they, in turn, ask questions of the student.

In order to apply to a graduate program, you should have completed an undergraduate degree in fashion design or a similar subject. A portfolio that demonstrates your aptitude in sketching, drawing, illustration, conceptual development and execution will be required. The application process is different for each school, but generally consists of filling out an application, paying an application fee, providing official transcripts, a résumé, submitting an autobiographical statement and a statement of interest (the area within fashion design that you plan to study, the type of research you plan to conduct, and your career goals upon completion of the graduate program), turning in two recommendation letters from faculty, and completing a personal interview with a member of the faculty. Once you complete a graduate program in fashion design, you will be ready to enter the job market as an advanced professional fashion designer.

Continuing Education

In order to remain competitive, fashion designers must always be on the cutting edge of their trade, staying on top of the latest technologies and refreshing their skill set. Continuing education nondegree courses (on a for-credit or noncredit basis) provide an opportunity for individuals to brush up on certain skills, such as textile technology; earn a certificate in specialties such as haute couture sewing techniques, CAD for fashion design, or draping; or learn something new. It is a great way to expand your skill set and improve your portfolio. These courses can also be helpful in career transition (e.g., from fashion to accessory design), and present a forum to make new friends, develop your business network, and give you additional knowledge to cultivate your design talent and advance your fashion career.

Continuing Education Units (CEUs) are a nationally recognized standard of measure for noncredited courses defined as 10 hours of participation and provides proof of completion. The International Association for Continuing Education and Training (IACET) offers the most industry-wide accreditation of CEUs. In certain countries, such as Canada, the term Continuing Education Credit (CEC) is used instead.

Continuing education courses are taught by professors, teachers, or industry professionals who offer a real-world point of view. Individuals may take continuing education courses as a prerequisite to enrolling in certain associate of applied science degree programs. Most schools have continuing education information sessions so that you can find out more about the program offerings prior to enrollment or you contact the school's continuing education department and ask for a bulletin to be sent to you in the mail, or view their courses online through their website.

In addition to taking individual continuing education courses, an individual may choose to receive a certificate program in a particular specialty. Certificate programs provide basic teaching and training for individuals who are interested in learning about a particular aspect of fashion design. They are considered less demanding than a traditional degree program, as it is part-time, non-credited and carries no admissions requirements. It is a great way to expand your skill set and improve your portfolio. Core courses as well as fashion specific classes are covered. The core course provides students with a foundation to begin a career in fashion design, engaging the student in topics ranging from color, pattern, form, clothing construction, including sewing, pattern making and draping, fabric sourcing, textile technology, sketching, clothing history, fashion marketing, and consumer behavior. For additional information on certificate program offerings, contact the school's continuing education department and ask for a bulletin to be sent to you in the mail or view the certificate programs online.

Spring 2012 Pamella Roland Advertising Campaign.
PHOTOGRAPHER: NIGEL BARKER, 2011.

Illustrated by Izak Zenou for
Henri Bendel. COURTESY OF
IZAK ZENOU.

3 The Job Market

Fashions fade, style is eternal.

—Yves Saint Laurent

CANDIDATES SEEKING WORK IN FASHION DESIGN need to demonstrate technical acumen, a propensity for creative thinking, and a business mindset. Fashion designer hopefuls should be armed with an impressive portfolio, a beautifully presented résumé, polished interviewing skills, endless energy, sublime enthusiasm, and tremendous positivity. Now that you are aware of the educational requirements needed to begin a fashion design career, it's time to review the decisions you will need to make once your college education is complete and you are ready to begin your job search. In this section, you will determine your design specialty, create marketing materials for your job search, and learn how to land your dream design job.

Determining Your Design Specialty

Since the fashion industry is so highly segmented, it is advantageous to determine your design specialty so you can maximize your job search. So how do you find your place in the crowd? You will need to take into consideration the many factors that will help you ascertain your design specialty. They include the following: 1) job category, 2) product category, 3) work environment, 4) fashion market, and 5) type of designer. Now let's take a look at each of these categories in further detail.

JOB CATEGORY

There are five different job categories: (1) freelance employee, (2) part-time employee, (3) full-time employee, (4) independent consultant or contractor (self-employed), and (5) business owner.

"Whisper of the Wind" by Dipika Lakshmi, 2010. COURTESY OF DIPIKA LAKSHMI.

Chado Ralph Rucci Fall/Winter 2012 Ready-to-Wear Collection. Fragmented Printed Cashmere Suit. PHOTOGRAPHERS: DAN AND CORINA LECCA. COURTESY OF CHADO RALPH RUCCI.

Freelance Employee

A freelance (or temporary) employee is a person who provides services to an employer independently in exchange for compensation on a nonsalaried basis. There are two different freelance job categories: temporary and temporary-to-permanent (also termed "temp-to-perm"). A temporary job is a nonpermanent position with an open-ended or set time-frame, while temp-to-perm is a nonpermanent position that is intended to become a permanent job at some point in time, either known or unknown. Freelancing gives you an excellent opportunity to learn more about the work environment and to see if the job is the right fit, prior to accepting the job in a full-time capacity. The downside is that you typically do not receive the benefits of working full-time for a company, such as health insurance, 401K, and paid vacation.

There are two different ways to begin a freelance assignment. You can become an independent contractor or work through an employment agency. As an independent contractor, you are considered self-employed and are responsible for finding freelance work on your own. If you work with an agency, you will become an employee of that agency once placed in a freelance job.

There are a variety of reasons why people choose to freelance. Many individuals are "career freelancers" and freelance as their only means of income, going from project to project. Others freelance in-between full-time jobs, either after a job loss or during a job transition, or as a source of income while simultaneously starting their own business. Those who are unsure of the area of fashion design that they want to specialize in can choose to test-drive different companies, experience various work cultures, while gaining exposure to different types of design positions, to help determine their career direction. Freelancing also offers flexibility while allowing you to choose only those assignments that you feel are the best fit for your background. Freelancing affords you the opportunity to build your network and hear about possible job openings within the company or elsewhere. Those not needing steady income (e.g., a stay-at-home parent with a salaried spouse) can freelance instead of building a long-term career.

Employment agencies either specialize in freelance-only job placement or offer both freelance and full-time job recruitment in fashion design. Freelancing sometimes pays higher than a similar full-time job, since employers don't have to factor in such benefits as health insurance, 401K, and paid vacation. In some instances, employment agencies offer health insurance at group rates to their employees who have worked for a certain length of time. Some freelancers may even be eligible for sick, holiday, and vacation pay, depending on the policies of the employment agency, as well as time and a half for overtime hours exceeding forty hours per work week.

An Interview with Ricardo Charles, Freelance Fashion Designer

Fall/Winter 2011 women's sportswear sketched by Ricardo Charles. COURTESY OF RICARDO CHARLES.

Where did you go to college, and what degree(s) did you earn?

❯ I received two degrees, a bachelor of fine arts in apparel and textile design from Michigan State University and an associate's of applied science degree in fashion design from the Fashion Institute of Technology in New York City.

List all of your internships, and please briefly discuss what sort of tasks you were assigned.

❯ I've interned at very *Devil Wears Prada*-esque companies, which were very intimidating, and the complete opposite. My first internship was at Jill Stuart, which I obtained on my own. It was very exciting! The following summer, my professor had a connection with a runway designer and asked if I wanted to intern there, and of course I said yes. I really enjoyed this internship. The designers/staff trusted my skill set very much, so the tasks were truly design-oriented. I was able to sew muslin mock-ups, create, fix, and adjust pattern pieces, and drape.

Do you feel that your internships sufficiently prepared you for a full-time job? If so, how? If not, why?

❭ My internships were very designer-based and most jobs are not at the designer price point. Many companies didn't care that I knew how to properly marrow two pieces of fur together or that I knew how to hand-stitch. Many companies want employees who are more computer and real-world savvy.

Please discuss the various freelance jobs you have held and what sort of tasks you were assigned.

❭ My first freelance job was at Izod working on U4ia (a textile CAD program) designing stripes for their polo tops. Next, I worked at Club Monaco completing tech-packs, which included flat sketching by hand, beadwork lay-out packages, and reviewing lab dips. After that, I worked for the Calvin Klein Intimates line working on Illustrator. The next job was at Macy's Merchandising Group, in which I designed Fair Isle sweaters and used Illustrator for presentations. Then I went back to Club Monaco doing the same work for a short project. My last freelance job was in fabric operations at Ralph Lauren for the Lauren by Ralph Lauren line.

Have you found it difficult to find a job? If so, what challenges have you faced?

❭ When I graduated from college and began looking for employment the economy wasn't doing too well, so jobs were scarce. I went to an interview at a company and found out that 34 other people were interviewing for the same position. Right then and there I knew I had a slim chance for being hired. Once I received my first freelance job, the rest became easy. I began making connections and building a more impressive résumé.

What made you decide to start a career in fashion?

❭ I work through imagination and art. I knew when I was younger, I couldn't do something that was too business-oriented or a job that seemed mundane. My senior year of high school, I saw a random fashion show online from Christian Dior's Spring 2004 Haute Couture Collection and immediately fell in love with the lavishness of the garments.

It takes a lot of courage and ambition to decide to move to New York alone and pursue one of the most challenging careers in one of the most competitive cities. How were you able to take the plunge?

❭ I was young and foolish, but in a good way; my naiveté helped me take the leap to New York. Also, I have two degrees in design so I know I was only useful here and maybe Los Angeles, but I am not L.A. material.

What is your ultimate dream job and what do you think it takes to land it?

❭ Creative director of womenswear at any mid-market to high-end brand, like Club Monaco, Kate Spade, Calvin Klein Collection, or Oscar de la Renta. It takes a mixture of good talent and connections. Knowing the right people in this industry helps. I hear of so many people receiving jobs because they knew somebody.

What has been the most rewarding part of working in fashion?

❭ Seeing products that I created in a store is the most rewarding aspect of working in fashion. In my first freelance job, I created a myriad of stripe patterns for Izod polo shirts. About a year later, Macy's Herald Square in New York showcased a huge display in their flagship store and in all the windows for the INDY 500, and I saw some of my stripes in the visual display. Little did those shoppers know that I created what they were purchasing. It was a very proud moment for me.

Looking back on the path you took to get here, would you have done anything differently? If so, what?

❯ Yes. I would have completed all of my schooling in New York instead of splitting it up like I did.

What sort of glamorous and fun things were you exposed to by working in fashion design?

❯ The most glamorous thing I have seen took place during my internship at Jill Stuart. Her show was held at the New York City Library, and a few celebrities attended, including model Tyra Banks, fashion photographer Nigel Barker, singer Vanessa Carlton,

and activist Lauren Bush. Another glamorous moment took place as a volunteer. One day I was sitting in class at F.I.T. when someone from *Vogue* came into our classroom and asked if anyone wanted to volunteer for an event. She didn't mention what it was for, so most people didn't volunteer. I did. We wound up volunteering for the Council of Fashion Designers of America (CFDA) Kenneth Cole GALA sample sale hosted by *Vogue*. This was not your ordinary sample sale. It was 100 percent red carpet. The sale was meant to raise money for AIDS, and the products were donated by various designers. Our job as volunteers was to basically help everyone there with their shopping spree. Celebrities in attendance included Kate Moss, Naomi Campbell, Anna Wintour, Bette Midler, Ralph Lauren, Michael Kors, Dita Von Teese, and Mary-Louise Parker.

WORKING WITH AN EMPLOYMENT AGENCY

Building strong relationships with employment agencies is important, as they can be excellent partners in helping you to obtain both freelance and full-time jobs. Here are some guidelines for how to best work with an employment agency.

1. *Register with various employment agencies.* Most employment agencies ask job seekers to submit an online application that you can access through their website so you can be added to their database. Registering consists of uploading your résumé, and answering pertinent questions regarding your job search, such as your desired position and salary level.

2. *Prepare for an informational interview.* Some employment agencies will ask you to come in for a face-to-face interview prior to submitting your résumé for any jobs. This gives the agency the chance to meet you in person to discuss your career objectives so they can place you in the most appropriate job based on your background and experience. At that time, you may also be asked to fill out a freelancer agreement. A typical freelancer agreement covers topics such as client confidentiality and at-will

employment. You may also be asked to fill out tax forms, such as the W-4 (employee tax withholdings) and I-9 forms (work authorization). You will also be given the option to fill out a direct deposit form (electronic transfer of your paycheck to your bank account). During the interview, you will also present the agency with your updated résumé and portfolio. Be sure to have a sell sheet for your portfolio (a summary featuring several items of your work from your portfolio) that you can leave with the recruiter.

3. *Await contact by the agency for a job opening.* The agency will email or call you when a position that matches your background becomes available. They will give you information about the company, the job responsibilities, the length of the assignment (if it is a freelance job) the rate (hourly, weekly, per project or salaried), and any other pertinent aspects of the assignment. They may also ask you more in-depth questions about your background that specifically relate to the job responsibilities, to ensure that you are the right fit for the job. After the recruiter explains the job responsibilities, you will be asked if you would like your résumé submitted for the job. If you accept, the agency will submit your résumé for the position. An agency will not send your résumé to a company without contacting you first.

4. *Await contact by the agency for a job interview.* The recruiter will call you if the company would like to interview you. Always make yourself available for the timeslot given, as the company is usually under a time crunch to get the position filled. The agency will then confirm all of the necessary interview details.

5. *Prepare for the interview.* You should prepare for an interview you receive through an employment agency just as seriously as you would any other interview. Prior to going on your interview, the agency will likely remind you not to discuss salary or hourly wages with the client under any circumstances, as the agency handles this aspect of placement.

6. *Call the agency after your interview.* The agent you have been working with will usually ask you to contact them after the interview, to let them know how it went. It is highly recommended to make the call right after your interview ends, even before you get home, to show your enthusiasm.

7. *Agency will contact you if you booked the job.* The agency will contact you if you got the job, and will communicate all the necessary details. Ask any questions you may have at this time, and be sure you are clear about where you need to report, and what is expected of you. The agency will also further explain any of their policies for new hires.

8. *Keep in touch with your recruiter.* Remember to always stay in contact with your recruiter in between freelance assignments or full-time jobs to let them know you are in the market for a position.

◄◄ Chado Ralph Rucci Fall/Winter 2012 Ready-to-Wear Collection. Fisher Fur and Braided Leather Cardigan with Grey Flannel Pant. PHOTOGRAPHERS: DAN AND CORINA LECCA. COURTESY OF CHADO RALPH RUCCI.

◄ Fashion designer Paul Hernandez with his own creation for the Make a Wish Foundation, 2011. COURTESY OF PAUL HERNANDEZ.

Part-Time Employee

Part-time jobs are generally few and far between in the fashion industry, and are generally best found by using the advanced search option on online job-seeker websites. You will usually find a handful of listings using this search method.

Full-Time Employee

Full-time work is the most popular job category amongst fashion designers, and most full-time job opportunities come with benefits, including health insurance, paid vacations, and 401K plans, and, on occasion, clothing allowances. The biggest detriment is that you are usually classified as an at-will employee and can be fired or discharged at any time, for any reason. Your job will also be at risk during recessions and economic downturns. In some cases, higher-level fashion designers will be offered contracts outlining provisions for job termination, which usually differ from those of an at-will employee.

Self-Employed

There has been an increase in the demand for self-employed fashion designers in the industry, ranging from consultants to contractors. The company hires the consultant on a project basis

Look 25 of the Spring 2012 Peter Som Runway Collection.
PHOTOGRAPHER: DAN LECCA. COURTESY OF PETER SOM.

and either pays an hourly rate (including time and half pay for any work week exceeding forty hours) or a project fee. The consultant may be in the office as often as a full-time employee or may have the flexibility to schedule his or her own hours. Independent consultant jobs are usually not posted on public websites and are often obtained through word of mouth, networking, or previously formed relationships.

Business Owner

It is an aspiration for many fashion designers to launch their very own collection. As a business owner, you have the luxury of being your own boss, yet you hold the burden of having to successfully operate your business on your own or with a small team until it is built. No longer can you go to the company attorney to handle all of your legal issues or to the finance department for all of your monetary concerns. Each and every decision falls on your lap, but all of your hard work goes directly into the building of your company, and the rewards can be tremendous. For further information on launching your own fashion collection, see Chapter 5.

PRODUCT CATEGORY

Once you've determined your job category, the next step is to determine the product category that most appeals to you. Do you want to design apparel or accessories? Once you've answered that question, get really specific. If you chose apparel, do you want to design women's sportswear separates or boys' swimwear? If accessories, do you want to design women's belts or men's wallets?

WORK ENVIRONMENT

Once you've determined your product category, the next step is to determine the work environment that you feel best suits you. As an aspiring fashion designer, you have the option to practice your craft in many different work settings. Do you feel more comfortable working for a large international apparel manufacturer with branch offices all over the world or a small design firm? When you work for a larger corporation, you will most likely begin your career working in a segmented product category, such as women's sweaters. When you work for a small design firm, you will be expected to take a more hands-on approach, generally giving you the opportunity to design across several product categories and to take on greater responsibilities. Keep in mind that compensation can be lower working in a smaller, recently established firm, due to budgetary constraints. However, working for an up-and-coming designer can give you the opportunity to get in with the company from the get-go and help build it into a more prominent brand.

FASHION MARKET

Once you've determined your work environment, the next step is to determine the fashion market segment that you would like to design. There are twelve different fashion market price points: (1) one-of-a-kind, (2) haute couture, (3) bespoke, (4) designer, (5) bridge, (6) better, (7) contemporary, (8) secondary, (9) moderate, (10) private label, (11) mass, and (12) discount. You can refer to Chapter 1 for a complete description of each.

TYPE OF DESIGNER

Once you've determined your work environment, the next step is to determine the type of designer you would like to be. There are six different types of designers: (1) apparel, (2) accessories, (3) footwear, (4) technical, (5) CAD, and (6) textile. You can refer to Chapter 1 for a complete description of each. Within their chosen areas of specialty, fashion designers typically follow a specific career path for advancement. To find out typical salaries for each position in the following list, refer to the section on negotiating your job offer in Chapter 3 for a list of salary resources:

Design Assistant: This entry-level position is a typical first fashion design job for recent college graduates and most designers start out as a design assistant. It can be more administrative than design-focused, but it oftentimes includes creative tasks, such as researching new design concepts; layout and creation of storyboards; maintaining fabric, trim, and color libraries; and assisting the design team with their workflow, including daily administrative tasks, such as creating design binders and making copies. In some cases, a design assistant will be brought in as the right hand to the head designer or creative director—a wonderful opportunity to hone his or her skills and learn from the best.

Assistant Designer: The next level up from the design assistant is the assistant designer, who assists the designer in all the steps of the design process. Tasks may include research, development and execution of designs; flat sketching; creating technical packages; setting up line sheets; fabric/trim sourcing; attending fit meetings and communicating fit comments to overseas factories; tracking prototypes, strike-offs, and lab dips; and managing the overall sample approval process.

Associate Designer: The associate designer is oftentimes given creative input and a truly participative role in the actual design process, as well as handling certain design related tasks in the absence of the designer. This added responsibility prepares the associate designer for a future head designer position. The associate designer will serve as a liaison among the design, technical design, product development, and merchandising teams to ensure cohesive information flow.

In some companies, associate designers can assist in identifying seasonal fashion direction and merchandise trends; competitive shop the market; give design approval on lab dips, strike-offs, prototypes, and samples; and participate in fit meetings and advise comments to factories via "tech pack" submissions.

Designer: The designer, or head designer, participates in the entire fashion design process, often while overseeing a design team, consisting of design assistants and assistant designers, as well as design interns. The designer collaborates with the senior designer and design director to develop the line direction, while working with all cross-functional teams to exchange viewpoints, leverage proficiencies, and streamline the product development process. Domestic and international travel is often required. The designer usually reports to a senior designer or the design director.

Senior Designer: The senior designer is one step ahead of the designer, with responsibility for communicating brand direction, including seasonal concepts, and fabric, trim, color and silhouette ideas to the design team. This is a truly cross-functional role, as the senior designer will interact with many departments in addition to design, including fabric/trim development, merchandising, production, the sample room, and sales, ensuring that all departments are partnering effectively to deliver a collection that is consistent with corporate brand strategies and saleable to the target market. The senior designer may manage individuals from any of these departments and reports to any of the senior design leaders from the design director to the chief creative officer. International travel to fabric and trade shows, mills, factories and branch offices, and for research trips is customary.

Design Director: The design director leads the entire product development process, by building the collection from concept to market launch, including the supervision of several direct reports, from interns, design assistants, and associate designers to the heads of design, patternmakers, drapers, and the sample room manager and sample room assistants. This position is also usually responsible for projecting retail prices, target margins, and costing with the merchandising and costing teams, as well as participating in marketing and selling initiatives. The ability to manage a deadline-driven time and action calendar is essential, as well as having an eye for trends, a strong color sense, fabric and print sensibility, and a capability to conduct fittings. International travel to fabric and trade shows, mills, factories, branch offices, and for research trips is common. The design director is expected to have prior management experience and will typically be responsible for performance evaluations for all direct reports.

Senior Design Director: The senior design director is one level up from the design director, and uses his or her in-depth knowledge to create innovative designs that are true to the brand aesthetic. A senior design director's primary responsibility is to maintain the highest quality, function, and fit of the product and to onboard the design, merchandising, production, sales, and sample room team so that all individuals are working together to uphold brand integrity and exceed corporate expectations.

International travel to fabric and trade shows, mills, factories, branch offices, and for research trips is common. The senior design director will have prior management experience, a proven track record of delivering timely collections from concept stage to production, and will typically be responsible for performance evaluations for all direct reports.

Vice President of Design: The vice president of design is a common promotion from design director or senior design director. This role oversees all aspects of design, including multiple product categories, in compliance with all corporate brand initiatives and strategies. This position commonly reports to either the president of design or the

Chado Ralph Rucci Fall/Winter 2012 Ready-to-Wear Collection. Black Reptile and Tulle Motor Jacket. PHOTOGRAPHERS: DAN AND CORINA LECCA. COURTESY OF CHADO RALPH RUCCI.

CEO of the company and is considered a senior member of the corporate executive management team. He or she must have a proven ability to lead and manage an entire design and product development team. The vice president of design will have prior management experience, will typically have a full international travel schedule, and will be responsible for performance evaluations of all direct reports.

Senior Vice President of Design: Along with the vice president of design, the senior vice president of design has a solid understanding and proven track record of consistently turning designs into products that turn a high percentage sell-through. The senior vice president of design will have prior management experience, expected to travel internationally, and will be responsible for performance evaluations of all direct reports. Like the vice president of design, this position commonly reports to either the president of design or the CEO of the company and is considered a senior member of the corporate executive management team.

Creative Director/President of Design/Chief Creative Officer: The creative director, president of design, or chief creative officer is the highest-level creative position in a fashion house or apparel/accessories manufacturer. The main objective of these executives is to formulate concepts and give tactical and strategic direction to the various design directors of each product category, to ensure that designs are carried out to their specifications. Their role is to determine what designs should be executed, what will be appropriate to the target market, and how the concepts will be applied, to ensure that all products remain true to the brand image and that the bottom-line sales objectives of the company are reached. All design positions report into this role, whether directly or indirectly, and this role reports to the chief financial officer, chief executive officer, or founder/owner of the company.

Once you have chosen your different categories and determined your design specialty, you can target your job search strategy accordingly. Keep in mind that you may not be offered your ideal job right away. It is of utmost importance to gain experience, no matter what type of job opportunity comes your way, especially when first starting out. You'll always have time to target your search more specifically later on in your career.

Personal Branding

Now that you've decided the best career path to take, it's time to develop a personal branding statement (PBS). A PBS is a message that clearly and concisely outlines your strengths and talents, while demonstrating what differentiates you from the competition. Simply put, it represents who you are, what you stand for, and what you bring to a company. It allows you to stand out as a leader, and it influences how others perceive you. Once you create your PBS, it will become the central theme in all the marketing tools you use to obtain a job—your résumé, your business card, and the way you present yourself during interviews and at networking functions. Everyone in the market for a job or those currently holding a job should develop a personal brand for themselves.

During your job search, a PBS will help differentiate you from the competition by carefully conveying a strategically thought-out message pertaining to the value you can bring to a company. Once you land the job, your PBS will serve as a catalyst for your continued success. If upper management has an understanding of your potential, you will more than likely become a stronger candidate for promotional opportunities and career advancement. Personal branding is especially important during tough economic times, when competition is fierce and thousands of people are vying for the same job.

As a job seeker, your goal is to "sell" your skills to a potential employer, and at any given moment, you may run into someone who can help you land a job or lead you to a job opportunity. With a personal branding statement under your belt, you will be prepared to get across who you are, what you can offer a company, and what you are looking for in a short period of time. For a hiring manager, a PBS will answer the question, "Should I hire you?"

Oprah Winfrey, Madonna, and Donald Trump all have used personal branding to contribute to their success. And within the fashion industry, so have Ralph Lauren, Tommy Hilfiger, Michael Kors, Betsey Johnson, Oscar de la Renta, and virtually all successful fashion designers. Not only did each of them differentiate themselves from the competition, but they did so in way that makes them exceptional. For example, Ralph Lauren invented the concept of lifestyle advertising. Not only does he sell the customer his clothes, he sells them the luxury lifestyle behind those clothes. His advertising allows those viewing it to visualize themselves living the life of the models in the advertisement—sailing in Newport or living in a stately countryside mansion. He delivers a consistent message that is carried out not only in his ads, but in the merchandising of his stores and shops within the department stores, and in the visual displays of his store windows across the globe. His message is consistent and clearly gets across to his target customer.

Grace Gardens "2056 Collection" from the Kara Saun runway presentation, 2006. COURTESY OF KARA SAUN.

Advertising agencies create catchy taglines for products that become ingrained in our minds over time. They convey something about the product that benefits us and encourages us to purchase it. If we do actually benefit from the product, we will continue to buy it, which creates brand loyalty. In the same way that advertisers brand their products, we have to act as advertisers for our own individual brand and create that same loyalty in a potential employer with our personal branding statements. Remember to update your PBS as your career advances, to stay current with what you can best offer a company.

PERSONAL BRANDING BY CHRISTOPHER J. BILOTTA, PRESIDENT OF RESOURCE DEVELOPMENT COMPANY, INC.

Since Tom Peters first coined the term "personal branding" in a 1997 *Fast Company* magazine article entitled "The Brand Called You," the concept has exploded. Peters said that we are the CEO of our own company and our most important job is to be head marketer for the brand called "you."

Standing out from the crowd has become an increasingly difficult task in today's age of information overload. Given our hyper-competitive, 24/7 world, where everyone is vying for attention, it can be argued that the proverbial 15 minutes of fame has been reduced to 15 seconds, which leaves precious little time to make the right impression. Personal branding is a powerful means to achieving one's goals. By differentiating yourself and showcasing your unique value through a clear and consistent message, personal branding provides the tool to reach your target market and separate yourself from the competition.

As a fashion designer, your personal brand is about building a solid reputation within the industry, establishing yourself as a designer of choice, and increasing your perceived value versus your competition. Your profession inherently gives you an excellent platform to differentiate yourself, since fashion is all about being distinct. When you think about the high-profile brands that are part of our everyday life, their tagline is what helps make them unique and memorable. To draw on a prominent example, consider "Nothing comes between me and my Calvins" by Calvin Klein. Here are steps to help you start creating your personal branding statement:

1. Conduct your own personal branding survey. Ask five people, including clients, associates, coworkers, business acquaintances, friends, and family, to choose three adjectives they feel best describe you. Ask them for words that quickly pop into their minds.

2. Conduct this same exercise again, only this time ask yourself the question and compare the results with step one.

3. Group the adjectives into categories based on your personality, competencies and unique value.

4. Take the best characteristics from each category and use them to describe your brand.

For example, your personal brand statement might read:

A visionary and innovative fashion designer combining instinctive feel, dramatic flair, and an eye for critical detail, I excel at creating unforgettable styles that inspire people to dress their best and help build long-lasting customer loyalty based on elegance, comfort, and quality.

Building trust and credibility are the keys to success in any marketing effort. As people begin to see your name and become aware of the benefit and knowledge that you offer, you will become known as someone whose expertise is valued. Your brand will make a permanent impression, and you will be remembered. Whether you are looking for a new job or striving for career advancement in your present job, your personal brand and how you market it will help widen the gap between you and your competitors. Creating marketing materials that break through the clutter is essential. Your résumé, portfolio, personal website, business cards, and other collateral should all be designed with a distinctive look, feel, and message focused on the brand vision.

As the aforementioned Peters also said, "We all have brands worthy of remark." By developing and marketing your personal brand, you can accrue multiple benefits, including enhancing your own self-awareness, clarifying your goals, increasing visibility and presence, and creating staying power.

Portfolio Development

A fashion designer's portfolio is a powerful artistic tool—providing a synopsis of your most cherished work and a chance to reveal your own distinctive design interpretations. A professional portfolio (referred to often as a "book") features the work created by a fashion designer and is an essential tool in demonstrating one's range of artistic talent and skill level during the interviewing process. It can also be used to present to a potential investor if launching your own collection. It can include designs created during college, an internship, a freelance assignment, a full-time job or any other independent or substantial project, and should be a compilation of only your finest work. Even though a designer is required to have both a résumé and a portfolio, your portfolio will be the focal point and what hiring managers will concentrate on most during an interview.

Eco denim mood board for Ethical Fashion Show in Paris. TIERRA ECOLOGIA, 2005.

If you are a recent graduate, employers will understand that you have limited work experience and therefore a smaller number of artistic samples, so concentrate on showing any designs, illustrations, sketches, and mood boards you created as a student for class projects or during a college internship.

PORTFOLIO SELECTION

There are several steps that go into creating a portfolio. The first step in the process is to determine the type of portfolio that is going to best showcase your work. A bound portfolio is a must have for anyone in a creative role and can be purchased at any major art or office supply store. Make sure the dimensions of your portfolio case are in line with the size of your sketches, illustrations, and designs. Recommended sizes include 8" x 10", 9"x 12", 11"x14" (the most commonly used size), 14"x17", and 16" x 20". Other available options include zippered presentation cases, nonzippered, spiral-bound (some offer removable binders), easel styles, and custom-crafted portfolios. Most portfolios come with a 3-ring binder, which allows the user to place designs in individual sheet protectors, which are then placed in binder rings. This is an extremely professional way to show your work.

Keep in mind that your final case choice is first seen before your actual work and therefore will be assessed along with the contents of your portfolio, so choose the one that best reflects your design aesthetic. Keep in mind the color, texture and detail of each case before finalizing your selection.

It is also critical for you to have a digital presence or an e-portfolio. You can create your own website (by purchasing a domain name) to display your design work, or you can create an e-portfolio by using a free online portfolio website (a listing of online portfolio website companies can be found in the Appendix). Be sure to list your website's URL on cover letters, in the contact section of your résumé, on the title page of your portfolio, and on your business card. This will give potential employers an opportunity to view your work online when deciding whether to call you in for an interview.

Occasionally, you may need to send a potential employer, a copy of your portfolio ahead of time in a packet along with your résumé. In such cases, it is a good idea to have a few compact disc ROM (CD-ROM) versions of your portfolio on hand. You can purchase blank CD-ROMS at any major office supply or computer store.

STRUCTURE

The traditional portfolio includes a title or introductory page (a unique description about you, including your name and logo; your personal branding statement, your e-portfolio URL); four to six design concepts, along with corresponding materials that show how you formed the concepts, including fabric and color swatches (cut evenly with pinking shears) and trims; flat sketches (specs can also be included); and illustrations. After you've completed all of your design concepts, as well as showing both the inspiration behind them, and all the steps in your process, you can then include school awards, contest winnings, and any press and recognitions you may have received.

Your portfolio should be focused and show a range of product categories, price points, and seasons targeted to a particular customer base. Be sure to use self-adhesive, pre-cut lettering or computer-generated typeface (a creative, yet simple font ensuring legibility) for titles, themes, and any sort of labeling throughout your portfolio. Begin and end your portfolio with your most impressive work, to create interest, set the tone, and appeal to the viewer.

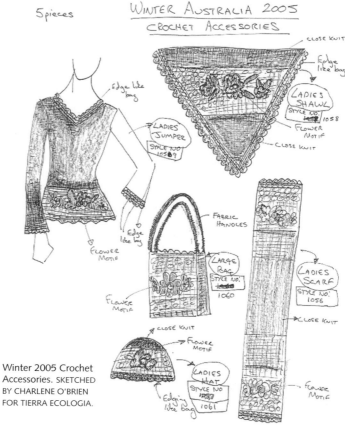

Winter 2005 Crochet Accessories. SKETCHED BY CHARLENE O'BRIEN FOR TIERRA ECOLOGIA.

Pre-Fall 2012/2013 jersey punto milano melange with lingerie-inspired details of tulle and lace trimmings, sketched by Marta Buscaroli. COURTESY OF MARTA BUSCAROLI.

CONTENT

It is important to develop a well-rounded portfolio by including a variety of media, including flat and technical sketches and illustrations created by hand and computer, digital art, graphic design, and artistic renderings. You should also include fabric, trim, and color swatches to accompany your sketches, in order to give a complete overview of the collection you created. Include any items that inspired the design, for example, a photograph of a texture or a painting. A photograph of a presentation or mood board may also be included. A presentation or mood board is a visual tool used to communicate the feeling of a concept. It contains an overview of different coordinated groups of apparel or accessories, and should include sketches, illustrations, fabrics, trims, color palettes, tear sheets, or any other items that inspired the design concept. Accessories designers can include swatches of raw materials, colors, finishes, hardware, detailing (such as a particular stitch used), as well as flat and technical sketches, illustrations, and photographs of the finished product in their portfolio.

When interviewing, most companies expect to see examples of the types of products they manufacture represented in your portfolio. A sportswear company will not get much out of seeing a portfolio that only includes eveningwear designs. So make sure you thoroughly research the product line(s) that the company makes, and include design ideas based on those product offerings. Your interviewer will be measuring your creativity level, drawing/sketching ability, conceptual development ability, and trend awareness. You also should create a sell sheet, which is a one-page document showing a summarized pictorial representation of your work (a portfolio overview) that you can leave with the interviewer when your interview is over. This will be sure to make a lasting impression!

Lastly, it is vital that you keep your portfolio updated with your most recent work, so continue to add content to your portfolio as you progress in your career.

Sketched by Peter Som for the Spring 2012 Peter Som Collection. COURTESY OF PETER SOM.

Mood board for Steve and Barry's by Jenny Lew, 2007. COURTESY OF JENNY LEW.

What Should Every Fashion Designer Include in His or Her Portfolio?

❯ For a job interview, your portfolio serves as tangible evidence of your professional history, the synthetic proof of who you are and how you have impacted the firms you have worked for in the past. Its magic resides in the ability to articulate concepts and tell a story without words. The perfect portfolio is clear, striking, elegant, minimal, simple, and breathtaking. To have an impactful portfolio, you need to study in-depth the nature and the history of the firm you are applying for and create the story you want to tell. A candidate who is flexible and not characterized by a rigid style is rare and therefore very much appreciated, both from a philosophical and practical standpoint. The same kind of flexibility can be practically applied also to the portfolio creation process, by developing modules of contents and messages and by blending and combining them together, into a slightly different story that is particularly engaging to the firm [where] you are applying. Fashion designers create value by crafting dreams that are made of sophisticated style, meaningful appearance, and a sense of belonging. An in-depth understanding and management of the aesthetic elements that can make those meaningful dreams come true into a collection and in a brand cannot be conveyed just by your portfolio during an interview; interview experience is holistic, and the portfolio needs to be in line in a consistent way with your personal image as well. Your style, the selected dress code, and

What Should Every Fashion Designer Include in His or Her Portfolio? (Continued)

your body language are communicating implicit messages that need to be in perfect harmony with your words, your portfolio, and with the values of the company you want to join.

Elisa Padrin, Designer, Yves Saint Laurent, Milan, Italy

❯ Keep it short and sweet! No one wants to look through pages and pages of drawings and inspiration boards. Editing is key; include the work that you feel is the best, and always put your best projects first and last. When it comes to interviewing for jobs, it's always good to include a project that will correspond to the house aesthetics. This way you can show the diversity of your skills and also your commitment. Lastly, make it about you, as it will always work better if it feels right to you!

Kinga Malisz, Womenswear Designer, Prêt-à-porter, Nina Ricci, Paris, France

❯ Every designer should always have great visuals of the actual product they designed. Another suggestion is to create a digital version of the portfolio as it's always appreciated.

Antonio Giussani, Senior Men's Shoe Designer, Christian Dior, Paris, France

Illustrated by Izak Zenou for Henri Bendel, 2007. COURTESY OF IZAK ZENOU.

❯ A portfolio is a very important aspect of the interview process for any fashion designer. As an entry-level designer wanting to break into fashion, a portfolio gives a snapshot of your creativity and skill set to a prospective employer. Emerging designers should always include an inspiration page, fabric and color selections, illustrations, and flats. Photos of your work are always a great addition to your portfolio because they illustrate your competency in other facets of design, including draping skills, sewing skills, production skills, etc. While your portfolio is an extension of your own personal aesthetic and creative abilities, make sure the content can blend with many different styles and markets. Be prepared to present your portfolio while interviewing, and practice presenting it prior to any

Untitled sketch by Kinga Malisz, 2010. COURTESY OF KINGA MALISZ.

Pre-Fall 2012/2013 androgynous silhouettes by Marta Buscaroli. COURTESY OF MARTA BUSCAROLI.

scheduled interviews. Always present your portfolio in a concise manner that conveys your inspirations, abilities, and your added value to the company. One last important note is to make sure to always keep your portfolio current and up-to-date.

Danielle Benson, Director, Fashion Division, Taylor Hodson Fashion, New York, New York, USA

❭ A designer's portfolio should be personal, fun, new, and unique, yet very technical. The best way to present your work relies on the right balance between creativity and practical implementation. Spend a lot of time creating it and present your sketches, along with the details, including accurate fabric research, color palette, technical details, and flats.

Marta Buscaroli, Senior Freelance Womenswear Designer, Emanuel Ungaro, Paris, France

❭ A fashion designer's portfolio should be made up of two essential parts. The first part should contain commercial work to show the viewer of your portfolio that you can understand the brand and design outside of yourself. The second part should be a personal section that shows how an idea is born. Demonstrate how you get through the creative process to a finished garment. And last but certainly not least, keep it tidy!

Remember, your portfolio is a direct reflection of your professional and creative self.

Alisha Adams, Product Recruiter, Lululemon Athletica, Vancouver, British Columbia

❭ Every designer's portfolio should tell a story. What inspired the design? Your portfolio should include your inspiration through to final product. You are presenting an edited version of your creativity, and you want to make sure that you can show your thought process for your design, whether it is a running shoe or an entire couture collection.

Bevy Reyes, Global Director of Creative & Design, Janou Pakter, New York, New York, USA

❭ While the current trend is to make use of modern technology, it is important to recognize that there is a time and place for its use. That being said, when meeting with a fashion designer, we want to see a physical portfolio, not to just be sent a link to view examples of work. The physical portfolio is always more of interest and more expressive of originality. We would be happy to go to a link following the interview for further examples of talent. Next, we want to see recent work. While spectacular school projects may serve as trophies for the candidate, we are more interested in seeing actual paying

What Should Every Fashion Designer Include in His or Her Portfolio? (Continued)

examples. If the candidate is applying for a first job, creative work done solely for the purpose of showcasing talent specifically for the interview with us is greatly appreciated and positively regarded. If a candidate is currently working in children's wear, but hoping to obtain a position in men's, we expect to see examples appropriate to the position. The "introduction" to your skill, the first works in your portfolio, should be work you are most proud of, but should be creative, spontaneous, and appropriate to what we are looking for.

LeeAnn Claridge, Director, Human Resources, Mark Edwards Apparel Inc./Sixty Canada/Want Agency/Group of 3/MEJK Apparelab, Montreal, Quebec, Canada

❯ A fashion designer should first and foremost have a clean, fresh, and updated portfolio. When interviewing, they should make sure that they have current trend ideas represented that relate to the company's product line and their target market. Designers must also have illustrations and photo work in their portfolio. It is important to have both hand sketches and sketches done on Illustrator to show potential employers. Extra copies of the résumé should be kept in the portfolio as well.

Fran Gellis, Manager of Fashion Division, Winston Staffing, New York, New York, USA

❯ A winning portfolio should include work samples from past employers, internships, or project work. In our experience, a combination of inspiration pages, hand sketches, technical drawings (by hand or in CAD), swatches, and images of final products best showcases a designer's abilities and understanding of the design process. What our global fashion clients are looking for in design candidates is the ability to successfully adopt and interpret their specific brand DNA and deliver "brand right" product. Designers should keep this in mind when putting together their portfolios. The goal should be to show as much diversity and breadth in working with different aesthetics, silhouettes, fabrica-

tions, and classifications as possible. In the case that past work experience is limited or candidates have mostly worked on one specific style or product (e.g., eveningwear) and they want to show a broader skill set, we also encourage personal projects that will give a better idea of the candidate's own aesthetic and personal style and taste. The candidate should present work that is not only item based, but that shows the designer's ability to put together complete collections. While creativity is key, more and more fashion clients want designers with a "merchant eye" and the ability to successfully marry creative and commercial needs, so showcasing the thought process behind the creative work is also important. Finally, having an online version of their portfolio that can be shared with companies and recruiters virtually is a must-have in today's digital world.

Theresa Fuchs-Santiago, Search Director, Martin & Heads!, New York, New York, USA

❯ Your portfolio shows your design process and includes concept/mood boards, including fabric swatches, color concepts (in yarn, ribbon, paint, chips, etc.), magazine tear sheets or printouts from current/recent runway shows, stills from old movies, vintage references, architectural photos, pictures from foreign countries, and anything that inspires your designs for each theme you're presenting. Presentation is everything, so make certain it is neat and organized. If you are a great hand illustrator, then your book should showcase that and provide a few figures that give an overview for each theme. If you have trouble illustrating, then find another way to present your designs (on a stylized hanger or modern looking mannequin form, or create flats that are not stiff but have movement). Include samples of flats (front and back) and technical drawing capabilities. Don't use fancy borders and backgrounds on your work, as it is distracting. When you're out of school for a few years, take out your senior runway project and school work. Keep it fresh and forward-looking. Keep several copies of your résumé in the back of the book.

Emily Koltnow, President, Koltnow & Company, New York, New York, USA

❯ A designer's portfolio should include representation of all the skills that they use on the job or can bring to an employer's business. Paired with creativity should be a display of a designer's business sense and knowledge that they can create a product that will sell. Inspiration, mood or concept story, ability to roughly sketch ideas on paper, and the ability to make these creative drawings come to life are all general points that can define what can exist in a portfolio. The designer can show their on-the-job skill set in their portfolio by including any number of the following items or tasks: concept ideas, inspiration, mood or trend, thumbnail sketches, croqui sketches, hand and computer illustrations/sketches, flat sketches or technical renderings, development of the garment (including samples of fabric, trim, or color), line sheets, full collection presentation, prints, patterns, graphics, embroidery layouts, and special skills. A portfolio should be chronological in the design and development process.

Alicia Fazio, Managing Director, fourthFLOOR Fashion, New York, New York, USA

❯ Nothing shows off a designer's natural talent and ability quite like a hand sketch. If possible, include a technical sketch and an image of the finished product. You may also want to include inspiration for a particular piece in your portfolio.

Dione Katelhut, Executive Director, The Fit, Portland, Oregon, USA

❯ A designer's portfolio is their most prized possession: a reflection of their experience and talent. Within a portfolio, there should be a variety of work, ranging from hand-drawn sketches through to CAD-based design work, depending on the level of the market they are designing in (e.g., high-end de-

sign houses expect hand drawings). Including mood and trend inspiration/boards is key to set the theme seasonally and show how the person builds their research and collates their ideas and thoughts prior to designing a collection. Seasonal projects either from their current employer or personal work reflecting their own ideas, in chronological order with the newest pieces at the front, should follow each board. Illustrative work is often used after each collection to show the full range line-up and overall seasonal look. Depending on the product area in focus, a couple of specs sheets should be included at the back of the portfolio to demonstrate a technical understanding of the product. A portfolio is usually one main book; however, some designers prefer to have one main portfolio plus a sketch and press book.

Salma Sodawala, Consultant, Design, Technical, Production & Sales, Henry Fox Recruitment, London, England, United Kingdom

❯ I believe the most essential part of the portfolio is to have photos of your strongest pieces and sketches from your collections. Also, it is very important to include all the articles about your collection or yourself (newspapers, magazines, and online blogs), as these are assets for your brand. Of course, if you have celebrities wearing your collection at different events, make sure to include these images because this particular factor will help you to build your brand faster.

Marcus Kan, Fashion Director, Ukamaku, Toronto, Canada

❯ A fashion design portfolio is an important tool for any designer to showcase their best work, and each designer has a unique design perspective based on several aspects such as color, audience, season, etc. The portfolio is a tool to communicate your design sense to the world. A portfolio is essential if you are applying to a design school or if you are looking for work with a prospective employer. Your portfolio highlights your fashion skills, such as your fashion and color sense, sketching ability,

What Should Every Fashion Designer Include in His or Her Portfolio? (Continued)

trend forecasting ability, textile knowledge, visualization, and so on. Different skill sets are required for different work profiles within the fashion industry, so be sure of which segment you wish to enter before starting. Your portfolio is a reflection of your design style and a statement of your capabilities. Make it interesting and enjoyable to flip through, and present it in a way that shows you learning and growing with every new assignment you have done. This impresses clients and gives you a strong brand image when pitching for work.

Supriya Ghurye, Freelance Fashion Designer, Bangalore, India

❯ It's always important to show your best work in your portfolio rather than every single project you've completed in school or in your previous jobs. You should demonstrate your process in your portfolio as well, by showing how you get inspired, where you got your inspiration, and how you formed your ideas. Simplicity with strong images is always a plus.

Tugce Ozocak, Designer, Beymen, Istanbul, Turkey

❯ Having a beautiful portfolio with all your creative ideas is expected, and every designer should have one. In order to make your portfolio special and set you apart from others, you should take the design collection that you are most proud of and present it from inspiration through to retail sales. Show the collection from design concepts to finished samples, including all public relations, points of distribution, and what financial contribution your collection made to the overall company.

Michael Beckwith, Founder, Encore Jobz, Blufton, South Carolina, USA

Every fashion designer should always include technical work to support the fabulous illustrations in their portfolio. A fashion designer's portfolio should be a combination of creativity and technical knowledge to represent a completely rounded

fashion designer. It is very important to show garment construction and material knowledge, as well as creativity and design skills. Samples of a "tech pack" should always be included, as it displays technical knowledge and background. It is very important to show garment construction and material knowledge, as well as design skills in a portfolio. A successful fashion designer not only designs great pieces but is able to execute the designs into reality.

Connie Byun, Women's Outerwear Designer, New York, New York, USA

❯ I personally believe less is more, so you should show only your best creations. You want them to be clear, eye catching, up-to-date, and personal. A portfolio should also show pictures from finished products, so people get a realistic impression of your skills, capacities, and achievements. Including a certain element of surprise and variation is good to hold interest. Furthermore, I believe in the importance of the actual packaging of your portfolio. A professional, well-made portfolio always adds an extra element to your presentation. See your portfolio as an investment in your future because when it really comes down to it, this is the tool which can give you new job opportunities!

Halewijn Bulckaen, Print Designer, H&M, Stockholm, Sweden

❯ It is important for a fashion designer to show how their mind works and where their inspiration came from, as well as the end result. It is as much about the process as it is about the final piece, and also [demonstrates] whether their skill set complements that of the rest of the team and how the business is structured.

Chloe Lonsdale, Director, MiH JEANS, London, England, United Kingdom

❯ Your portfolio is a representation of you: your style, your hand, your organizational abilities, the direction you want to go in your fashion design

the most important attributes a designer must have (from the style, cover, and layout to the selection of paper). It should be consistent and show that you have thought of every detail possible.

Jen Muegge, Designer, Handbags and Accessories Designer, Treesje, Los Angeles, California, USA

Designed by Jen Muegge for Anne Valérie Hash. COURTESY OF ANNE VALÉRIE HASH.

Spring/Summer 2010 MiH JEANS Collection by Pierre Bijork and styled by Chloe Lonsdale. COURTESY OF MIH JEANS LONDON

career. Make sure it makes an impact and is not mundane. It is important to show the process. Show a trend board, a freehand, colored sketch of each design, and a colored CAD to show your abilities using Illustrator and Photoshop. Your designs should also show movement and dimension.

Charlene C. Burke, President, CC Burke, Ltd., Bronxville, New York, USA

❯ The most important element that a designer should think about before developing a portfolio is the type of design and work they want to have in their portfolio (i.e., haute couture, luxury, ready-to-wear, contemporary, or mass market). For example, luxury brands look specifically for hand sketching and concept development. However, once entering into other markets, Illustrator and Photoshop skills are an absolute essential. The one key factor that remains a constant is proper layout and presentation. Pay very close attention to detail, as this is one of

❯ Every fashion designer should include in their portfolio samples of the different stages of their creative process. Start with mood boards which show where the ideas came from and how they were interpreted and then translated into the final product. Materials and sketches should also be included. Final sketches can be colored or outlined, depending on your personal style; I normally mix both techniques, which makes it visually stronger. Lastly, add a few examples of technical specs and photos of the finished product, showcasing them in the best possible way.

Ana Borges, Senior Footwear Designer, Jaeger, London, England, United Kingdom

Spring/Summer 2010 Juan Antonio Lopez Collection by Ana Borges. COURTESY OF ANA BORGES.

Creating a Résumé that Pops

It takes a mere 30 seconds for a potential employer to decide whether to continue reading your résumé or to toss it in the "no" pile. With hundreds and sometimes thousands of people vying for the same position, it is essential to ensure that yours stands out from the rest. The best way to do this is to create a well thought-out résumé (made by you or a professional résumé writer) that is presented in the most impressive way possible. So how do you make this happen?

DETERMINE THE TYPE OF RÉSUMÉ YOU NEED

The first step is to decide the type of résumé that is best suited for your career background. There are three basic types of résumés: chronological, functional, and a combination of both. The chronological résumé lists your work experience by company, title, and dates of employment, listing the most recent employment first. This format works best for those who have had little to no gaps in employment and who generally followed a direct career path. It is the most commonly used and widely accepted format and is preferred by hiring managers because it clearly demonstrates your work history and growth potential, and provides an easy-to-follow snapshot of your work experience. It is important to note that employment gaps do stand out with this format, and it also emphasizes frequency in job changes. It is recommended for anyone pursuing a job for which you have a consistent record of position advancement. It is not recommended for individuals who have jumped from job to job and generally held each position for less than one year or for those with large gaps in their job history.

A functional format categorizes your résumé by different skill sets in various categories, and also lists your education, and achievements rather than each individual job. There is very little focus placed on employment history. Examples of skill sets are "Management," "Fashion Design Experience," "Team Building," and "Technical Package Creation." Under each section, you would describe your responsibilities, skills learned, and accomplishments achieved. The employment section, including names and locations of companies and dates of employment is brief and listed on the bottom of the page or eliminated altogether. This format highlights skills and achievements relevant to your career objectives and shifts the focus away from possible negative aspects of your background, such as long gaps of unemployment, which may eliminate your chances of getting an interview. Disadvantages to this format include the fact that lack of dates of employment may make hiring managers suspicious, work experience is not directly linked to specific companies and positions held at each company, and it is difficult to determine job responsibilities held in each job. It is recommended for those with large gaps in their job history, individuals who have held the same job over a long period of time with different companies, those who are trying to change positions within the industry, as well as anyone who is trying to return to work after a prolonged absence.

The combination résumé is a mix of both the chronological and functional formats. It lists work experience by skill sets and also includes employer name, using reverse-chronological dates of employment. Advantages include the fact that your accomplishments are highlighted upfront, and you eliminate any potential suspicion from hiring managers, since employment dates are included. It is also effective for freelancers and consultants who want to transition back to full-time work. In terms of disadvantages, this format will typically not be in chronological order and can be confusing to the reader. Additionally, some hiring managers will still think you are trying to conceal something negative because they are so used to seeing chronological résumés.

Chado Ralph Rucci Fall/Winter 2012 Ready-to-Wear Collection. Trapunto Grey Flannel and Feather Dress. PHOTOGRAPHERS: DAN AND CORINA LECCA. COURTESY OF CHADO RALPH RUCCI.

DECIDE THE LENGTH

The second step to create your résumé is to decide its length. Résumés are usually one to three pages long, depending on the number of years you have been in the industry. You can determine the most appropriate length based on certain criteria. Consider using a one-page résumé if you have had less than five years of work experience, are a recent college graduate or entry-level job seeker. However, if you fall into any of these categories, but have significant internships, summer jobs, regular work experience, pertinent extracurricular activities, certifications, volunteering, and/or leadership roles that justify a two-page résumé, go for it! You may use a two-page résumé if you have five or more years of work experience. All résumés that exceed one page should be numbered at the bottom of the page. Be sure to list contact information on the second page in the same place you put it on the first page. You do not need to list your address again, just include your name, phone number, e-mail address and url for your online portfolio, if applicable. A three-page résumé (or more) is appropriate if you are a senior-level fashion designer or above with a track record of impressive accomplishments and increasingly progressive job responsibilities.

Look 28 of the Spring 2012 Peter Som Runway Collection. PHOTOGRAPHER: DAN LECCA.

ADD PERTINENT SECTIONS

The third step in the résumé creation process is to add relevant sections. There are a variety of key components that every résumé should encompass. The heading, typically placed at the top center of the page, includes all of your pertinent contact information, such as your first and last name (add your middle name or middle initial if you desire), address (optional but preferred by most hiring executives), including apartment number if applicable, phone number (home and/ or mobile), e-mail address and the url for your online portfolio, if applicable. Whether you decide on left, center, or right placement depends on your personal preference, but center placement is most common. Be sure the heading is bold and in a larger font size than the rest of your résumé. Experiment with different font sizes until you come up with the most aesthetically pleasing fit.

Contrary to popular belief, you should not include an objective statement in your résumé. An objective states what type of job you are seeking, which is of little relevance to a hiring executive, who is more interested in knowing what you can bring to the table. Your personal branding statement (PBS) should replace the objective, and can be placed directly under the heading. Many people are not aware of the importance of the PBS, or have not even heard of it, so by including one, you will stand out among the competition. Your PBS can stand alone or be listed above your qualifications summary. A qualifications summary (also referred to as a summary of qualifications, summary of skills, or profile) is a recap of your relevant skills and proficiencies and is optional. If you add this to your résumé, it should be located under your contact information.

Your work experience should be listed in reverse chronological order, with your most recent job held listed first. This section should include the name and location (both city and state) of the company, title of the position you held, dates of employment, and job responsibilities, highlighting your accomplishments.

In your education section, the highest-level college degree should be listed first, followed by any continuing or adult education courses, certificates, or degrees, with the most recent listed first. Do not list your high school education unless you chose not to attend college. The order in which you list this information is based on your own inclination; however, most adhere to the following layout:

Fashion Institute of Technology—New York, New York
Bachelor of Fine Arts, Fashion Design, August 2011

If you haven't yet graduated from college, you can still use this format, just add "expected graduation" before the month and year of your planned graduation date. List all computer-related experience in this section, including expertise in word-processing software (Word, WordPerfect, etc.), spreadsheet knowledge (Excel), database management (WebPDM, Access, Lotus 123), e-mail programs (Outlook, Outlook Express), presentation software (PowerPoint), industry related software (Lectra, Photoshop, Illustrator, CAD), and any other pertinent computer expertise that relates to the position you are seeking. In this section, you can also list honors that you think would impress potential employers. Extracurricular activities are optional and are only recommended if you list those activities that relate to the fashion industry or are a recent graduate with little to no work experience. You may list professional organizations that have some relation to the fashion industry or somehow relate to your career goals (membership affiliations for a particular sector of the industry such as IACDE, the International Association of Clothing Designers and Executives). Hiring managers are already aware that references are available upon request, so there is no need to include a statement to this effect on your résumé.

Make sure your résumé is easy to read and easy to follow as you want to ensure that anyone who reviews it, finds it pleasing to the eye. You can accomplish this in a number of ways. You can start by fully justifying the text. This aligns the text to the left and right margins, adding extra spaces between words when necessary, which creates an overall clean, organized, and symmetrical format. Choose a common font. You can play it safe and stick to the more commonly used fonts such as Arial and Verdana, or give it a slightly creative edge by using a font such as Century Schoolbook or Futura Bk. Don't use overly fancy fonts on your résumé, because you don't want it to be illegible. Be sure to avoid using full sentences, since résumés are not written in sentence form, but rather in short phrases. Instead of using articles, such as "an," "a," and "the," you can use action words. In place of using the pronoun "I" to begin a sentence, use an action word to list your accomplishments. Your objective is to create and present a streamlined résumé to potential employers. Review the following list of sample action words to determine the most fitting for your résumé.

Sample Actions Words Table

Achieved	Closed	Developed	Helped	Maintained	Prepared	Registered
Acquired	Collaborated	Directed	Hired	Managed	Presented	Reorganized
Adapted	Collected	Eliminated	Identified	Marketed	Prioritized	Revamped
Adjusted	Combined	Enforced	Illustrated	Merged	Produced	Reviewed
Advised	Compiled	Ensured	Implemented	Modified	Projected	Revised
Advocated	Completed	Established	Improved	Monitored	Promoted	Scheduled
Analyzed	Composed	Evaluated	Incorporated	Negotiated	Proposed	Secured
Appointed	Conceptualized	Exceeded	Increased	Operated	Proved	Selected
Approved	Conducted	Executed	Initiated	Ordered	Provided	Simplified
Assigned	Consolidated	Expanded	Inspected	Organized	Publicized	Sold
Assisted	Coordinated	Expedited	Integrated	Outlined	Purchased	Spearheaded
Authorized	Created	Facilitated	Introduced	Oversaw	Received	Supported
Budgeted	Customized	Fashioned	Involved	Participated	Recommended	Tested
Built	Delivered	Formed	Joined	Performed	Recorded	Trained
Cataloged	Demonstrated	Founded	Launched	Photographed	Recruited	Updated
Categorized	Designed	Generated	Led	Planned	Redesigned	Wrote

Use bullet points after action words to neatly outline your job responsibilities and accomplishments. Be consistent by following the same format for each job listing. The most common approach is to arrange the information from most to least important, as follows: Title, name of employer, city/state of employer, dates of employment. However, you have to decide what format works best for you. You may want to list the name of the employer first and your title second. Make certain that you keep the same format consistent right down to the smallest details. Do not list one date as "6/2008" and then list another date as "6/5/08." Review the following before-and-after example that utilizes these layout rules:

Before:

> I came up with various standard operating procedures in the design department which allowed for productivity to increase by 40 percent on a monthly basis.

After:

- Implemented standard operating procedures in design department raising overall productivity to 40 percent monthly

In addition to presenting a concise and easy-to-follow résumé, it is important that you present factual information. Any kind of dishonesty on your résumé can cost you your job, both prior to being hired and after you are given the offer. It is very common these days for companies to fact-check the résumé and background of a potential hire. This is usually done at the same time that the references are being checked.

Chado Ralph Rucci Fall/Winter 2012 Ready-to-Wear Collection. Black Tiered Feather and Lace Gown. PHOTOGRAPHERS: DAN AND CORINA LECCA. COURTESY OF CHADO RALPH RUCCI.

You also want to be specific in describing your responsibilities and, whenever possible, list measurable accomplishments. Instead of stating a general accomplishment, use specific details to demonstrate accomplishments, as follows:

Before:

> I designed many dresses for the women's dress division.

After:

- Designed evening gowns for women's dress division that had an average sell-through of 93 percent per quarter at retail

Once you have completed building your résumé using the aforementioned steps, conduct a spelling and grammar check. After using the spell check tool, meticulously and thoroughly proofread your résumé. Look out for spelling and punctuation errors and grammatical mistakes (keep present jobs in the present tense, past jobs in the past tense). A grammatical or spelling error on a résumé gives the hiring manager a clear message that you are not detail-oriented, and you will most likely not be called in for an interview. Additionally, it would be beneficial for you to have a family member or friend peruse it to offer opinions and feedback.

These days, most résumés are submitted via electronic mail. Rarely will a company ask you to send a résumé to a mailing address, as it is just too time consuming. You should save your Word document in a variety of versions to accommodate every type of submission requirement. They include the Word 2007 version (.docx format), the Word 97–2003 version (.doc format), as well as a PDF. A PDF or Portable Document Format is a standard for document exchange created by Adobe that enables any user who has the software to open this type of document without relying on an operating system specific to a particular user.

Networking Your Way to a Job Offer

Research has shown that approximately 75 percent of all jobs are obtained through networking. Networking is the process of building connections to form a mutually beneficial business relationship. Networking, like a business deal, is a collaborative effort that requires a win-win situation for both parties in order for it to work effectively.

The old adage "It's not what you know, but who you know" still holds true. However, it is not solely "who you know" that gets your foot in the door, as your experience and knowledge will still play important factors in your success. If you are new to the industry, you may not have your network immediately established. Don't be discouraged as you can certainly get a job without a network. In order to build your business network, you will need to tap into already established contacts and develop new ones. This is an ongoing process and should be a prime focus for you throughout your career. There are a variety of methods you can use to build and grow your network, which are outlined as follows:

Leverage your personal contacts. Go through your contacts database and get in touch with everyone you know, even if they do not work in the fashion industry. They could know someone who does or who has connections with someone who works in the field. Let them know you are in the market for

Illustrated by Izak Zenou for Lancôme.
COURTESY OF IZAK ZENOU.

a job, and give them a brief summary of what you are looking for and what you can offer (by relaying your PBS). Contact former colleagues in any of your past jobs, not just your last one. The industry is small, and they may know of a job opening or at least someone you can contact who may be able to lead you to an opening (perhaps they have moved on to a new company and know of a current opening there).

Become active with your university alumni association. Most cities have area alumni associations you can join, and in doing so, you can gain additional contacts, perhaps of people who are either in the fashion industry or know people who work in it. Your best bet is to do an internet search to see if one exists or to contact your university's alumni department for further information.

Go to industry trade shows and events. There are many different industry trade shows and various events to attend that happen throughout the world. Infomat (www.infomat.com) puts out a calendar for fashion-related events and trade shows throughout the world. They cover such shows as Magic in Las Vegas (nearly 100,000 attendees) and the Chicago Menswear Collective, as well as Shirt Avenue in Milan. ENK International Trade Events is a fashion industry mainstay in New York and puts out a calendar of apparel and accessory tradeshows, which can found on their website at (www.enkshows.com). Fashioncalendar.com is yet another excellent online fashion event listing. Attending trade shows and events puts you in direct contact with other people in the industry.

Become a member of professional organizations and associations. There are several fashion-based professional organizations and associations that oftentimes enable you to be part of a prestigious group of people whose members include the biggest names in fashion. These

All looks from Panos Emporio. COURTESY OF PANOS EMPORIO.

groups offer networking opportunities, lectures, seminars, roundtable and panel discussions, and other events that enable the people of the fashion industry to come together in a variety of forums and venues. A listing can be found in the Appendix.

Join fashion career networking websites. There are countless professional networking sites that enable you to join an online fashion community and network with others in the fashion industry. Some have job listings and offer a career development focus, while others enable you to share knowledge. A listing can be found in the Appendix.

Join professional networking websites. Professional networking sites are being established each day by the dozens. You can find, be introduced to, and collaborate with professionals in the fashion industry who can help you to accomplish your career goals. Some offer fee-based membership, which offers extended benefits. A listing can be found in the Appendix.

Participate in social networking websites. There are a plethora of online, no-fee social networking sites that allow you to make not only friends but business connections as well, thereby providing possible job leads. A listing can be found in the Appendix.

Volunteer. There are various ways you can volunteer and, in doing so, gain valuable experience while making lasting connections in the fashion industry. You can volunteer for charities such as Dress for Success, or you can volunteer at various fashion weeks if you live near the city hosting them. It takes a lot of work to make these shows happen, and as a result, the people and agencies that put on fashion weeks need volunteers to help set up each show. The only way to gain entrance into the shows is either by invitation or by volunteering (when available). So it is not surprising that volunteer status has become coveted—so highly desirable, in fact, that some people plan their vacation around fashion week just so they can volunteer when they are in town. Go to the fashion week website that interests you and contact their volunteer office for additional information. Many fashion week organizations have Facebook pages that publicize their volunteer opportunities.

Go out on a limb. Expanding your network can happen when you least expect it. You may be in a social situation when you come across someone whom you wind up networking with, or you may be out to brunch with family when a relative suggests a contact for you. Be open to these opportunities as you never know what may come out of it.

Attend networking events. Everywhere you look, there is a networking event going on somewhere in your town or the nearest big city; you just have to know where to find them. Fashion networking events happen through fashion associations; through fashion-related organizations such as Gen Art (www.genart.org); through Meetup (www.meetup.com), which has various fashion Meetup groups; and through company events and other industry events. CharityHappenings.org is an excellent online resource listing various charity fundraising events (many of which are fashion related) happening on a monthly basis in major cities.

Izak Zenou for Henri Bendel, 2010. COURTESY OF IZAK ZENOU.

It is of particular importance to know how to get the most out of attending a networking event. The ability to converse and communicate effectively is one of the key factors to being successful in any position you hold. Business networking allows a person to build new relationships, generate career opportunities, and discover job leads. No matter what type of business function you are attending, be it a cocktail reception, seminar, conference, or other, you need to master the fine art of working the room.

While walking into a room full of strangers can be daunting, the last thing you want to do is cling to the person who accompanied you, or fail to get up the nerve to speak to anyone else in attendance. When you attend a business function, you are being given a wonderful opportunity to meet an array of different people. So how do you most effectively maximize this opportunity? Using my three-pronged work-the-room approach (before, during, and after the event) will help you network like a pro. Remember, standard business etiquette always applies.

BEFORE THE EVENT

Dress impressively. How you present yourself is everything. You will be meeting people whom you may ask to help you in some way, so looking the part will give them more motivation to assist you. You should wear something ¾-parts fashionable and ¼-part business. Emphasize your best physical features, and make sure your overall look is distinguished.

Boost your confidence. Confidence never goes out of fashion and is only going to help make your networking function even more of a success. Remind yourself of your top three career accomplishments, attend a spin class, or do whatever it takes to give yourself that "I'm so fabulous" feeling before you walk out the door.

Calm your nerves. Ease your mind and remember any anticipation you may feel usually subsides once you arrive at the event. You may want to listen to relaxing music, deep breathe, meditate, or take a bath by candlelight to help relax you.

Practice your personal branding statement. Make sure you can describe what you do in 10–15 seconds. You want to be able to pique someone's interest enough so he or she will want to speak with you further at a later scheduled date.

Prepare conversation starters ahead of time. Armed with ice breakers such as "I don't believe we've met, I'm Jack" or "Great event, have you been to one before?" will allow you to effortlessly ease into dialogue with other people at the event.

Bring business cards. Don't forget to bring enough business cards with you so you won't run out. It won't bode well for you if someone asks for one and you do not have any. Answering a card request with, "I'm sorry, I forgot them" can be rather awkward and it's best to be prepared. You can either get business cards made or make them yourself, describing in five words or less what you do. There are many online sites that offer free business cards (www.vistaprint.com) and business cards with a fashion design theme (www.zazzle.com).

DURING THE EVENT

Check your coat. Holding onto your coat may suggest that you are on your way out or aren't going to be staying long, and could result in others not approaching you. Be sure to check your coat, tote bag, or briefcase so that you are hands-free when you exchange business cards or interact with others at the event.

Introduce yourself to the host/hostess. It is always good to get to know the host of the event. Offer a compliment on how well it was put together or how delicious the food is to show your gratitude.

Smile. Relax and try to feel at ease if this sort of event gives you tension. If you are smiling, you will appear more approachable, thereby increasing your chances that people will come up to you.

Scan the room for people you may know. It's always easier to talk to someone you know at the event first, before moving on to those you don't know. Scope out the room and see if anyone looks familiar. Once you begin conversing with those you know, you'll feel more courageous about introducing yourself to new people.

Relay your personal branding statement. Remember, you are there to sell yourself; however, do not communicate your PBS until you feel that the conversation is at the ideal point for doing so. People do business with those whom they like and trust. Once the trust has been built, jobs can be offered.

Ask people about themselves. Everyone loves to talk about themselves. It feels good to be able to boast about what we are doing or what we have accomplished. Show genuine interest in the conversation, and ask probing questions about what they do and what challenges they face in their roles specific to the design process. You can offer some ideas or suggestions to help them work more efficiently and ask them to keep you in mind if they hear of any job openings.

Don't talk to one person for too long. Chances are the person whom you are speaking to is also interested in meeting other people at the event, so be sure to give equal time to different guests throughout the course of the event. Remember to get a business card from people you've talked to before you leave, if you see any potential. And it's always a good idea to jot down a note or two on the back of the business card that helps you remember important points of the conversation that you had with that person so you can follow-up effectively.

Illustrated by Izak Zenou for John Lobb. COURTESY OF IZAK ZENOU.

AFTER THE EVENT

Contact your new connections. You should send an e-mail to the people that you met at a networking function within a week, but preferably within one to three days. Tell them how much you enjoyed meeting them, and reiterate what you have in common. Bring up a personal anecdote that you may have shared at the event. Recap how you feel you can best work together. On occasion, send them an interesting article or tidbit that relates to what they do. Investing in them at this level will hold their interest and help to build your new relationship. Ask them to lunch or for 15 minutes of their time on the phone to talk about job leads or job opportunities.

Add new contacts to your contact list. Gather all of the contact information that you gained at the networking event and add it to your contact list so the information is readily available when you need to access it.

Tried-and-True Job Search Strategies

There are as many approaches you can take to find open positions in the ever-competitive fashion industry as there are PANTONE colors. They can be divided into two categories: the direct method and the indirect method. The direct method provides you with direct access to available jobs, for which you can immediately apply, through job listings located in trade publications, through employment agencies, on fashion career websites, on general career websites, and on company websites. The indirect method employs more of a networking approach and allows job seekers to connect with people at career expo and job fairs, industry trade and fashion shows; through professional organizations, associations, and councils; at fashion events, through nonprofit organizations, professional networking websites, and social networking websites; and through personal contacts, college placement offices, and alumni associations.

Connections that you make through indirect methods allow you to build your business network, and doing this can provide possible job leads. The indirect method is just as important as the direct method because it not only leads you to potential jobs, but often lets you tap into people in your network as a way in the door. This provides you with a leg up on the competition and may even help you identify job openings that have not yet been, or will never be, publicly announced. The following is a comprehensive listing of resources that fall under both the indirect and direct methods for obtaining employment in the fashion industry.

DIRECT METHOD RESOURCES

Trade publications. Trade publications are an excellent resource for job seekers because they specialize in listing fashion design positions in the classified section. Nontrade newspapers will occasionally print fashion job listings in the career section of their website. However, most newspapers have now partnered with online job banks to post their job listings.

Employment agencies. Employment agencies (also known as job recruiting companies, executive recruitment firms, executive search firms, talent agencies, or headhunters) act as the liaison between the company trying to fill an open position and the job seeker. Their goal is to match the right employee with the right job. Employment agencies can be excellent partners in your search for the ideal job, as they have preestablished relationships with apparel and accessories companies in the industry and are usually the first to know when jobs become available. Most employment agencies specialize in either temporary staffing or full-time job placement, but some offer both.

Fashion career websites. There are several online fashion career websites that allow you to search fashion-only jobs. Some sites have extended features such as the ability to post your résumé online, receive career advice articles, and receive e-mail alerts for jobs that match your background; some also allow hiring managers to contact you when they are interested in discussing a possible job opening.

General career websites. There are a large number of online job banks that, for no fee, allow you to search for jobs in your area, post your résumé, and educate yourself with career articles and advice, and also allow hiring managers to view your résumé and contact you with job openings.

Company websites. Apparel/accessory manufacturers and retailers have current job openings/ boards listed in the career section of their website. Company websites that do not list their job openings generally provide an e-mail address where you can send your résumé. This is typically found in the "contact us" or "careers" section of the website.

INDIRECT METHOD RESOURCES

Career expos and job fairs. Career and job expositions (expos) put on by local businesses bring job seekers and representatives from companies together under one roof for the purpose of networking and discussing job openings. In some cases, mini interviews are conducted at the company booth, so be prepared for this possibility. Obtain a list of the companies who will be in attendance, and research them ahead of time. You can research the Internet for career fairs in your area. Don't forget to bring plenty of résumés! Fashioncareerfairs.com is a great resource for a popular career fair held in New York and Los Angeles.

Industry trade and fashion shows. There are many different industry trade and fashion shows and various other events that happen throughout the world. Refer to the section on "Networking Your Way to a Job Offer" for listings. Attending these shows allows you to network in person with other fashion industry professionals.

Professional organizations, associations, and councils. Joining professional organizations, associations, and councils not only affords you the ability to attend networking events, panel discussions, and cocktail receptions with an extensive network of other fashion industry professionals, but oftentimes permits you access to their individual job boards. Membership affords you the opportunity to participate as an insider in the professional fashion community. There are many different associations that are specific to various sectors within the industry, and there are also general fashion associations that anyone in the industry may join. Regardless, membership in one or more associations is an effective way to network and should be an integral part of your job search repertoire. A complete list of professional organizations, associations, and councils can be found in the Appendix.

Spring/Summer
Collection illustrated
by Christina Kwon
and inspired by Zaha
Hadid, 1997. COURTESY
OF CHRISTINA KWON.

Fashion events. Fashion events that are social in nature can be an effective vehicle for professional networking, so whenever you go out, be prepared with your PBS and a steady supply of business cards. Fashion-related events that are social in nature are typically hosted by online groups that meet in person, as well as membership-based clubs. One of the largest international fashion events is Fashion's Night Out (FNO). FNO is the brainchild of *Vogue* editor-in-chief, Anna Wintour, and is a series of store events that occur throughout the world, bringing together celebrities, musicians, fashion designers, models, editors, and shoppers for fun promotions, exciting giveaways, and late shopping hours. The idea stemmed from a need to kick-start the economy, by encouraging people to shop and feel good about giving back, as proceeds go to various charities (www.fashionsnightout.com/fno-worldwide).

Nonprofit organizations. There are many networking opportunities that exist when one associates with a nonprofit organization, including junior council membership, event attendance, volunteering, and participation in online communities.

Professional networking sites. There are countless professional networking sites that enable you to join an online fashion community and network with others in the fashion industry. New professional networking sites seem to be constantly established by the dozens. All of them offer networking opportunities through the posting of professional profiles containing various forms of background information. Most offer the ability to join various industry-related and job-related groups, and allow you to maintain your privacy by choosing which areas of your profile are visible to the public, and which ones are restricted. You can find these resources in the Appendix.

Social networking sites. There are numerous online, no-fee social networking sites that allow you to connect with friends. These sites should not be discounted when it comes to a job search, since you never know who can help lead you to a job opening or a business connection. Sites vary as to the methodology that can be employed for job searching, since the technology and features of each site are different. You can find these resources in the Appendix.

Personal contacts. When in the market for a job, leverage your personal contacts by meticulously searching your Rolodex and contacting everyone you know to inform them you are seeking employment. It is important to contact people you know who are not in the fashion industry, as they may know, do business

Illustrated by Izak Zenou for Galeria Korea. COURTESY OF IZAK ZENOU.

Mohair and faded silk silhouettes mood board by Marta Buscaroli. COURTESY OF MARTA BUSCAROLI.

with, or have connections with someone who works in the business. Contact former colleagues in any of your past jobs, not just your most recent one. The industry is small, and they will more than likely know of a job opening, someone you can contact who has a lead for a job opening, or someone who can help you in some similar way.

College placement offices. Most universities operate college placement offices or career guidance centers that help matriculating students and alumni with job placement, and offer some sort of job board or job listing. Check with your alma mater to find out how you can take advantage of their services and offerings.

Alumni associations. Alumni associations usually have a presence in most major cities and in many smaller cities around the country. The good news for people who reside in a large city is that there is often a large, active alumni group established in the area for affiliates of many colleges and universities. Most offer networking events and a chance to mingle with fellow alumni. Usually, the alumni club will have a website where you can find a job listing or a classified section permitting you to post an ad (usually at no cost), listing the type of job you are seeking. Most importantly, you can network with other alumni to find out about possible job leads. Your university website will generally have an alumni association listing by city, state/town/province, and country where you may look up the chapter nearest you.

Perfecting the Job Interview

Let's face it: Job interviewing is a nerve-racking experience. It is not always easy to converse with someone you haven't met before, while trying to sell yourself and prove you are the best candidate for the position in a relatively short amount of time. We've all heard the sound bite: "You never get a second chance to make a first impression." You will be judged on your appearance, how you present yourself, if you fit in well with the company culture, if you would represent the company well, the contents of your portfolio, your experience, your skill set, and how well you speak. Once an impression is made, it's very difficult to change it. Knowing ahead of time what to expect in an interview can help alleviate some of the nervous tension you may experience, and help you to win over your interviewer.

PHONE INTERVIEWS

Employers use phone interviews as one method of recruiting candidates for employment. Oftentimes they are used to screen applicants in an effort to narrow down the pool of candidates who will be invited for in-person interviews. Or, if a company is unsure of your qualifications, they will use a phone interview to decide whether to move forward with a face-to-face interview. They are also commonly used to curtail the expenses incurred for out-of-town applicants. In any case, do not make the mistake of thinking they are any less significant. You must prepare in exactly the same way you would for an in-person interview, and remember, your goal is to land a formal, on-site interview.

Create an outline. Prepare the same outline that you would prepare for an in-person interview. Thoroughly research the company background, history, product line, and competition, and jot down several pertinent questions. For all the items you should research prior to your phone interview, see "Research the Company" in the "Before the Interview" section which follows.

Keep a copy of your résumé in front of you. Be sure to have a good working knowledge of your résumé. When interviewers ask you to describe your past experiences, you will easily be able to take them through it, especially if it is within arm's length.

Dress in a professional outfit. The fact that you are not seen doesn't mean you should wear your favorite pajamas and a bathrobe for your phone interview. Doing so can put you in a casual mindset, which in turn can have a negative impact on how you portray yourself to the interviewer. Dress the part and you'll feel the part!

Make sure it's quiet. Turn off your cell phone. Shut your door. Remove any pets from the room. Turn off the radio and television. You want it to be as silent as possible so you can concentrate and hear everything that is being mentioned or asked of you. Clear away any possible distractions ahead of time, and ask others not to disturb you during that time (unless it's an emergency).

Don't chew gum. Some people have a habit of chewing gum and forget to get rid of it before engaging in a phone interview. Don't overlook this important tip.

Keep a glass of water nearby. You may get thirsty or start coughing during the interview, so it's a good idea to have a glass of water handy to prevent any excessive coughing that could interfere with the interview.

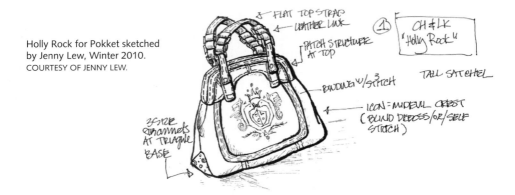

Holly Rock for Pokket sketched
by Jenny Lew, Winter 2010.
COURTESY OF JENNY LEW.

Give concise answers. Phone interviews generally go a little quicker than in-person interviews, so it's important to get your point across in a timely fashion and focus on articulating exactly what you want to say. Don't leave out any important information, but be direct.

Be enthusiastic. Enthusiasm does indeed come through on the phone. Be excited and fervent about the job. A little animation goes a long way, and your eagerness will surely rub off on the interviewer.

Take notes. Take notes throughout the phone interview, and write down specifics about the job as it is being described to you. You may not remember certain details about the position later on, and you can easily refer to your notes to help jog your memory.

Ask questions. Prepare a list of questions about the job ahead of time, and jot down any additional questions you may have during the interview. Be sure to ask them before the phone interview comes to a close. This will show your interest level. Refer to the sample list of questions that can be found in the "Before the Interview" section under "Your Background."

Find out next steps. If you are interested in the job, tell the interviewer that you are excited by the opportunity and would make an excellent candidate for the position. Ask if other candidates are going to be interviewed and when they are expecting to make their decision. Ask when you should follow up, or find out if they would prefer to get in touch with you when they have made their decision.

Thank the interviewer. Thank the interviewer for taking time out of his or her schedule to speak with you, and reiterate your interest in the position. It is also critical to send an e-mail to the interviewer to thank him or her again, and to relay your qualifications for the position.

IN-PERSON INTERVIEWS

Congratulations! You just landed an in-person interview. You have probably sent out countless résumés, and now a company is interested enough to explore your credentials further in a more formal setting. All your hard work has paid off and the moment has arrived to make your mark. It is important that you approach the interview process from the interviewer's perspective. The hiring executive will use the interview to find out how you stand out from the competition, if your background/experience suits the position, and if you have the ability to jump right into the role and make an impact in a short time frame.

Fall/Winter 2012 Diego Binetti Collection. PHOTOGRAPHER: ADAM WEISS.

Interviewing, these days, is akin to being thrown into a snake pit. You can be eaten alive if you are not properly prepared. So how can you ace the interview, beat out the other candidates, and score the ultimate job offer? There are a multitude of things that you should do prior to your scheduled interview.

Before the Interview

Memorize your résumé. You should commit to memory the most important aspects of your résumé and be able to verbally walk your interviewer through it during an interview, without having to read it word for word. It is certainly okay to glance at it occasionally, but you want to be able to speak intelligently about your work history in a free-flowing manner. You should also be prepared to substantiate gaps in your résumé. While in between jobs, did you freelance or consult? Volunteer? Get another degree? Take continuing education classes? Care for an aging grandparent? Were you spending your days looking for a full-time job, which can be a job in and of itself? Were you fired or laid off? Be prepared to explain yourself, as this is a frequently asked question.

Gather your references. You will need to furnish at least three business references when being seriously considered for a job. First put together a list of prospective references who you believe would speak highly of you. Stick to people who have had direct exposure to your work and performance, such as a previous supervisor. Then, you should contact your prospective references and ask if they would grant you reference permission. Contact your confirmed references once the company you are interviewing with informs you that they are beginning their reference checks. Let them know the name of the person (including their title and company name) that will be contacting them and brief them on the position for which you are interviewing.

Spring/Summer 2012 embroidered, printed, and gathered silk dress for Emanuel Ungaro by Marta Buscaroli. COURTESY OF MARTA BUSCAROLI.

Research the company. At this point, you will want to thoroughly research the company, inside and out. Simply put, do your due diligence. An interviewer will either come straight out and ask you what you know about the company or will speak about the company during the course of the interview, and, either way, you should have background knowledge so you can respond accordingly. Use the following resources to find out background information:

1. **Company website.** You can find a lot of background information of a company on their corporate website. This is the most useful tool for finding out information about your prospective employer. Some fashion companies have two separate websites: one for the general public/ customer base and a corporate website for career seekers and shareholders. Both are useful, but you will want to concentrate on the corporate site. Sometimes a PDF of the annual report can be viewed or downloaded, so be sure to take advantage of this if available. In addition to the basic background information that will be provided, check for a press section to learn about recent articles about the company in the news. More than ever, hiring managers are looking for designers who have both a creative and a business sense, so it is important for you to be on top of the business aspect which can be found using the aforementioned resources.

2. **Online company background resources.** Online resources for business listings include Hoover's Online, Edgar Online, PR News Wire, and Manta. Each has easily searchable websites to perform company background research.

3. **Internet search engines.** Conduct a general Internet search using a search engine, such as google.com or bing.com, which will typically produce a significant number of articles from various sources.

4. **Trade publications.** Industry publications such as *Women's Wear Daily* (WWD) publish articles daily on the latest news in the fashion industry. You can also search their archives for past articles on a particular company (a fee may apply).

5. **Library.** You can visit your local library, which will have several publications and sources to research. It is especially helpful if you have a nearby business library, which may be able to provide more direct and thorough information.

6. **Colleagues.** It is always good to get background information whenever possible by asking colleagues if they know anything about the company, management, staff, work culture, or any

other pertinent information they can pass along to you. The more you ask, the more you know and the better prepared you will be. If you happen to know someone who is working at the company you are applying to, be sure to let the hiring manager know this in the interview, as it may help you get hired.

Here are the key items you should research, as follows:

- **Company history.** When researching a company, you should know the year the company was established, the company timeline, their annual revenue, and whether the company is publicly traded or private. If it is publicly traded, learn the stock exchange and be familiar with the stock symbol.

- **Designer background.** Companies are generally corporate based (Phillips-Van Heusen Corporation) or designer label based (Zac Posen). That is not to say that designer-based companies are not corporations, but there are definite instances where there is no actual designer behind the name of the company (Ann Taylor). When there is, as in the case of Donna Karan, you should be knowledgeable about the designer's background and schooling, how the designer got started, other companies the designer worked for, his or her design sensibility, and so forth.

Spring/Summer 2012 Eros shirt and Eros shorts from Panos Emporio. COURTESY OF PANOS EMPORIO.

- **Company milestones.** Companies are proud of their milestones, and you should be able to identify their biggest achievements. Try to find out about their future goals, and if you do, figure out how you can fit into those objectives.

- **Key players.** Interviewers will frequently mention and speak about the C-level executives, such as the chief executive officer (CEO), and the chief creative officer (CCO), or other executives in upper management, such as the creative director, with the assumption that you know whom they are speaking about. Don't fall prey to discounting this important but often overlooked item.

- **Mission statement.** The mission statement is the purpose of the company's existence and is a vital part of the company's core values and structure, so familiarize yourself with this information. If the company is publicly traded, the mission speaks to upholding the shareholders' expectations. Knowing what the company stands for and why they exist is important.

- **Brand identity.** Brand identity is defined as how the brand is perceived by consumers. It is important for you to have a grasp on this, as well as how they differentiate themselves from their competitors. For Ann Taylor, it is all about updated classics. Tommy Hilfiger's brand identity is classic American sportswear.

■ **Future company goals.** Research future goals of the company. Perhaps the company has a revenue goal for the next fiscal year, or they are introducing a new brand. You should be able to speak about these initiatives and how you can fit into the company's long-term strategies. If you were not able to find out this information, ask about this during your interview. Perhaps they are planning to launch a new children's line and you have relevant experience in that product category.

■ **Product line specifics.** Research product specifics, such as price points for the product categories you would be responsible for if offered the job. Are they considered a contemporary designer, or are they at the designer level? You should have a sense of what they specialize in, what products they offer, and how often they produce collections.

Spring/Summer 2012 Jessie and James Collection. PHOTOGRAPHER: GIOVANNI MARTINS.

■ **Branch office and store locations.** Be on the ball about the various office and store locations throughout the country, and globally, if applicable. Pay particular attention to new and future planned store openings. Be able to speak about this information during an interview, saying, for example, "I think it's fantastic that the company is planning to open a store in Moscow next spring. The market in that region is booming."

■ **Media coverage.** Reference any recent media coverage that has taken place, both on television and in print. "I just saw your new print campaign that Fran Lebowitz shot for *Vogue*. Using Christy Turlington to show off the collection really drove home the new image of the company." Or you can discuss recent articles that you read in a particular newspaper, or online. "I just saw the article in *Women's Wear Daily* that your company is planning to introduce a new diffusion label in the fall. Since I've participated in new product launches in the past, I really see myself being part of this exciting launch in a promotional capacity." This not only speaks to your experience, but also to the fact that you are knowledgeable about what the company is doing in the market, you are a forward thinker, and you are capable of fitting into the structure of the company.

■ **Current events.** Make sure you stay informed of industry news and current events, especially pertaining to your specialty, by reading industry trade publications and other news sources. You should be aware of any new laws regarding importing, exporting, overseas shipping, and tariffs, and any other facts of relevance specific to your sector.

Shop the brand. A crucial step in preparing for your interview is to shop the brand. To really impress your interviewer, go to various retail establishments where the product is sold and get up close and personal with the collection. Feel the fabric, look at the fabric content and retail price, determine if the merchandise is marked down or if it is selling well. You may even want to talk to a sales associate in the department to field these questions.

Know where you're going. You may want to map out your route ahead of time. Be sure to figure out what method of transportation you will be using, the appropriate schedule, and any other pertinent information that will ensure your timely arrival.

Practice. Practice. Practice. In addition to learning the important aspects of your résumé, prepare

NUNCIA FLAVIA AMMIRATA
fashion designer

Sketch by Nuncia Ammirata. COURTESY OF NUNCIA AMMIRATA.

answers to commonly asked questions so you don't get stumped during the interview. You want to try to avoid mistakes that will throw off your confidence, such as jumbling your words or pausing too long when answering a question.

Research the interviewer. It is a good idea to find as much background information on the interviewer as possible. Search LinkedIn, Plaxo, and Jigsaw for your interviewer's profile, and then look at previous companies he or she has worked. Perhaps you've both worked for the same design studio in the past, which you can bring up during the interview as a commonality.

Make an outline. You've already researched the company, now it's time to put your findings down on paper. Create an outline as a Word document that you can print and bring with you to the interview to use as a reference. I recommend that you develop a template that you can tailor (add and take away sections, depending on the company and job at hand) and print for each interview, using the following basic format:

Company Background

- Interview details
  - Name of company
  - Company address, including floor and/or suite
  - Date and time of your interview
  - Name of your interviewer, title, and phone number
  - Name and phone number of the person you were told to ask for once you arrive, if other than your interviewer
- Company history
  - Year the company was established
  - Company timeline highlights
  - Major milestones
  - Designer bio (if applicable)
  - Company profile
  - Mission statement
  - Management team (list top executives and titles, including the CEO and senior design management)
  - Brands
  - Product sectors
  - Office locations (domestic and global)
  - Whether company is privately owned or publicly traded
- Company/product line specifics
  - Competitors
  - Press/editorial coverage
  - How the company is viewed by the target customer, the general public, and yourself, such as "classic," "contemporary," "modern," "nontrendy"
  - Where the product is sold (company stores, department stores, specialty stores, online portals)
  - Why you want to work for the company
  - What the company or designer is known for
  - The company or designer's inspiration for the current season's collection

Your Background

- Key strengths
  - Personal Branding Statement (PBS)

- Education
- Past work experience accomplishments
- Work ethic summary statement (e.g., loyalty, punctuality, etc.)

- Management style (if applicable)
  - Your management style description (e.g., democratic)
  - How long you've been a manager
  - How many people have reported to you in the past
  - Your direct reports' titles and general responsibilities
  - Direct report performance evaluation approach

- Sample questions
  - How did you get your start in the fashion industry?
  - Whom does this position report to?
  - How many people work in the department?
  - What are some of the skills necessary for someone to succeed in this job?
  - What are the biggest challenges that someone in this position would face?
  - What are the performance expectations of this job?
  - How does the design process work for your company and what role will this position have within that process?
  - Do you expect your designers to sketch by hand or by CAD or both?
  - In what countries do you currently manufacture your products?
  - Is this a newly created position? If not, why has this position become available?
  - What product categories is this position responsible for?
  - Are there direct reports? If so, how many and what are their roles?
  - Is there travel? If so, where and how often?
  - What is the typical career path for this position?
  - Are there any specific pressing issues that need to be addressed right away?

Gold plaque brand logo for Autumn/Winter 2011 Molly Pryke Footwear. PHOTOGRAPHER: MOLLY PRYKE.

- What are the main priorities for this role?
- Does the company often face budget cuts and lay offs?
- Who do you consider to be your greatest competitor?
- Do you have any reservations regarding my fit for this position? (This allows you the opportunity to address any concerns the company may have and to disprove them.)
- What is your timeline for making a decision regarding the hiring of this position?

Day of the Interview

Be prepared. Have plenty of up-to-date copies of your résumé on hand as you never know how many people you will be meeting with once you are there. Remember to bring your portfolio. Also, bring a writing device and a notepad. You should also bring a "work history" sheet that outlines names, addresses, and telephone numbers of past employers, as well as at least three business references, in case you are asked to fill out a job application. Have the full name, title, address, phone number, e-mail address, type of relationship (colleague, boss, etc.), and length of time you have known each reference. Have the address of the company handy, and know exactly how to get there.

Dress the part. We've all been told that an interview is not the place to make a huge fashion statement. This only holds true if you are in conservative industries like banking or law. However, in creative fields like fashion, you should not only dress to impress, but dress the part. Ideally, if you can wear an entire outfit or at least some items that were made by the company that you are interviewing with, by all means do so. This is an easy way for the interviewer to connect with you and see you assimilating well into the corporate culture. However, keep it simple and don't overdo it. And always create a professional look. Try your best to emulate the brand aesthetic when appropriate. If you are interviewing at Ralph Lauren and you can look as if you just stepped out of one of their advertisements, you've got it made. If you are interviewing for a denim company,

Watercolor dress from Panos Emporio. COURTESY OF PANOS EMPORIO.

don't wear jeans, but rather wear an upscale, tailored version of a sporty look. If you are a man and are interviewing at a company like Brooks Brothers, wear a suit.

Be punctual. Make sure you leave plenty of extra time for traffic or transportation delays, especially if it is during the early morning or afternoon rush hour. You should arrive 15 minutes before your scheduled interview time. You never want to make your interviewer wait for you or cause any disruption to his or her schedule. If you do find yourself running late, be sure to place a call to the interviewer to apologize and let him or her know when you will be arriving.

During the Interview

Greet the interviewer. Greet your interviewer with a firm handshake, enthusiastic smile, and direct eye contact. Using direct eye contact shows that you are confident, engaged and ready for the interview to begin.

Stay calm. Mild nervousness is a natural reaction to a job interview, and interviewers will understand

Spring/Summer 2012 Afrodite dress, Panos Emporio. COURTESY OF PANOS EMPORIO.

this. What you need to avoid is obvious signs of over-anxiousness such as a shaky voice, sweaty palms, constant tapping of your foot or your fingers, and overuse of the word, "um." Meditating or breathing deeply for as little as 10–15 minutes prior to the interview can help prevent this from occurring.

Act professionally. Remember not to chew gum, slouch in your chair, stare out the window, or talk extensively about personal topics. If you find you share a common interest with your interviewer, such as a love of golf, use it as an ice breaker.

Show your personality. Everyone has a distinct persona that is unique to them. Let yours show through in the interview. Keep in mind that interviewers meet many different people every day, so there is value in standing apart from the rest. Injecting a little humor can go a long way.

Use appropriate body language. During the interview, it is of utmost importance that you use correct body language. If you say one thing and act another way, you are likely to confuse the interviewer. If you are communicating your enthusiasm for the job, don't cross your arms as you are saying so. An easy way to avoid this is to use mirroring techniques. If your interviewer leans forward, you should lean forward slightly. Once the interviewer leans back, you should do the same. This psychological mimicking actually helps the interviewer to feel more at ease with you.

Be flexible. Some interviews last ten minutes, some last for hours. Some interviewers are very organized; some ask you haphazard questions with no rhyme or reason, and some interviewers may be running late. Your job is to remain happy, composed, and positive no matter what you are thrown. Your adaptation skills will be much appreciated.

Show your enthusiasm. In a hiring manager's eyes, enthusiasm equates to motivation, and everyone wants to hire someone with a high level of incentive.

Sell yourself. Three basic traits that an interviewer looks for in a candidate are ability, willingness, and manageability. It is your job to prove that you possess these attributes, by providing specific examples and illustrations.

Demonstrate your track record. Impressing a potential employer is no longer just about your education and experience. Rather, you need to bring specific examples of past accomplishments to the interview. Demonstrate how you accomplished a specific task under budget and ahead of deadline or how you saved or made money for your previous employer. It is a bonus if you can actually show examples of your work (kept in a binder with sheet protectors). It can be as simple as examples of forms you created to establish standard operating procedures, or a spreadsheet demonstrating how your designs increased sales in your department. Anyone can talk the talk, but when you back up your statements with tangible proof, you'll be ahead of the game and will stand apart from your competition.

Be politically astute. Don't bad-mouth any past colleagues or bosses. You should always speak positively about past jobs and supervisors, giving off the attitude that every position you've held was a great learning experience and benefited you in some way.

Answer questions directly. One of the most common mistakes interviewees make is to ramble on without ever answering the question at hand. If you are unsure of an answer, pause and take a deep breath to gather your thoughts. If you are absolutely blanking out, simply tell the interviewer that you'll have to think further about that question and will be happy to get back to him or her. However, this option should be your absolute last resort.

Be prepared to explain employment gaps. This is a biggie and proves to be a sticking point with a lot of potential employers. Perhaps you took off time to care for a sick relative, you were looking for work in between jobs, or you experienced a lay-off. Whatever the reason, explain it clearly, confidently, and truthfully. Try to quickly move the conversation to what you learned from the experience and how it will help you in future jobs.

Don't discuss salary. As the saying goes, "There is a time and place for everything." Bringing up salary before a job is offered to you can appear presumptuous. Your focus should be on selling yourself and getting the job offer. Once you do, a salary discussion will naturally follow. This also holds true for bonuses, stock options, vacation time, or any other employee-related benefits.

Take notes during the interview. Notes will certainly come in handy when you need to review aspects or expectations of the job for your thank-you letter or for a second interview. Note taking shows that you are taking this opportunity seriously.

Ask questions. An interview is a place to figure out if the position is a proper fit for both the interviewer and the interviewee. Don't hesitate to ask questions about specific details, responsibilities, and expectations of the position. Use the outline you created prior to the interview to ask all of the pertinent questions listed, as well as any additional questions that arise during the interview. You can refer to "Make an outline" in the "Before the Interview" section.

Find out next steps. If you are interested in the job, tell the interviewer that you are excited by the opportunity and would make an excellent candidate for the position. Find out if other candidates are going to be interviewed and when they are expecting to make their decision. Ask when you should follow-up or if they prefer to get in touch with you when they have made their decision. Be sure to get business card of each person that you interviewed with for easy follow-up.

Thank the interviewer. Thank the interviewer(s) for his or her time. Give the interviewer a firm handshake and a warm smile, and wish him or her a fantastic day.

After the Interview

Send a thank-you note. Taking the time to send a thank-you note to your interviewer is a crucial step in the process. Some interviewers view this as a test, and if you don't follow up, you don't get the job. Ideally, you should send an e-mail thank-you on the day of your interview or within a few days. This shows you are serious about the position, and your enthusiasm will not go unnoticed. Most companies these days will not look down upon an e-mail thank-you letter; however, you can assess this on your own. The letter should summarize your qualifications and state why you are a good fit for the job. The overriding feeling should be positive and uplifting. This is also a good time to say anything that you forgot to mention in the in-person interview. Don't forget to proofread your thank-you letter before sending it out. After your initial follow-up, if you do not hear back from the company within a week (or within the specified time frame given), e-mail (preferred) or call your interviewer to obtain a more direct response. Your follow-up methodology should be consistent, but not overbearing. I like to go with the "one touch-base per week" rule.

Don't put all your eggs in one basket. As much as you may want the job you just interviewed for, you cannot rely on only one company to give you an offer. You may be the perfect candidate and have the exact qualifications that the company is looking for, but still not

Style: Losna. SPRING/SUMMER 2012 FABIOLA PEDRAZZINI COLLECTION.

get the offer. Maybe they had to put the position on hold, hired an internal candidate, or felt you were just not the right fit. Your goal is get your résumé out there, interview with as many companies as possible, and try to get multiple job offers. This will give you the negotiating edge you'll need when it comes down to decision-making time.

SECOND AND SUBSEQUENT INTERVIEWS

Landing a second interview is much like being a NASCAR driver coming down the home stretch in a race—you're almost at the finish line. Regardless of whether or not it leads to a job offer, you should feel elated, proud, and filled with an extra boost of confidence. Being asked to come in for a second interview shows serious interest on the part of the company and indicates you've played your cards right so far.

Second (and subsequent) interviews characteristically fall into two categories: Either final approval is still needed before an offer can be extended, or the decision has already been made and the company wants to make sure they've made the right choice. Either way, you can expect more in-depth questioning and a thorough dissection of what you are capable of bringing to the table. Now it's up to you to close the deal.

All of the previous tips still apply, however, the following rules represents additional guidelines to follow for second or any subsequent interviews:

Before the Interview

Know the agenda ahead of time. Some companies will present you with an itinerary prior to your interview listing the names and titles of all the people you will be meeting with by time slot. If not, it is a good idea to try to find this information out.

Prepare for more in-depth questioning. Because you are a serious contender for the position, there will be a more intense and complex level of questioning to evaluate your skills, accomplishments, personal character, and competency level. Be well versed on specific examples of how your past experiences or schooling (if you are a recent graduate) can help you to succeed in this new role.

Spring 2008 Randolph Duke Couture, Los Angeles Fashion Week.
COURTESY OF RANDOLPH DUKE.

Plan for the possibility of several interviews. Second interviews usually run differently than your initial interview, in terms of the number of people you meet with and the length of time the interview will last (in some cases, it can last half a day or an entire day). You will likely be meeting some of the same people and several new people, including department heads, managers, senior-level executives, and/or other staff or colleagues that you will be working with on a day-to-day basis. You will also generally meet with your potential direct supervisor and his or her supervisor, if you haven't already. If it is at all possible, it is good to conduct research on the individual people that you will be meeting with, to get a background of what they do in the company so you can relate to them better. The general rule is that you will interview with the people with whom you will have the most interaction in that particular job. So if you are interviewing for an assistant designer position, you will generally meet with the associate designer, designer, senior designer, technical designer, design director, senior design director, vice-president of design, creative director, president of design, and/or chief creative officer. Be prepared with specific questions for each of them. It is not uncommon for a company to interview a candidate on two, three, four, five, six, and sometimes seven or more different occasions. And it is also not unusual for a company to interview you a total of six or seven times in one or two settings.

Prepare for different interview formats. Your interview may be conducted in a panel interview format, in which case you'll meet with several people at one time. If this is the case, you should always address everyone on the panel, not just the person who originated the question. The meeting could involve breakfast, lunch, or dinner, so brush up on your business dining etiquette. You may be given a company tour, and, in doing so, will be introduced to even more people so try your best to remember everyone's names as you are introduced to them.

Be sure to wear a different outfit. You are way too much of a style maven to commit the faux pas of wearing the same interview outfit twice, so no further explanation is needed for this tip.

Autumn/Winter 2012 New Choicez Collection. PRODUCTION: MERLIN PENGEL AT BLACK PEPPER, AMSTERDAM. HAIR AND MAKE-UP: BARBRA OLIEMANS. MODEL: NATASHA ROGER FROM D&A MODEL MANAGEMENT. PHOTOGRAPHER: GIOVANNI MARTINS.

During the Interview

Answer questions in more depth. You are in serious contention for the position at hand, so in order to prove that you are the best candidate for the position, you need to answer questions with more thought, wisdom, and profundity.

Bring up what you didn't say the first time. If there is anything you forgot to mention, during the first interview, or something you would like to clarify, ask or further explain, bring it up this time around.

Ask more probing questions. Questions posed to your interviewers should include greater insightfulness on your part. This is your opportunity not only to make a big impact, but to fully understand what would be expected of you in this role.

What Skills Do You Seek When Hiring a Fashion Designer?

❯ There are several skills I look for when hiring a fashion designer, including their passion about fashion and their willingness to learn and grow, their accuracy, consistency, and creativity in their portfolio, the amount of experience they have, and if they hold a degree in fashion design. In addition, I want to know if they understand the timely sense of trends, market direction, and deadlines, that they possess excellent verbal and written communication skills, they are a strong team player with a willingness to try new approaches, have an ability to sketch free-hand and computer based, have a strong fabric and color sensibility, are proficient in Adobe Illustrator, Photoshop, and Excel, are aware of current trends and can bring in new ideas and push the current ideas to the next level, have brand-appropriate taste level and dress brand-appropriate in the interview, and are humble and flexible.
Bernd Kroeber, Design Director, BCBG Max Azria, Los Angeles, California, USA

❯ I look for someone who can take full responsibility of the design department. A good designer is involved in every aspect of the process of creating a

Sketch by Bernd Kroeber. SPRING 2012 MANOUKIAN COLLECTION, A DIVISION OF BCBG MAX AZRIA.

Fall 2009 Opera Coat
by Gilles Montezin.
PHOTOGRAPHER: MARK
DREW.

collection, including the making of runway samples until the last button! I also seek a designer who has a good sense of style, color, and proportions, as well as extensive knowledge of clothing construction. I seek a person who can inspire others to collaborate and work together as a team. The whole experience has to be playful, joyous, and pleasant!

Gilles Montezin, Designer, Gilles Montezin, New York, New York, USA

❭ When hiring a fashion designer, I always look first for their ability to interpret the latest fashions in relation to our business. I don't care if someone's portfolio is impeccable and absolutely fabulous; I need to know that you can translate your idea to reality. I also look for people who have taken the time to become knowledgeable about our company and our product (what kind of product we manufacture, our price range, and our target customer). I also look for designers who can explain how they feel they can make a difference in our design department. I want to work with people who are hungry to learn and at the same time are willing to share their experience. People who want to make

a difference and believe in themselves are the best candidates for me to hire.

Betsy Carlo, Design Director, Girls, Squeeze Jeans, New York, New York, USA

❭ There is more to being a great fashion designer than just the ability to be creative. When hiring, we look for someone who can think outside the box, express their individual creativity, and who can just as easily translate someone else's idea into a unique and creative design. We look for someone in tune with current trends, as well as a good communicator, both in verbal expression and in comprehension. It is important for the designers we want to hire to clearly understand what the company is looking for and create designs and trends that are on one hand unique, but also in line with the look the company is aiming to achieve. We look for CCIAO: Creativity, Communication, Intuition, Autonomy and Outside-the-box thinking!

LeeAnn Claridge, Director, Human Resources, Mark Edwards Apparel/Sixty Canada/Want Agency/Group of 3/ MEJK Apparelab, Montreal, Quebec, Canada

What Skills Do You Seek When Hiring a Fashion Designer? (Continued)

❯ The skills I look for when hiring a fashion designer are creative vision and execution. I look for designers who have the vision of fantasy or the journey of the customer and where it takes them. I look for ingenuity and savvy when it comes to executing creative ideas. I seek the skills of forward fashion thinkers who also possess the knowledge of real-world society and a level of practicality of function.

Miguel de Contreras, Designer, Miguel de Contreras, LLC, New York, New York, USA

I look for a fashion designer who has the combination of creativity and excellent product knowledge, with a solid technique. Another very important trait is that the person must remain very curious and possess a great vision.

Fabiola Pedrazzini, Owner, Fabiola Pedrazzini, Milan, Italy

Fall/Winter 2012 Line and Dot Collection mood board by April Oh. COURTESY OF APRIL OH.

Style: Ros. FALL/WINTER 2011 FABIOLA PEDRAZZINI COLLECTION.

❯ When it comes to being a fashion designer, being creative is a must, as well as being an acute observer. Drawing skills and knowledge of sewing techniques and garment construction are also very important.

April Oh, Design Director, Line & Dot, Vernon, California, USA

❯ Knowledge of other languages, someone who can always be on time at work, someone who can be as objective as possible, someone who can manage their workload and their technical drawing skills are all important traits I seek.

Nuncia Ammirata, Freelance Fashion Designer, Florence, Italy

❯ I personally like to see a designer's hand drawings rather than computer drawings, since hand sketches have so much more personality. Great work ethic and organizational skills are very important.

Aram Lee, Creative Director, Kooba, New York, New York, USA

❯ The skills I look for in a fashion designer include the capacity to get things done under pressure, knowledge of Illustrator and Photoshop, ability to troubleshoot and come up with creative solutions to problems, confidence and assertiveness with new ideas, familiarity with market and industry news, capability to provide solutions, aptitude to sew on an industrial machine and by hand, and comfortable with draping and pattern making.

Emily Tischler, Designer, Catherine Malandrino, New York, New York, USA

❯ When I first meet a fashion designer, I will always ask to see some of the best pieces from their latest collection. I will ask the designer to explain the strength of their collection. Then I will also want to review their lookbook and promotion materials, as this will give me an idea if this designer is on the right track (appropriate target market, quality of the campaign images, etc.). It is a bonus if they have interned at a fashion designer's studio because this will help the designer to market their brand. Finally, I will ask the designer about their five-year plan. If they can explain this, I feel more certain they are taking their career seriously.

Marcus Kan, Fashion Director, Ukamaku, Toronto, Canada

❯ A fashion designer needs to understand how to translate passion into workable designs. No customer is going to seek something that represents her past, as she wants something that will express her present desire and her future aspirations.

Panos Papadopoulos, Owner/Designer, Panos Emporio, Gothenburg, Sweden

On her: Adele Dress. On him: Brightman shirt and Panos pant from Panos Emporio. COURTESY OF PANOS EMPORIO.

❯ Innate creativity, versatility, composure, eagerness to learn, and someone who is easy to work with are qualities I seek in a designer. Even if you are highly talented, most people will be turned off if you are difficult to work with. A versatile designer who can keep their composure and deliver quality work during high-pressure times will become a key player within the team. Being open to learn is also admirable at any level. I know many designers who at some point lose perspective and hinder

What Skills Do You Seek When Hiring a Fashion Designer? (Continued)

growth because they lose the ability to be humble enough to learn from their peers. A designer who is constantly growing and showing new and fresh ideas is someone I always trust to be a source of inspiration.

Raquel Caruso, Design Director, Steve Madden, New York, New York, USA

❭ What I seek in hiring a designer is creativity and someone who is able to step out the box; someone who understands the product, but who is also able to show sizzle. I am drawn to a person who knows how to take over a design and revamp it into something new and different. I like when a designer can take elements from music or sports, and create a theme.

Shawn Campbell, Design Director, Birdy and Grace, Greenwich, Connecticut, USA

❭ When I need to hire a designer, I find the most important skills that I look for are willingness to learn, enthusiasm, desire, humble attitude, positive thinking, as well as basic design skills, such as sketching, organization, and knowing how to present yourself.

Mina Cha, Accessory Design Manager, Milly, New York, New York, USA

❭ I look for a candidate who has a fashion design degree. Candidates who have only worked at one place for an extended period can sometimes have a narrow view and be less flexible. Designers should post their portfolios online, so it is easily accessible. I don't like attitude or ego, and I don't like designers who don't have much to say. I also like designers who can show a personal style. I want candidates to be enthusiastic about themselves, the market that the job is in, and the company where they're interviewing. Designers that come off as aloof towards any of the above are potential red flags. If the job is in a specific market, too, a personal connection to that market is a big plus; if I'm hiring someone to

design yoga apparel, it helps if they practice yoga, which would be that "personal connection" to the product that they'd be responsible for designing. Overall, I would like the potential candidate to be educated, detail oriented, enthusiastic, humble, prompt, a good communicator, professional, creative, versatile, flexible, efficient, and have applicable experience.

John Nite, Design Director, Under Armour, Baltimore, Maryland, USA

❭ Good CAD design skills are essential. Also important is someone who has a good eye for upcoming trends and can demonstrate how they could execute these trends to final products. In addition, I look for impeccable communication, organization skills and someone who is constantly searching for newness and innovation.

Yuko Iida, Senior Designer, Marigold Enterprise, Ltd., London, England, United Kingdom

❭ When hiring a fashion designer, it is important that this person is creative, environmentally conscious, and takes a great interest in society. It is also important that they have an open mind to follow new trends, not only in fashion, but in music, movies, television, and literature. The designer should be able to express their ideas in their drawings, have a sense of precious details, and have good knowledge of patternmaking and sewing.

Katarina Dzale, Owner/Fashion Designer, Obilje/Katarina Dzale, Zagreb, Croatia

❭ It is sometimes difficult to evaluate someone based only on their portfolio. I look for cultural and intellectual proximity. It is my strong opinion that fashion must be inspired by different environments, not necessarily self-referential, and I'm always very pleased when, during a job interview, we discuss cinema, arts, photography, illustration, and society.

Gianni Cinti, Creative Director, Awesome Design Studio, Turin, Italy

❯ I look for artistic talent and style, a good sense of color, and an optimistic personality. Being able to function as part of a team is key. For my company, I have hired industrial designers as shoe designers. I find they have good technical skills and understand shape, volume, and three-dimensionality; they are able to think from 2D sketches to 3D products. A good candidate would be able to convey details to factories or sample rooms without the kind of sketches that are too filled with attitude. I would not hire a person who could only sketch like an illustrator.

Jamie Lawenda, Vice President of Design, 2568 Shoes/Sendra Shoes, New York, New York, USA

❯ I look for enthusiasm, a true love for what they do, and a great aesthetic.

Stella Vakirli, Vice President of Men's Outerwear, Weatherproof, New York, New York, USA

❯ The designer's aesthetic is the most important skill I seek. However, the designer should have knowledge of all of the different aspects of the product development cycle, including initial design research, fabric selection, patternmaking, construction, fit, sampling, costing, production, retail price, sales, and distribution. A good designer should be able to master both hand illustrations as well as computer-rendered sketches. The designer should be a team player, valuing every person who is involved in the process, whether it is assistants, patternmakers, cutters, sewers, tech team, production team, merchandiser, buyers, all the way to the customer. I seek designers who have experience, as well as a conviction to learn. I look for a creative, passionate, organized, respectful, positive designer who is a team player, has initiative, leadership, and a sense of urgency.

Monet Lugo, Senior Fashion Designer, Guess, Los Angeles, California, USA

❯ When I hire a designer, I look at their experience and try to find someone that will fit in my world as closely as possible. You should show relevant work for each brand you are applying, not just your best work.

Amelia Teniere-Buchot, Head of Design, Bershka (Inditex Group), Barcelona, Spain

Negotiating the Job Offer

Now that you have perfected the interview process, it's time to learn the ins and outs of negotiating a job offer. One of the most important things to do before you begin any sort of job offer negotiation is to educate yourself on the process. Many people tend to focus their efforts on interviewing and do little to prepare for the negotiating process, which is of equal importance. When it comes to having a salary conversation with a potential employer, it is important that you have a set range in mind, based on market research you have conducted. If you give a number too low, you can lose the potential to make more money, and if you give a number too high, you can price yourself out of the running. Overselling and underselling your worth are both unviable options and can easily be prevented.

In addition, there are many factors other than salary that are open for discussion and should be included in the negotiating process to determine your final compensation package. So what is the key to getting it right? You must hone your negotiating skills to maximize your total professional worth, both monetarily and in terms of perks and benefits.

Determine if the job is the best fit. Before you begin the salary-negotiating process, you have to look at the big picture, as there are many things to consider before accepting a job offer. From job advancement potential, company culture, and location to job title and the total compensation package, you need to evaluate all of the factors, not just salary alone. Once you've concluded that you would like to join the company in the role you are being considered for, you can proceed to the next steps.

Determine your market value. There are four major factors for determining your market value: your education, experience, the industry standard, and your unique selling proposition. Keep in mind this figure will increase as you gain more experience and as cost of living increases, so it will be a constant work in progress and will change as you climb the corporate ladder.

Grace Gardens "2056 Collection" from the Kara Saun 2006 runway presentation. COURTESY OF KARA SAUN.

Education. Most fashion design positions require a minimum of bachelor of fine arts degree. Most jobs do not require advanced degrees. Your salary will be proportionate with your education level, which is typical in most fields.

Experience. Hiring executives in the fashion industry are concerned with your experience level more than anything else. Since there is very little on-the-job training in most fashion design positions, companies seek people who are experienced as reassurance they'll be able to quickly jump in and make an impact. So the more direct experience you have, the better off you'll be. However, if you are just starting off, there is only so much experience you can acquire. Different jobs at different levels have different requirements. As a general rule, design assistants/assistant designers require 0–3 years of experience, associate designers 4–5 years, designers 6–9 years, and senior designers, directors, and above 10+ years.

Industry standard. Most companies have a set salary structure for each position they offer based on job status/level, responsibilities, education, and experience, defined as the industry standard. However, you will rarely be able to gain access to this information, as it is strictly confidential. If you don't already know the typical salary range for the position, you are seeking, it is best to find out.

Salary research sites. There are various salary research sites online that you can access to get a better idea of the appropriate salary range you should be categorized into, and what the going market rate is for the job you are seeking. One such site is Salary.com. Salary.com is one of the most popular salary research websites and combines data from hundreds of professionally conducted surveys of corporate human resource departments.

Salary statistics. There are agencies and resources that provide salary statistics and surveys for compensation planning. The United States Bureau of Labor Statistics is the principal fact-finding agency for the federal government in the field of labor economics and statistics, and may offer salary insight. The Economic Research Institute (ERI) is a salary survey resource that offers cost-of-living comparison data and executive compensation survey data.

Salary calculators. There are also various online salary calculator sites that can be used to assess typical salaries for different jobs. Remember, these sites give general information; do not go solely by these figures, as they tend to underestimate current salary offerings.

Spring/Summer 2012 printed multi layered and raw cut skirt on large tone-on-tone scarf top for Emanuel Ungaro by Marta Buscaroli. COURTESY OF MARTA BUSCAROLI.

CBsalary (Cbsalary.com) is a comprehensive salary center founded by careerbuilder.com that provides you with various salary tools. These tools include a salary calculator that allows you to search for the average salary paid for a position by city, and state. They also offer a premium salary report that is tailored to your amount of experience, education level, and company size. In addition, they have a salary advice section that offers tips on how to manage and negotiate your salary.

PayScale, Inc. (Payscale.com) is a popular tool for calculating salary.

Glassdoor (Glassdoor.com) is another helpful site that asks its users to post their salaries anonymously. This website allows visitors to find out the salary for different jobs at various companies.

Job listings. Look for job listings on various websites and in classified ads, which will sometimes list the salary or salary range offered for a particular job.

Ask colleagues. Ask colleagues and other people you know in the industry if they are aware of going rates for the job you are seeking. Industry associations and employment agencies sometimes put out job surveys and publish the results. There are different variables such as economic conditions, company size, geographic location, and other demographics that need to be factored into the process. These sites give general ballpark figures and should in no way be used as an absolute.

Determine your unique selling proposition. The final factor in determining your market value is your unique selling proposition or personal branding statement (PBS). You are already familiar with what a PBS is, so now it's time to put it to good use. When negotiating salary, you should emphasize any above-and-beyond skills that you possess in the form of experience, accomplishments, education, awards, certificates, recognition, connections, or anything else that makes you unique and sets you apart from your competition.

Britney Spears in Randolph Duke Couture dress at the 43rd Annual Grammy Awards, held at the Shrine Auditorium and Expo Hall, Los Angeles, California. *INSTYLE* MAGAZINE, 2000. COURTESY OF RANDOLPH DUKE

Consider all factors. Salary is not the only component to consider when negotiating your total compensation package. Your success rate in receiving these perks will depend highly on your position rank within the company, among other factors, such as what you can offer a company.

Sign-on bonus. Any bonus that you receive, such as a sign-on bonus, is just that, a bonus, and will not be figured into your base salary. Keep in mind that future performance evaluations and subsequent raises will be built around your base salary.

Early performance evaluation. You would typically have to wait upwards of a year to receive a performance evaluation when joining a company. Instead, you can negotiate an early performance evaluation within three or six months, with the chance for an increase in base pay and title. If the company will not agree to an early performance evaluation, you can try to negotiate a title change, approximately three to five months into the job.

Additional vacation time. Most U.S.-based companies offer their employees the standard two weeks' vacation time each year. While we are far from receiving the amount of vacation time our European counterparts receive, it can't hurt to ask for an in-between. Here you can negotiate both the amount of vacation time you would like to be granted and when it can be taken since there is a typical trial period that must pass before it is allowed (usually three months).

Early medical benefits. Medical benefits are usually received only after your three-month trial period has ended. In some cases, the trial period may even extend to six months. You can ask to receive early medical benefits after two to three months on the job.

Year-end bonus. Year-end bonuses are generally not given unless you are in a sales capacity. However, if your position has a direct influence over total revenues, as most senior level fashion design positions do, you can ask for a year-end bonus based on your performance or on your division's performance as a whole.

Miscellaneous perks. There are countless additional perks that can be figured into your total remuneration package, including clothing allowance, company car, gas, public transportation allowance, gym membership, use of executive clubhouse, and use of executive chef during business hours, to name a few. Remember that if you don't ask, you don't get, but use your best judgment.

Spring 2012 Pamella Roland Advertising Campaign. PHOTOGRAPHER: NIGEL BARKER, 2011.

Illustrated by Izak Zenou for Henri
Bendel, 2007. COURTESY OF IZAK ZENOU.

4 The Fashion Design Process

There's only one thing in life and that's the continual renewal of inspiration.

—Diana Vreeland

A DESIGNER'S JOB CONSISTS OF A COMPLEX JUGGLING ACT, balancing both the requirement to develop creative concepts that translate into trend appropriate and wearable fashions targeted to a specific customer base, and satisfying sales and merchandising by coming up with a collection that produces a strong retail sell-through.

There is a multitude of ways to approach the design process that can vary by company and designer. Fashion design classes will teach or have already taught you the elements of design, including line, shape, value, form, texture and space, as well as the principles of design, including proportion, rhythm, balance, emphasis, and unity. This chapter serves as an overview offering a summary of the major steps (the order of these steps may vary) in the fashion design process, including conceptual development, patternmaking, sample creation and finalization, presentation, and hand-off. Each step is outlined in the following section.

Conceptual Development

The first step to create a design is to conceive of the ideas or concepts for the collection, which will convey a clear-cut fundamental theme or narrative. This is done by conducting research, and drawing upon inspiration. Some designers conduct their own research, while others depend on trend reports published by fashion forecasting companies. Trend reports indicate what styles, colors, fabrics, trims, and embellishments will be fashionable for a particular season and product category (you can refer to the Appendix for a listing of trend and color forecasting companies).

Nicolette Dennis

Knits and woven looks for the contemporary market. ILLUSTRATED IN MARKER AND COLORED PENCIL BY NICOLETTE DENNIS, 2010.

In addition to research, designers draw upon their inspiration for
the season and incorporate it into
their design concepts. Inspiration
can come from anywhere—places,
people (style icons, actresses, actors, celebrities, musicians, and
everyday people), art, films, music,
architecture, landscapes, photographs, magazine tear sheets (clip-
pings), historical costume references, and objects represent just
a few examples. Clothing, whether
historical, tribal or contemporary
can be a source of inspiration for a
designer. For example, the "military
look" taken from a military uniform
has sparked inspiration for many
collections that we have seen hit
the runways.

Entire collections can be ig-
nited and built around a particular
material (silk), idea (hope), texture
(tweed), or color story (burgundy).
Sometimes a fashion story can be
created around only one central
premise. For the Fall 2012 collec-

Spring 2010 watercolor floral painting by Raquel Caruso. COURTESY
OF RAQUEL CARUSO.

tions, designers found their inspiration in this very way. For Cushnie et Ochs, inspiration came
from "skin;" for Tracy Reese, it was "Baroque;" for Jenny Packham, it was "Film Noir;" for
Tommy Hilfiger, it was "Military Prep;" and for Tadashi Shoji, it was "Opulence."

At this point, all research and inspiration is gathered, and initial sketches and illustrations
are created by hand or by computer. Computer-aided design (CAD) is an excellent tool that enables designers to translate their hand sketches into digital versions. Fully detailed flat sketches
showing fabric, trim, embellishment and color usage, button placement, seam lines, and points
of measure can be created quickly and easily through CAD software such as Lectra. Designers are
then able to review various versions of concepts so that fewer prototypes have to be made up in
each design, saving both time and money.

During the entire design process, design will meet with the heads of merchandising, production, sourcing, and sales to receive their feedback or recommendations for how to build the line. For example, merchandising will advise best/worst sellers by color, by product category and merchandising objectives, such as the number of units per garment that they would like to see produced.

Mood board created by Jenny Lew. COURTESY OF JENNY LEW.

Designers then visit fabric mills, fabric agents, and/or fabric trade shows to review the seasonal fabric collections and decide which fabrics to use. From their selections, they narrow down their choices and sometimes make customized changes in color or print or pattern layout. Designers choose color palettes based on colors that have done well in the past, the ship date of the product, what is trending at the time, and the particular season for which they are designing, generally sticking to the brighter colors for spring/summer and the more neutral colors for fall/winter. The designer will then create a mood board (presentation board) or a rig wall, which is a presentation that collectively shows all inspiration, concepts, themes, and sketches for the line, as well as corresponding fabrics, trims, and colors for each silhouette.

At this time, a first edit is conducted, in which the designer

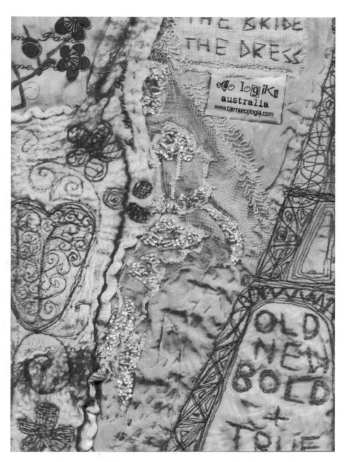

Paris mood board for Ethical Fashion Show in Paris, 2009. COURTESY OF TIERRA ECOLOGIA.

or design team will eliminate concepts that do not work cohesively with the line. The designer will then decide which concepts he or she would like to see in sample form. Sample yardage is purchased by either a fabric manager, fabric buyer, or the design or production team.

Patternmaking

Patternmaking, pattern cutting, or pattern drafting, is the creation or making of patterns. A pattern is the original paper or cardboard template from which different parts of the garment are traced onto fabric before they are cut out and assembled. In the United Kingdom, it is more common for this process to be called pattern cutting or pattern drafting, and in the United States, it is more universally referred to as patternmaking.

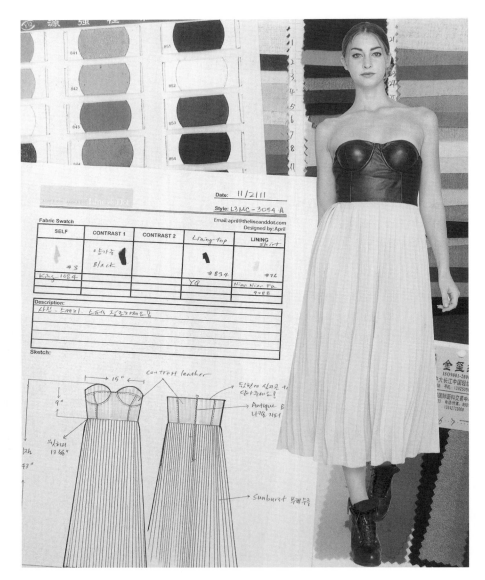

Fall/Winter 2012 Line and Dot Collection by April Oh. COURTESY OF APRIL OH.

The first pattern, known as the sample pattern is made in the sample room of a design studio or fashion company. It can be made out of paper or lightweight cardboard. Production patterns are fully detailed and made on heavy cardboard since they will be sent to a factory for manufacturing purposes. They need to be durable as they will be used over and over again for the grading process. Draping offers an option to pattern making and involves draping the fabric directly on a dress stand.

The actual drafting of a pattern is usually done by a skilled pattern maker and can be done by hand or by computer using a software program. The end result will be a graded paper pattern used for sewing. Using the designer's sketch or drawing, the pattern drafter will create a template known as a block or slope and add straight and curved lines based on body measurements. Fabric is cut from the block to form a mock up or toile.

Once the different shaped pattern pieces are completed, they will be made into a toile (term that originated in Europe) or muslin (term that originated in the United States). A toile is made out of muslin, a cotton woven fabric that is typically unbleached or white in color and is used for fabrics with more drape and fluidity. Calico is also an unbleached, plain woven textile (often unfinished) and is used to mock up more structured garments. Since muslin or calico is inexpensive, it is used to test the fit of the garment, avoiding costly mistakes that could be made with the actual, more expensive fabric being used. It should be as close as possible to the weight of the actual fabric so that it most closely resembles the structure of the garment. Finishes (seams, edges, facings, openings) will be applied to the toile, and then will be fit on a model. At this time, overall line and balance can be evaluated and any issues can be corrected before proceeding to a final sample. In addition, the end result of producing a toile is to refine the pattern template.

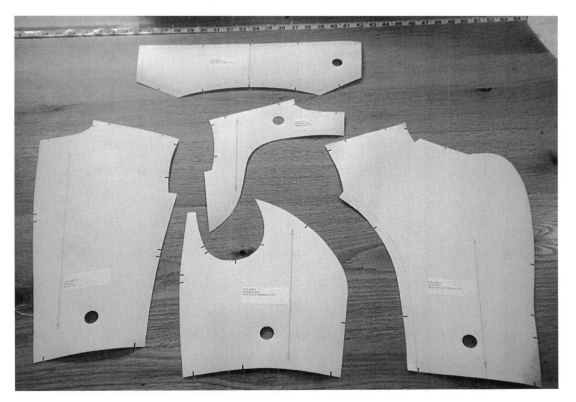

Bodice and collar pattern. COURTESY OF ANDRY OSHLYKOV.

Skirt sample from the Autumn/Winter 2011/2012 Katarina Dzale Prêt-à-Porter Collection. COURTESY OF KATARINA DZALE

The next step is pattern grading, which is a vital aspect of patternmaking. It is the process that adapts a basic pattern to a range of sizes, while preserving the fit and style of the original garment.

Sample Creation

The next step is to have the first sample prototype sewn. At this time, a "tech pack" (technical package) is created by the technical designer so that a sample or several samples can be made. A "tech pack" includes a technical drawing, or flat sketch of the garment, shown as both front and back views (and side views, if applicable), which shows completely finished dimensions; specifications, such as topstitching; label details and placement; trim component placement, such as zippers and buttons; stitching details; graphic placement; pattern or print details, shown by the repeat of the pattern or print and exact placement on the garment or accessory; embroidery and trim details and corresponding artwork; wash or special treatment details; a spec sheet, which includes the graded spec measurements; fabric and lining utilization, indicating what fabric(s) are being used (including sample swatches) including all colorways and color combinations; and a bill of materials (BOM) listing all of the individual items that are used to make the product, including season and style #. The tech pack is then sent, usually via FedEx, UPS, or DHL (for speedy delivery) to the factory or sample house that is making the sample.

A marker and grader will also lay out, mark, and cut the fabric to form the different parts of the garment. "Marker makings" is the actual full-size printout that shows how the styles are cut on the fabric. The marker and grader will also calculate and document the yields and maintain fabric inventories. The contractor with whom you are placing your bulk production order will often make your samples (this has the added benefit that the contractor can cost your garment for production), or you can go directly to a sample maker. The first sample is usually two to three times the cost of a garment being mass-produced for bulk. The factory or sample house will send the finished sample to the designer for review.

Sketched by Peter Som for the Spring 2012 Peter Som Collection. COURTESY OF PETER SOM.

Finalization, Presentation, and Hand-Off

The designer will need to fit the sample on a model, and a technical designer will sit in on the fit meetings and will note any changes that need to be made. The changes will be communicated back to the factory so that a second sample can be made for review. This process continues until the sample is approved. Once all samples have been finalized and made, design will usually present the collection to various departments, including merchandising, sales, public relations, marketing, and production. Each of these departments will then move forward with their respective tasks to prepare for the finalization of the collection.

Merchandising will cost the garment, and assign the number of SKUs that are needed in the line building process. Public relations will generally work with marketing to prepare their advertising and promotional campaigns, and present the line to the press and buyers by way of trunk and fashion shows. The sales team will schedule appointments with buyers and wholesale accounts to show the collection. Design will then complete their hand-off to production so that they can place the bulk orders with the factory.

Illustrated by Izak Zenou for Henri Bendel. COURTESY OF IZAK ZENOU.

5 Launching Your Own Fashion Collection

When in doubt, wear red.

—BILL BLASS

BEING WILLING TO COMMIT TO THE INTENSE AMOUNT OF TIME, energy, money, and resources it takes to launch a collection is an essential requirement in making the decision to launch your own collection. Today's most successful designers interned, apprenticed, and worked for many years for other designers, honing their craft and learning the business firsthand before starting their own companies. Vera Wang worked for Ralph Lauren; Donna Karan for Anne Klein; Raf Simons for Jil Sander; and Marc Jacobs for Perry Ellis. Along your journey, you will probably encounter pitfalls, drawbacks, and snags. These are nothing more than tests. Embrace these challenges, face them head-on, take on a "no guts, no glory" attitude and you will likely be rewarded.

This section in not meant to be comprehensive in nature, but rather serves as an overview. Following these guidelines will help facilitate the ultimate dream of launching your very own fashion label.

Writing a Business Plan

The first step in launching a collection is to write a business plan. A business plan outlines a strategic approach for creating a business, and includes all the steps necessary to execute it. It should include the executive summary (focusing on the strengths of the overall business plan), a market analysis (description of the industry, target market, pricing structure, competitive analysis), company description (mission statement and the PBS for your company), organization and management (staff structure), marketing and sales strategy, description and benefits of your product line, funding request (if you are seeking funding from an investor or a bank loan), and financial projections. For help writing a business plan, you can take out a book from the library on business plan writing, purchase a book on this topic, use reliable Internet resources, or contact the Small Business Administration (SBA) at www.sba.gov.

Illustrated by Izak Zenou, Personal Collection, 2009. COURTESY OF IZAK ZENOU.

Choosing Type of Ownership

Next you will choose the type of ownership or business structure for your company. Each business structure carries different tax and legal implications, so research the one that is best suited for your company. A sole proprietorship is an unincorporated business owned and operated by a single individual and is the most common type of ownership in the United States. As the sole owner, you make all the business decisions; however, if the business fails, you bear all of the responsibility. A partnership is a business that is owned and operated by two or more people. There are three basic types of partnerships: general (all partners have limited liability); limited (one partner has limited liability; and at least one partner has full liability); and a joint venture (general partnership for a limited period of time). A corporation (referred to as a C corporation) is an independent legal entity owned by shareholders. An S corporation (referred to as an S Corp) is a special type of corporation in which shareholders in the business, not the business itself is taxed. A limited liability company (LLC) provides limited liability (as the name implies) and is not taxed as a separate business entity. Instead, all profits and losses are absorbed by each member (the owners of an LLC are called "members").

After deciding your ownership, you should begin thinking about your company location. Whether you plan to work from your living room at home or lease your own design studio in an office building, you will need to choose the location that fits your budget, purchase insurance to cover your property and inventory in case of damage or theft, and lease or purchase any necessary equipment so you can get started on doing what you do best—designing!

What Was Your Greatest Challenge When Launching Your Collection?

❭ When launching the Kara Saun Collection, I'm blessed that the typical challenges a new designer faces in terms of media presence and raising capital were offset by my appearance and visibility on the TV series *Project Runway*. Having the privilege to show at *New York Fashion Week* was huge. Although *Project Runway* was a tremendous boost to my career, like any aspiring designer, there was an even a greater amount of work to be done once the show was over. We went on to launch an amazing sophomore showing that was well-publicized and garnered rave reviews.

Grace Gardens "2056 Collection" from the Kara Saun 2006 runway presentation. COURTESY OF KARA SAUN.

The collection was then sold to boutiques across the country. Sometimes your greatest challenge is figuring out how to successfully maneuver through all the many mishaps that will arise. For that, know who you are as a fashion designer and more importantly, as an individual. Know where on this fashion journey you truly want to be, and then take huge steps and leaps of faith in that direction.

Kara Saun, Fashion/Costume Designer, Kara Saun, Los Angeles, California, USA

❭ My greatest challenge is finding the balance between creating my own sense of identity and ultimately building a brand with integrity and values, while staying relevant and modern and delivering what the customer wants at any point in time. I monitor this daily, as it is so easy to lose a sense of oneself in an attempt to be what's hot now.

Chloe Lonsdale, Director, MiH JEANS, London, England, United Kingdom

❭ The most difficult aspect for me was how to finance my project. I came to London from France and had no idea where to look for help, so I worked very hard and saved but also had to borrow from family and friends to get the business started. Being self-employed isn't as glamorous as you might think, it involves a lot of hours and hard work.

Tina Lobondi, Founder/CEO, Tina Lobondi Collection, London, England, United Kingdom

❭ The greatest challenge is to make a better collection the following season! In addition, it was being able to establish a business in Tokyo. We have a huge following now, and I have shown in *Tokyo Fashion Week* and *London Fashion Week*.

Reem Alasadi, Designer/Director, The House of Reem, London, England, United Kingdom and Tokyo, Japan

What Was Your Greatest Challenge When Launching Your Collection? (Continued)

Reem Alasadi Collection. PHOTOGRAPHER: DEBORAH ANDERSON.

Anthi bikini from Panos Emporio. COURTESY OF PANOS EMPORIO.

❯ The greatest challenge was staying true to my instinct and convincing the media that I was on the right track. I was able to convince distributors and retailers as I traveled around Sweden with my first collection. But the media tended to think they knew best. When I went with curvy models, the industry found thin, figureless women more popular. However, to me, thin wasn't feminine. It was actually the public that embraced my use of the model Victoria Silvstedt, who has since gone on to do much bigger things which proved that I was right. After that, they began listening, a little. Without that public support, I wouldn't have made the impact I wanted. The lesson is to stay true to yourself and to stay true to your customers. Everyone else eventually comes around.

Panos Papadopoulos, Owner, Panos Emporio, Gothenburg, Sweden

❯ The biggest challenge is to visualize your dreams so that they can become realities. When you launch a collection, it is very important to understand that compromises will be required. It is critical to remain loyal to your vision. We have the tendency to forget that our designs are reflections of our inner selves. We reflect ourselves on to the canvas. The challenge that we have as artists is to recognize our unique style and to distinguish it from others. That is what will make you authentic, innovative, and genius.

Diego Binetti, Creative Director, Binetti, Inc., New York, New York, USA

❯ Realizing that you are suddenly a businessperson as well as a designer and knowing that in order to build your business, design, finance, marketing, sales, and manufacturing all have

Fall/Winter 2012 Diego Binetti Collection.
PHOTOGRAPHER: ADAM WEISS.

Hand silk screened "Cover Girl" dress from the Spring 2006 Sue Stemp Collection.
PHOTOGRAPHER: GREG KADEL.

to grow together, can be quite overwhelming. However I found people were very willing to help and be supportive when I first set out on my own. Everyone always loves something new! The launch of my collection was relatively easy, exciting, and fun. The greatest challenge is the second collection and all the defining decisions that you have to make in the first few months of business.

Sue Stemp, Designer/Owner, Sue Stemp, Los Angeles, California, USA

❯ Finding good people that believe in your same passion and who embody the drive to start something new was my biggest challenge. It takes a huge amount of trust to hire your first employee. Finding sales, marketing, and manufacturing professionals that believe in the same passion, vision, and product is key. It takes a collaborative effort of a team to take the collection and shape it into a brand. A good accessory recipe is made up of exceptional design, great manufacturing quality, and a good retail price. Finding the balance among these three things is not just a challenge at a launch of a collection, but a necessity to the longevity of your company. There is no question that a designer sometimes has to leave their personal style at the door in order to produce a successful product line that is profitable.

Shari Seidlitz-McCandlish, Creative Director/Owner, Geoni Studios, Los Angeles, California, USA

What Was Your Greatest Challenge When Launching Your Collection? (Continued)

❯ My greatest challenge when I was launching my collection was finding my manufacturer, patternmaker, leather supplier, zipper wholesaler, hardware supplier, and the platform to sell to my customer. I had to remind myself that my designs would never see the light of day if I did not have a customer to buy it. I didn't want to be obligated to have to manufacture so many pieces that I would have extra inventory sitting around. I basically didn't want to put myself out of business before I started. Designing with success is 50 percent creativity and 50 percent business. Sourcing with consideration to longevity is key and a large part of the foundation that your collection and business will be built upon.

Laura Dotolo, Principal, clutchbags.com, New York, New York, USA

❯ My greatest challenge was to find good quality individuals to work with me to build my brand. I have come across many people who were interested in collaborating with my label, but many were not professional enough or I felt didn't have the qualities for creating strong, long-lasting and positive synergies.

Alexis Reyna, Owner/Artistic Director, Alexis Reyna, Barcelona, Spain

❯ My first challenge was launching an eco-friendly collection. I wrote a business plan and one year later, I was ready to launch my first collection at Mercedes-Benz Fashion Week in Sydney. This collection was composed of recycled denim fibers made from factory off-cuts. At the time there was no eco awareness in the mainstream market, and it seemed it was not ready to embrace an environmentally friendly product. I never gave up with the concept and persevered on improving the product. My other challenge was educating the general consumer as well as the retailer on the benefits of purchasing an eco-friendly product. I explored retail-ers that would be interested in carrying the range, and I often faced rejection. I have been loyal to the eco concept where it would have been easier to just give up. I am so glad I have remained true to myself as an eco-designer against all odds.

Charlene O'Brien, Creative Director, tierra Ecologia, Perth, Australia

My biggest challenge was to bring together my design concepts within a clear framework and with unity.

Zuzana Kralova, Creative Director, Kralova Design, Madrid, Spain and Prague, Czech Republic

Fashion Design VII, Collection, "Where Everything Begins," Kralova Design, 2012. PHOTOGRAPHER: IVAN CLEMENTE.

❯ Money. Starting out, I knew I would not be able to create the ambitious collections I had in mind on such a small budget. I wasn't willing to cut out quality fabric and workmanship, so I had to reassess my line and decide what I could do without for the time being.

Rachel Rose, Owner/Designer, Rachel Rose, Brooklyn, New York, USA

❯ The greatest challenge was juggling all of the facets of being a one-woman show. Not only was I the creative director of my accessory line, I was the designer, marketer, public relations person, salesperson, bookkeeper, you name it. Once I got my feet off the ground and a few big stores under my belt (Henri Bendel, Patricia Field), I worked with a small showroom that helped with sales and growing my business. In hindsight, I learned so much from doing it all. Once I decided to work in the industry for an established accessory design company, I knew all of the facets of the business firsthand.

Christina Caruso, Creative Director/Founder, Christina Caruso, New York, New York, USA

Defining Your Brand

Once you have chosen your business structure, you will need to define your brand. In order to better define what this is, it is a good idea to create a unique selling proposition (USP). A USP or tag line defines what makes your brand unique and different from the competition. It will serve as the overall theme for your marketing campaign. In order to create your USP, first determine the biggest benefit that your collection can offer. Now determine what sets you apart from other companies who offer similar products. Next, identify what need your product fills in the marketplace. Now bring all of that information together in one concise sentence. Using a compelling USP will be the driving force behind the growth of your business startup. Implement it in all of your marketing materials, in your product labeling, including hang tags and in advertising campaigns for optimal customer recognition. You will also need to create a logo or some distinguishing brand feature to go along with your tag line.

Once you have determined your brand identity, you will then choose a business name. Choosing a business name is one of the most important steps in the process as it will reflect your brand identity and set the stage for how you are perceived in the competitive marketplace. Choosing a name is easier to do once you've defined your brand and target market and determined what is going to draw customers to your brand versus

Look 31 of the Spring 2012 Peter Som Runway Collection. PHOTOGRAPHER: DAN LECCA. COURTESY OF PETER SOM.

the others in the market. You should make sure that a similar name doesn't already exist by conducting a trademark search with the United States Trademark and Patent Office or the trademark office in your country. When selecting a name, consider if a domain name (website address) is available and if so, you may want to register the domain name so you can get your company website up and running in time for your launch.

You will also need to register your business name which is known as your "Doing Business As" (DBA) name through your state government. If you intend to incorporate your company, you need to check with your state filing office to see if the name you selected is already in use. At this point, you should find out if you need to obtain certain business licenses or permits to legally run your business. Contact your local, state and federal government regulating bodies to find out if these compliances pertain to your business.

An Interview with Maggie Norris, President and Fashion Designer of Maggie Norris Couture

What first led you to pursue a career in fashion design?

❯ When I was a little girl, I was so enchanted with dressing my dolls that I would fantasize that they were walking the red carpet or a princess in a foreign land. I started to design and construct all of their clothes. I was also inspired by movies such as *Breakfast at Tiffany's*, starring actress Audrey Hepburn. After learning more about legendary fashion designer Hubert de Givenchy (who designed her wardrobe for the film), my dream was to one day create beautiful couture as he did.

Prior to starting your own collection, Maggie Norris Couture, you were senior design director for the women's runway collection at Ralph Lauren. So many former Ralph Lauren employees like yourself have gone on to launch their own collections, among them Vera Wang, John Varvatos, and Reed Krakoff. To what do you attribute this?

❯ Ralph Lauren is truly an amazing creator and mentor, who inspired me to dream. Ralph Lauren Corporation is one of the greatest places for a designer to call home. From my first day there, I was surrounded by some of the most talented illustrators, artisans, patternmakers, and artists from around the world. It is an unparalleled creative environment. We were all encouraged and challenged to explore, research, and create in the flow for each collection. It is in this sort of environment that true artistry can flourish.

During the course of your fashion career, you spent some time working in Europe as the creative director for Mondi, a knitwear collection. Describe what that experience was like.

❯ The European experience at Mondi was exciting, and it proved to be an important opportunity for me. It gave me a more immediate connection to Italy, France, Russia, and many other surrounding countries. I would travel to these countries to do research and gather inspiration, and it was a chance for me to implement my own vision on the creative direction for an entire company that I had admired for so long. As the designer and creative director, I was able to put my stamp on every aspect of their collections, including eveningwear, accessories, sportswear, and active wear. While creating these collections, I partnered with legendary haute couture craftsmen such as Albert Lesage, the premiere Parisian embroiderer; Maison Legeron, the premiere Parisian provider of handcrafted silk flower appliqués; and legendary accessories designer Christian Louboutin for shoes. These men and women constructed wearable works of art. My first three shows were all made in Paris by craftsmen who have constructed for designers such as Christian Dior and Christian Lacroix.

The fashion industry is intrinsically linked to other creative industries, such as the art world and the entertainment industry. Have you had any experiences in which you were able to collaborate with another artist?

❯ One of my passions is the collaboration with artists, illustrators, painters, and photographers. I was searching for a painter who paints in the style of John Singer Sargent. After an extensive search, I found Nelson Shanks, who has painted a portrait of H.R.H., Diana, Princess of Wales, and His Holiness John Paul II, among others. It was an honor for me that he chose our "Ekaterina" couture corset to create a portrait of Kiera Chaplin, actress, model, and granddaughter of the great actor, director, and composer, Charlie Chaplin. Shanks also created another painting using our couture corset, called "Dragon Lady," which is being exhibited at the Russian Academy of ArTs in Moscow.

How does the design process begin for you? Do you begin with a theme or some form of inspiration, a silhouette or a recently discovered can't-live-without fabric?

❯ The inspiration for a design can come from almost anywhere. Every season I create a theme, where I can be in Russia one season and Paris the next, which allows me to explore all realms of my

"Dragon Lady" painting by artist Nelson Shanks, featuring "Ekaterina" corset by Maggie Norris Couture and Gilan earrings. PHOTOGRAPHER: JOSEPH DOLDERER, 2009.

research and imagination. Each client is unique. You have to spend time with them and hear their stories to understand them and create around their passions and needs. For some we draw from history; for others, we draw from classic cinema or great works of art. Trying to capture the essence of our clients' needs is our top priority.

You create one-of-a-kind garments for your clients, who range from high-profile businesswomen to socialites and celebrities. Please explain how this very intricate process works.

❯ First, I work very closely with our illustrator, Anna Kiper, developing every aspect of the design—be it color, draping, or even the attitude of the drawing—to best reflect the clients' wishes. We go through many phases of refinements, choosing fabric selections and design silhouettes before we produce the final watercolor to present to the clients. Once approved, it is ready to be developed and executed for a client as a one-of-a-kind couture garment.

How long does it typically take to complete a custom piece from concept to finalized garment?

❯ The typical time line for a couture corset can run as long as four or five months. First we create a design that has inspired us for the corset, which takes about two weeks. Then the illustration is created, which takes another week. The client will then come into my atelier for her measurements. The toile (a less expensive version of the garment, usually made of muslin, to test the pattern) is built, which takes two to three weeks. Then there is a second fitting with the client. The embroidery has to be laid out on the pattern and sent to Paris for the fabric to be embroidered. Depending on the complexity of the embroidery, it can take two months before it is returned to our studio. Two sewers will work full-time for three weeks before there is one final fitting with the client. Once the fitting is complete, we will spend two more weeks refining the corset. It will then be presented to the client.

Being able to obtain a celebrity clientele is the highlight of any fashion designer's career. How did you obtain your first celebrity client?

❯ I was fortunate to have the legendary editor and stylist Polly Mellen visit my atelier.

"Wong Liu Tsong" Silk Draped Skirt with "Nicole" Trench Jacket. ILLUSTRATED BY ANNA KIPER FOR MAGGIE NORRIS COUTURE, 2008.

She selected my haute couture constructed "Ambrosine" corset for actress Nicole Kidman for the cover of *Vanity Fair* magazine, as she was a stylist for them at the time. She began her career as the protégée of Diana Vreeland and later as an editor at *Harper's Bazaar* and *American Vogue*.

Different designers are inspired by different things. Where do you draw most of your inspiration from?

❯ Inspiration, for me, is exploring the classical designs of the past through photographers, films, paintings, music, literature, and architecture, as well as bringing inspiration through current contemporary works of art. Essentially it is about drawing from what is happening culturally in the world right now.

I have always described your creations as museum worthy. Have you partnered with museums to exhibit any of your pieces?

❯ We have showcased our couture in London at the Victoria and Albert Museum, as well as the FIT Museum in New York City and the Museum of the City of New York.

Irina Dvorovenko, principal dancer at the American Ballet Theater, wearing Maggie Norris Couture. ILLUSTRATED BY ANNA KIPER, 2011.

An Interview with Bibhu Mohapatra, Fashion Designer

Designer Bibhu Mohapatra with model wearing paprika satin asymmetric sleeve gown by Bibhu Mohapatra. COURTESY OF BIBHU MOHAPATRA.

Was there a pivotal moment in your childhood, growing up in India, upbringing, or at some point in your life that led you to pursue a career in fashion design?

❯ The pivotal moment for me came the day my mother taught me how to sew on our old Singer sewing machine at home.

After completing your master's degree in economics, you enrolled at the Fashion Institute of Technology (FIT) in New York. What propelled you to study fashion design?

❯ I have always wanted to be a fashion designer; it is only once I graduated with my master's degree in economics that I came to New York City to study fashion.

While still at FIT, you worked as an assistant designer at the design house of the iconic and renowned Halston. How did you land that position prior to receiving your design degree?

❯ One day I went to all the fashion buildings on Seventh Avenue and dropped off my résumés at some of my favorite designer offices. Some of the buildings were located at 500 Seventh Avenue, 530 Seventh Avenue, and 550 Seventh Avenue. Out of that effort I received two phone calls, and one of them was from Halston design studio.

During your senior year at FIT, you received the esteemed Critic's Award for Best Evening Wear Designer. What did you design to receive this honor?

❯ The design challenge was to create something out of white. I made a white double-faced wool and silk satin strapless gown with fabric flowers and feathers.

Upon graduation, you were the design director for a New York–based runway designer, where we worked together. I was always inspired by your raw design talent and penchant for maintaining the highest level of couture craftsmanship. Please describe what you took away from this role.

❯ Those nine years were some of the most important years in my career, where I learned a lot, shared my knowledge with others, built the team, and designed three collections a year. It was a great experience.

Before fully launching your own eponymous collection, you began designing custom couture evening gowns, cocktail dresses, and furs for a select group of private clientele in New York, Europe, and India. Please describe how this process worked and if you were the sole designer or employed a staff at this time.

❭ I rented a small room on the Upper West Side where I got a sewing machine and a cutting table and just myself as the sole worker. Later on I hired a sewer.

What led to the launch of your own collection? Please provide a summary of how you prepared for your launch.

❭ I have always wanted to launch my own brand of clothes, and in 2009 it was the time to finally do it. I raised some funds, worked on an inspiration and theme, and prepared a sixteen-look collection, which I showed to buyers and editors at the Bryant Park Hotel in New York.

What is your design philosophy?

❭ A successful design is a perfect balance of creativity and practicality.

How does the design process begin for you? Do you begin with a theme or some form of inspiration, a silhouette, or a recently discovered can't-live-without fabric?

❭ A theme first, then imagery, then draping and sketching, and ultimately I finish through editing.

Do you have a separate fabric team that globally sources your fabrics, or is this the responsibility of the design team?

❭ Currently, I do it all myself, but someday I dream to work with a fabric team to help me source incredible fabrics from all over the world.

As a fashion designer with a namesake collection, you partner with your executive management team and creative heads to ensure that all the steps of developing and selling a collection—such as design, technical design, merchandising, visual presentation, quality control, public relations, fashion show production, sales, and marketing—are successfully implemented and executed. How do you manage this process with your staff?

❭ More delegation and less micro-management.

Your collection is currently sold at Bergdorf Goodman and Neiman Marcus and in select specialty boutiques in North America, Europe, and the Middle East. What advice would you give to aspiring fashion designers who are pounding away at the pavement trying to land their first retail account?

❭ Show your work, creativity, eye for quality, but also show your business mind when you are presenting to buyers and retailers.

Do you have an international retail expansion strategy, and are you targeting a certain region for expansion, such as Asia, which has been and continues to emerge as a prominent retail market for the apparel industry?

❭ We are definitely targeting Asia and the Middle East, as well as Europe.

What role does social media play in the promotion of your brand and in staying close to your customer base?

❭ Twitter and Facebook are incredible tools to connect and stay in touch with my clients and supporters, and I am getting good at it.

Among your many recognitions, in 2010, you were a finalist for the Fashion Group International's (FGI) Rising Star Award for women's apparel. A few months later, you received the Young Innovator Award from the National Arts Club. The following month, you were inducted into the Council of Fashion Designers of America (CFDA), as an official member. In 2011, you received the Ecco Domani Fashion Foundation award. What did it feel like to receive such high accolades?

❯ It humbles me to see such appreciation of my work and propels me even more to work harder. I am very grateful.

Your blog is fantastic! It really enables people to get a behind-the-scenes feel for what you do every day, and gives the public a true sense and taste of what fashion design in the New York fashion industry is all about. Describe how it came into being and what prompted you to implement it.

❯ The blog is really an extension of my working life and experiences as a fashion designer in New York City.

What advice would you give to an aspiring fashion designer who is trying to launch his or her own collection?

❯ Work hard, believe in yourself, and fight for it.

How do you achieve balance between your career and your personal life?

❯ I achieve balance by getting away to my country house as often as I can. Nature balances everything.

Sketch of moss raven print ballet dress by Bibhu Mohapatra for the Fall 2011 Bibhu Mohapatra Collection. COURTESY OF BIBHU MOHAPATRA.

Do you have a favorite fashion quote?

❯ "Pink is the navy blue of India."—Diana Vreeland

Describe the ultimate perfect day for you.

❯ The ultimate perfect day is 72 degrees, a clear blue sky, a good breakfast, a day of draping and sketching, an evening with a good home-cooked meal and a glass of wine.

Protecting Your Designs

When it comes to launching your own collection, it is important to protect your work from unauthorized copying and infringement by taking all necessary precautions before marketing and selling your products. Review the following checklist to ensure that you have all your bases covered:

INTELLECTUAL PROPERTY CHECKLIST BY KAREN ARTZ ASH, PARTNER, NATIONAL CO-CHAIRPERSON, INTELLECTUAL PROPERTY DEPARTMENT, KATTEN MUCHIN ROSENMAN LLP, NEW YORK

1. Your Names, Trademarks, and Domain Names
   - Are your trademarks the subject of federal applications and registrations in all countries where your products are or will be manufactured or sold, where you currently distribute, where you have or may have licenses, and where you intend to sell in the future?
   - Have you had searches run and cleared on all of your primary and secondary marks, logos, and style names?
   - Do you have a proper watching service in place to identify potential infringers of your trademarks? This can be done by some regular Internet checking and updates, including a review of newly issued domain names and websites, and by perusing "flash sale" sites.
   - Do you regularly check e-Bay and similar sites to see if others copy your distinctive designs or names, or resell your products without authority or with improper or misleading information?
   - Do you take steps to protect your domain name(s)? This means objecting to registrations and uses by third parties that incorporate your name. It also means buying new top-line domains (e.g., .net) as they are available, so that others are precluded from doing so.
   - Do you have global/domestic protection for domain names? This is important if you intend to make international online sales and deliveries, or engage in a foreign brick-and-mortar business.
   - Do you have proper vendor and manufacturing agreements in place with those facilities that manufacture your samples and products? If so, do they have the proper indemnities in place and the proper control over disposition of products, labels, and trim? Are the other parties prohibited from copying your products?
   - Do you have the proper licenses and sublicenses in place? If so, have those licenses, or short-form versions of those licenses, been recorded in those countries where this is required?
   - Do you have the proper distribution agreements in place? This covers the circumstance where a third party buys already finished products and sells them to retailers.

- Are your trademarks recorded with customs border and protection services domestically and internationally to protect against the importation of goods that violate your registered trademarks?
- Do you use proper forms of trademark notice, for example, ™ or ® notices?

2. Copyrights

- Do you have copyright applications or registrations for distinctive, original ornamentation or fabric designs?
- Do you have proper "work for hire" and related assignment agreements with third parties that create designs, elements, trim, advertising, printed material, fabric designs, patterns, graphics, and photographs that you have commissioned or that will be used by you?
- Do you have copyright applications or registration for the graphics, text, and content of distinctive hangtags, pocket flashers, promotional materials, and label formats?
- Do you use proper copyright notices on your materials?

Sketched by Peter Som for the Spring 2012 Peter Som Collection. COURTESY OF PETER SOM.

- If you have engaged a photographer, design studio, web designer, or advertising agency, do you have the proper agreements in place, and will you own all work product and content?

3. Patents

- If you have invented a unique functional aspect of a product or a distinctively designed three-dimensional item, have you considered seeking utility or design patent protection, as applicable? You could then use the legend "Patent Pending."

4. Third Parties

- If you have sales agency agreements in place for third-party resellers in foreign countries, are you cognizant of the legal obligations associated with them upon termination?
- If you meet with third parties, such as potential financial investors, make sure that all of your material bears your name, a copyright notice, and a legend stating: "Confidential and proprietary business and design information."
- Try to have all of your applications for proprietary protection (trademark, domain names, patents, and copyrights) and a signed standard confidentiality or nondisclosure agreement in place before you show anything you consider proprietary to anyone else.

What Is the Best Way for a Fashion Designer to Protect His or Her Work from Unauthorized Copying and Infringement?

❯ A fashion designer must protect his or her intellectual property assets, as it is critical to building a business that can secure financing, support customer demands, and engage in marketing, manufacturing, advertising, promotion, and sales. First and foremost, the designer's name must be protected. This is the brand or trademark that identifies and distinguishes that designer from all others. It begins with the designer's personal name and might also extend to acronyms, first names, last names, phrases, nicknames, or a symbol.

Next order of business in establishing a solid basis for protecting a designer's name is securing Internet domain names in the relevant jurisdictions and on a proper top-line basis. The designer should also protect his or her distinctive graphic designs, fabrics, patterns, moulds, three-dimensional patterns, or materials used for making the product, trim (e.g., rivets, buttons), text, advertising, and similar types of materials. This could also include distinctive, source-identifying stitching, such as a pocket stitch design. In the United States, unlike in France, for example, there is currently no per se copyright protection for the garment design, itself. However, there are other means to protect and enhance recognition for distinctive elements (through trademark and trade dress protections and possible design patent protection, for example).

If a designer is using the services of a third party (an independent contractor, not an employee) to create any materials, proper "work for hire" and assignment agreements should be in place to ensure that the designer, and not the commissioned third party, actually owns the work product. If you have an employee, the proper protections should be included in the terms of employment or employee manual. Once the appropriate protections are in place, the designer should regularly take steps to monitor the Web and marketplace and take enforcement measures, as appropriate and cost-effective. In addition to taking steps to protect one's own proprietary rights, it is also important to make sure that the designer does not infringe someone else's rights, even inadvertently. This is typically addressed by conducting appropriate clearance trademark and, as applicable, patent searches. A good rule of thumb when looking elsewhere for inspiration is to put yourself in the place of the other party. If you would be upset by the "inspired" materials, then assume the other person would be bothered, too, and may explore legal action.

Karen Artz Ash, Partner and National Co-Chairperson, Intellectual Property Department, Katten Muchin Rosenman LLP, New York, New York, USA

❯ The best way for fashion designers [in the U.S.] to protect their work from copyright infringement is to register copyright for their designs with the United States Copyright Office. Designers can register their works electronically at www.copyright.gov. The process is straightforward and inexpensive. It is critical that designers register their designs before someone else copies them. Pre-infringement registration entitles the copyright owner to elect statutory damages and potentially to recover attorney's fees and costs associated with enforcing their copyrights. To ensure pre-infringement registration, designers should submit their designs to the Copyright Office prior to disclosing them to the public.

Dan Nelson, Partner, Nelson & McCulloch LLP, New York, New York, USA

❯ Fashion designers have no easy mechanism under U.S. law to capture the exclusive right for their creative fashion designs. As a result, fashion designers have to be more intentional in their creative

What Is the Best Way for a Fashion Designer to Protect His or Her Work from Unauthorized Copying and Infringement? (Continued)

expression so as to prevent unauthorized infringers from exploiting their works. With careful planning, however, fashion designers may be able to claim the exclusive right to their designs under copyright or trade dress laws and prevent others from seizing the goodwill that rightfully belongs to the fashion designer. How can a fashion designer acquire the exclusive right in the design set forth in an article of clothing? The answer is to make the design of the clothing item more like a "pictorial" or "graphic" work that could stand on its own if separated from the clothing. Courts in recent years have granted copyright protection to a pattern or design in clothing when the artistic qualities of the pattern or design can be separated from the utilitarian nature of the garment. If the design is marketable, independent of the utilitarian purpose of the garment, then the fashion designer may be able to assert a copyright interest and keep others from copying it. The other area of intellectual property law that may afford protection to the fashion designer is the law of trade dress, which protects the way a product design is "dressed up" for the public. If the purchasing public would recognize a particular product design as having a single source, trade dress protection may extend to the design and, under the Lanham Act, the owner of the design can prevent others from selling confusingly similar designs. How does one develop trade dress rights in a fashion design? Typically, trade dress rights are developed over time and through extensive advertising and marketing campaigns, and can be proven by putting on evidence of sales, advertising expenditures, and even consumer surveys. Examples of companies that have made substantial investments over time to develop trade dress rights in garments might include the Burberry plaid design, the pattern of Vera Bradley products, and the style of the Timberland Wheat Nubuck boot.

Jason Sneed, Managing Member, SNEED PLLC—Intellectual Property Legal Services, Davidson, North Carolina, USA

❯ There is no copyright protection for useful articles. This is a concept known as the "Useful Articles Doctrine." This doctrine states that if a work does not have a form that is separable form its function, it is generally not protectable via copyright law in the United States. A great example of this is a wedding dress. The creative "work" of the dress is one in which the form and function of the dress are the same in the eyes of the law. The law generally sees the dress merely as an object to cover one's body, so the form of the white fabric wedding dress is seen as united in whole with its function of covering the body. This is why fashion designs are generally nonprotectable via copyright law in the U.S. It is notable, however, that the elements of a fashion design that are separable from the function, such as a red rose embroidered on the train of a wedding dress, are generally protectable via copyright law as works of two-dimensional visual art. There have been several bills before Congress in recent years to try to extend copyright protection to fashion designs. None of these bills has been passed into law, but this is a development that may be on the horizon. Furthermore, what is not protectable via copyright law may still be potentially protected via a design patent. The patent process is typically much more costly and time-consuming than the copyright process, and therefore, design patents are often inaccessible to fashion start-ups without considerable funding. Therefore, trademark protection to protect the brand name of your apparel items is one of the best ways to protect your fashion designs. While a trademark will not protect the designs themselves, it will give the trademark owner the right to prevent others from using a name that is likely to cause confusion with your brand name in the minds of consumers. This helps to preserve the goodwill that you have spent considerable time and money developing.

Melissa Dagodag, Attorney, The Law Offices of Melissa K. Dagodag, Beverly Hills, California, USA

❯ Conceptually, designers need to think of themselves as a business and their creations as their assets. Once they start to take themselves seriously as a business enterprise, an awareness of the value of their business assets, shortcomings, and requirements will heighten. Without this business mentality, designers will be their own weakest link. Designers should surround themselves with professionals who have legal, business, or financial savvy, to assist them to map out the long- and short-term vision for their business. This kind of business planning is invaluable. The foundation of protecting fashion designs lies in intellectual property laws. Intellectual property laws provide a great legal and business tool to fashion designers, to help protect their creative ingenuity. From a legal perspective, strategies used to protect fashion designs will vary according to the different jurisdiction, as intellectual property laws are governed on a country-by-country basis. This is important to understand, as most fashion companies are globally based. Whereas some countries have developed intellectual property laws that are well-attuned to protecting fashion designs (some countries in Europe), other countries have been more conservative in the scope of protection of fashion designs. Intellectual property protection can serve a business purpose by protecting the identifying and distinctive parts of the brand. The more creative the designers are in protecting their fashion design, the greater the "brand monopoly" the designer will have in the marketplace. In Canada, distinctive aspects of fashion designs may be protected under trademarks, copyright, industrial design, and, in some instances, patent laws. Determining which avenue of intellectual property law is appropriate is dependent upon the subject matter and is determined on a case-by-case basis. Generally, the biggest obstacle lies in whether the aspect of the fashion design is functional and/or generic.

Ashlee Froese, Lawyer, Gilberts LLP, Toronto, Canada, and founder of CanadaFashionLaw.com.

❯ After putting a great amount of time and energy into their work, fashion designers should make protecting their unique designs a top priority. Even though the general shapes of clothing are not eligible for copyright protection, unique fabric designs, intricate patterns, and ornate decorative pieces like belts and jewelry are protectable. Creating and incorporating these types of original distinctive elements into a design [make it] more likely copyright protection will extend to a fashion designer's works.

Daliah Saper, Principal Attorney, Saper Law Offices, LLC, Chicago, Illinois, USA

❯ Generally, United States law does not extend copyright protection to fashion designs. However, there is a growing movement to extend copyright protection to fashion designs, at least on limited three-year basis, which arguably would provide the designer with a reasonable amount of time, given the short lifespan of fashion designs. Until the law is amended, designers should copyright patterns and artwork when possible and rely on other areas of the law to protect their designs. A designer should register his or her trade name, brand, logo, or symbol as a trademark with the United States Patent and Trademark Office. A designer should then actively review the marketplace to ensure that his or her trademark is not used with knockoff products. If protected designs, patterns, or trademarks are infringed upon, the designer should send a cease and desist letter to the infringer, demanding that the infringing action immediately stop. If that does not resolve the issue, a designer should initiate a lawsuit.

Terrence M. Dunn, Partner, Einbinder & Dunn, LLP, New York, New York, USA

❯ Copyright law, which prevents theft of creativity, doesn't protect useful objects such as garments. That's why malls are full of knockoff fashion, which can be devastating to emerging designers. "Trade Dress" law may offer some hope. Trade dress is a cousin to trademark, protecting any creative ele-

What Is the Best Way for a Fashion Designer to Protect His or Her Work from Unauthorized Copying and Infringement? (Continued)

ment that becomes a brand identifier, like Tiffany & Co's signature shade of blue. If a line's entire collection features the same whimsical pocket placement, for example, then customers might come to recognize the brand by the pockets. Lesson: if you come up with a great design element, include it in several pieces and make it yours. Lawyers for luxury brands have increasingly asserted as much in lawsuits against copiers. They argue, for example, that a successful shoe design is protectable trade dress because customers know who makes it. The copier, so the argument goes, isn't just misappropriating a pleasing design, but also improperly benefitting from the brand goodwill built by the originator, not unlike a true counterfeiter. So far, we don't know

how the courts will sort this out. If the public might mistake a knockoff for one of your pieces, consider invoking the protections of trade dress law. Also, watch how the law evolves in this area for further clues about protecting your designs.

David Alden Erikson, Founder, Law Offices of David Alden Erikson, Los Angeles, California, USA

❭ In the United States, register your work with the U.S. Copyright Office because that entitles the copyright holder to recover statutory damages and attorneys' fees for post-registration infringements. Protection should also be sought in foreign countries as well.

Joseph Mandour, President, Mandour & Associates, APC, Santa Monica, California, USA

Creating Accounting, Budgeting, and Bookkeeping Systems

Next you will want to create accounting, budgeting, and bookkeeping systems, including financial reports and projections. Proper accounting is essential in any business because it allows you to assess and keep track of the functioning of your business operations. The balance sheet and the income statement are the main financial statements that you will have to prepare when launching your business. The balance sheet is an outline of your business financials, including assets, liabilities, and net worth. Your income statement (profit and loss statement) shows your revenue (income) and expenses. A budget includes the revenue your company anticipates it will bring in and the money it expects to pay out as expenses (rent, salary, utility bills, advertising budget, etc.). A budget should be completed for the first year you are in business and should be adjusted for each consecutive year. The budget should be in working format and should be reviewed consistently and adjusted as necessary.

Every business needs to pay close attention to its accounting and bookkeeping records, which will track and store sales, cash flow: purchases, assets (expenses), and liabilities, inventory, as well as profitability on a yearly basis. Recording such transactions can be carried out by an actual accountant or bookkeeper, or if your budget doesn't allow, in the form of a computer accounting software program, such as QuickBooks. You can also take an accounting and bookkeeping class so you are better equipped to handle this aspect of your business. To run a well-organized business, these records need to be in order not only for tax purposes and recordkeeping upkeep, but so you can plan cost-savings initiatives, change sales or marketing strategies, or enhance the profitability of the company.

Once you have these systems in place, you can begin to explore funding options in the form of financing from loans, grants, and venture capitalists. In addition, each state and country have their own local, state and federal tax laws and as a business owner, you are required to pay taxes by certain deadlines so be sure to thoroughly research and ascertain your tax obligations.

Hiring Employees, Contractors, and Interns

Most designers initially handle all aspects of running a business themselves when first starting out. Once business picks up, staff can be hired. Before hiring employees, you need to obtain an employer identification number (EIN), also known as a Federal Tax Identification Number, from the U.S. Internal Revenue Service (IRS). If you are starting a business outside of the United States, check with your local regulatory body for rules and regulations. The EIN is necessary when reporting taxes and employee-related information to the IRS. Federal laws requires an employer to verify potential employees' eligibility to work in the United States, so as an employer, you must ask each potential employee to fill out the I-9 form or the employee eligibility verification form. Businesses with employees are required to pay workers' compensation insurance, so contact your state agency for details on registration. Businesses with employees are also sometimes required to pay unemployment insurance, so research the requirements with your state workforce agency (Department of Labor). Some states require businesses to provide disability insurance, so be sure to check with your state agency on the provisions relating to this. You will also be required by law to put up posters in the workplace that inform employees of their rights under labor laws. These posters are available at no cost from your state and federal Department of Labor. There are city, state, and federal tax filing requirements that can be obtained from the IRS. It is important to implement a structured and organized system for recordkeeping so that all of your requirements and forms are in one place and are easily accessible.

Hilary Swank wearing Randolph Duke Couture to accept the Best Actress Oscar for *Boys Don't Cry* at the 72nd Annual Academy Awards, held at the Shrine Auditorium and Expo Hall, Los Angeles, California. REUTERS, 2000. COURTESY OF RANDOLPH DUKE.

You will want to create a job description for each open position in your company, indicating detailed job responsibilities, expectations, salary and job requirements, along with whether it is a full-time or contract position. You can choose how much you want to spend on advertising these positions, or you may choose to obtain potential hires through word of mouth. It is a good idea to create an employee manual that outlines code of conduct and other important facts for employees. You may also choose to find a reputable company that can provide background checks of potential employees. For both full-time and contract employees, you may choose to bring on an employment agency that can do the hiring for you, for a fee, or you may choose to do your own recruiting. There are many agencies that specialize in fashion and accessory job placement.

Look 8 of the Spring 2012 Peter Som Runway Collection. PHOTOGRAPHER: DAN LECCA. COURTESY OF PETER SOM.

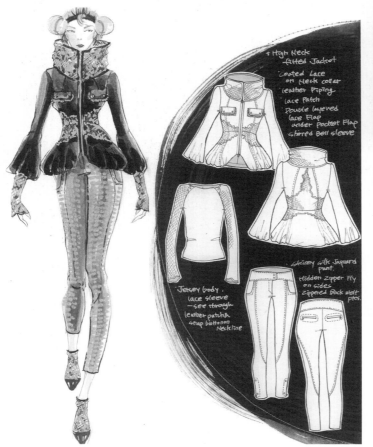

Fall/Winter Collection illustrated by Christina Kwon and inspired by Cremaster, Matthew Barney, 1996. COURTESY OF CHRISTINA KWON.

Hiring an intern is a cost-effective method of adding staff to your design team. You can work with the internship coordinators of major universities and fashion schools to make sure your company is included in their roster. You should decide if you want to offer a nonpaid internship and/or offer a small stipend. If you decide to offer a nonpaid internship, you may choose to offer the intern(s) a perk, such as a discount on your product line or entrance to the company sample sale.

Developing a Marketing Plan

The more exposure your line gets, the better off you'll be. Relationship building is a key component to promoting and marketing your brand. It is important to develop strategic connections with everyone who can become a partner with you to help promote and sell your collection, including editors, buyers, and retailers. There are numerous ways to promote your brand and to get the word out about your new collection, including trade and fashion shows, partnering with stylists, participating in open sees and fashion-related contests, social media outreach, and implementing a public relations strategy.

Spring/Summer 2012 Nanette Lepore Collection.
PHOTOGRAPHER: MARIA VALENTINA, 2011.

TRADE AND FASHION SHOWS

Trade shows such as Magic, GenArt, and Stylemax present viable opportunities in which you can show your line, build brand recognition, and make additional industry contacts, such as buyers from both small specialty stores and the larger department stores. If you have a budget to hire a sales representative to assist you at the trade shows, doing so will serve you well. You can also use fashion industry networking websites to try to find free student models, makeup artists, and photographers for your various promotional initiative who may be willing to work pro bono to add to their experience. Interns can always be used as assistants to help sell and promote your line.

Fashion shows provide a runway space for the debut of your seasonal collections to buyers, journalists, and the media. There are large-scale fashion shows that take place during various fashion weeks throughout the United States and the world that are costly and are meant for the more established designers, and there is the option of a lower-scale runway or trunk show. A trunk show is an informal presentation of a designer's collection and can take place on a small runway in a department store, boutique, or specialty store or in your own design studio or shared showroom. It is geared to an up-and-coming designer who does not yet have the budget for a runway presentation at a fashion week or in a more substantial establishment. You can seek out these locations as possible partners in your show launch.

An Interview with Fashion Director of Lincoln Center, Stephanie Winston Wolkoff

Portrait of Stephanie Winston Wolkoff. PHOTOGRAPHER: HANNAH THOMSON. COURTESY OF SWW CREATIVE.

Was there a pivotal moment in your childhood, upbringing, or at some point in your life, that led you to pursue a career in the fashion world?

❯ Many of my industry colleagues can vividly recall the moment they fell in love with fashion. It might have been the first time they encountered their grandmother's vintage Chanel bag. In that single instant, they "just knew." My journey was more gradual. I did not spend my childhood dreaming of fashion editorials or gala dinners. As the lone sister of two brothers, I grew up idealizing the basketball court far more than I ever acknowledged the runway, and yet, so many of the skills that I've honed over the past decades were learned when my wardrobe was more Nike than Michael Kors. I learned how to be a team player from my high school and college basketball teams. I learned determination and grace from the years I spent earning my black belt in martial arts. Most essentially, I learned how to deploy the most important accessory in my now extensive collection, my game face.

How did you prepare for your role as fashion director of Lincoln Center?

❯ I was asked by editor-in-chief of *Vogue* magazine, Anna Wintour, to become the ambassador in this position once the decision to relocate had been made. I moved into my office at Lincoln Center almost a full calendar year before Mercedes-Benz Fashion Week opened its doors at Damrosch Park. I came on board at that point because I knew, like the rest of the community, that this undertaking was about more than just a physical relocation. I saw the transition, to put it in Lincoln Center terms, as a curtain opening. To prepare for it, I held thousands of conference calls, met with hundreds of designers, and planned press conferences. I also commissioned new floor plans, updated databases, sent more e-mails than I care to remember, and considered investing in an air mattress, given the number of nights that I spent working late at the office.

Prior to your current position, you served as director of special events at Vogue *magazine, working one-on-one with editor-in-chief, Anna Wintour. She has been a monumental mentor and supporter of up-and-coming fashion designers. Are you able to carry out a similar focus at Lincoln Center? If so, what sort of programming is available to up-and-coming fashion designers who are trying to create a name for themselves?*

❭ Not a week goes by in which I don't reflect on how I can better serve the design community. One of my favorite aspects of this catch-all job is the extent to which I get to use my personal and professional contacts for the benefit of young de- signers. This past season, I facilitated a system of cost sharing that enabled four designers to split hair-and-makeup and all production costs. I've also introduced up-and-comers to corporations that are looking to support the industry, and I've been able to lengthen payment periods and strip padded budgets because I learned from the best. Anna has an eye for talent that I'd venture to say is unmatched, and once a designer is ready to show

their collection to the press and to the public, I feel lucky to be able to support them.

The fashion community is going to be able to experience a year-round schedule of exciting fashion-related programs and events at Lincoln Center. What can be expected?

❭ Lincoln Center is now the epicenter of fashion, and to continue the riveting energy of Mercedes- Benz Fashion Week, we produced a remarkable event this past October 2011 with an American icon, Ralph Lauren. *Lincoln Center Presents: An Evening with Ralph Lauren*, hosted by Oprah Winfrey, celebrated Mr. Lauren's renowned dedica- tion to culture, design, and his family. Jointly ben- efiting Lincoln Center and the Ralph Lauren Center for Cancer Care and Prevention, the event was the largest fund-raiser in the history of Lincoln Center and truly a memorable night for our industry. We are now in the process of creating a designer lecture series, as well as a fashion film series, to achieve our goal of keeping fashion on par with the arts and designing a platform for the public to fully experi- ence the complex, yet inspiring world of fashion at its best.

What advice would you give an aspiring fashion designer trying to launch his or her own collection?

❭ Succeeding in this business is not easy. No matter how talented you are, at some point someone will look at the work that you've poured your heart and soul into and simply say, "No." Because of that, my best advice to designers is to believe in your own work absolutely. Root your collections in your own experiences. Be genuine in your craft. I think the modern-day consumer values that sense of integrity. Make sure the clothing that you produce has it. And above all else, love what you do.

Are you seeing a higher percentage of non-American fashion designers showing at Mercedes-Benz Fashion Week at Lincoln Center? What benefits does showing here provide to the fashion designer who is not based in the United States?

❯ The borders that exist between countries and continents are almost invisible on the Internet. Online commerce doesn't and shouldn't care if you're in London, Paris, New York, or even Sydney, Australia, and I think designers are very aware of that. Even young designers are looking to introduce their collections to a global audience, and I don't think there is a single stage as international as the one that New York offers. The United States, and New York in particular, is still the best platform for diverse exposure. I'm so proud of that.

Where can fashion designers who are not based in New York go to learn more about what you do?

❯ With the success of social media and the Internet, an entirely new population is exposed to the work that we do. www.fashionlincolncenter.org is the nexus of our activity and communicates who we are to the industry and even the novice fashion devotee. Featuring live streams from runway shows, our calendar of events and upcoming initiatives, www.fashionlincolncenter.org is an incredible tool for promoting fashion programming at Lincoln Center.

Please provide an overview of the options that are available to fashion designers who choose to show at Mercedes-Benz Fashion Week in New York.

❯ Because Lincoln Center is a campus, housing a dozen constituent organizations, our spaces run the gamut in terms of size, aesthetic, and location. Ultimately, we're committed to facilitating the best and most beautiful shows in New York City during Mercedes-Benz Fashion Week, whether that means whisking invited guests up to Avery Fisher Hall's portico for Zac Posen's dreamy runway, or making sure that Norma Kamali can load her 3-D technology equipment into the David Rubenstein Atrium in time for her morning show. If a designer has his or her heart set on it, I want to make it happen. That's my structure.

During fashion week, I would imagine your schedule is nonstop jam-packed, minute-to-minute. What is a typical day like for you?

❯ The organized chaos that is Mercedes-Benz Fashion Week doesn't take too kindly to generalizations, so I can't say that there is necessarily any "typical" day. But my usual looks something like this: I begin my morning with the sunrise, at which point I'm almost immediately on my e-mail and reviewing my schedule. My John Barrett dream team, hair and makeup, shows up at my apartment to get me ready for the onslaught of photographs and interviews that I'll take and tape throughout the day. By 8:30, I've dropped my kids off for school and am en route to Lincoln Center. I don't pretend to be some kind of supermom, but those decidedly unglamorous moments are ones that I wouldn't sacrifice even for Mercedes-Benz Fashion Week. On any given day at the Tents and around New York, I'll squeeze in four to six shows and as many meetings. I like to carve out three to four hours in the afternoon to stay on top of contracts, press, and production schedules for the shows taking place on Campus. This year, I dropped into the CIRCA Accessories Salon within the Tents daily. The Salon, which invited a different designer each day to display his or her Spring 2012 collection in appropriate splendor at Mercedes-Benz Fashion Week, is an accessory-lover's paradise. Once I tear myself away from that, I generally try to sneak out of the Tents because, by evening, I'm ready to head home and tuck my children into bed.

Fall 2012 Rachel Roy Collection. PHOTOGRAPHER: RICHARD GLEASON.

You are truly a tour de force in the fashion world. Is there an insider secret to your success that you can share with the world?

❭ I don't think there's any one secret that leads, definitively, to success, but I can guarantee that you won't succeed unless you are willing to work. Late nights and early mornings are all wrapped up in the beautiful package that is this industry. Learn to love it.

What is the most wonderful aspect of your job?

❭ The people that I work with every day are the most talented, creative, and game-changing individuals in their respective fields. I collaborate with musicians, producers, designers, artists, actors, and icons. Because of them, I get to play a role in, literally, fashioning the most exciting, exclusive, and beautiful events in the world.

Not only are you a high-powered fashion executive, but you are married and have three children. How do you balance it all?

❭ Like every working mother, in every field, I do the best that I can. I don't think I strike a perfect balance, not least because I don't think a perfect balance exists. Everyone who works with me knows that my kids come first. Both motherhood and my career are aspects of my life that I've chosen to make a priority. Balance, for me, is a day when I go to sleep feeling like I haven't compromised on either one.

What is your favorite quote?

❭ There are two quotes that I always come back to, and both have had a great influence on my life, and they are, "Love what you do and do what you love" and "We are all perfectly imperfect."

Describe the ultimate perfect day for you.

❭ During the summer, when we trade weekends in the concrete jungle for Saturdays by the beach, I get to watch my three children run around the deck, drip ice-cream all over everything, and play games of make-believe together. Seeing them in action, from sunup to sundown, makes for genuinely perfect days.

FASHION STYLISTS

Fashion stylists are great partners for fashion designers as they can help to create buzz and promote your brand. Many stylists are skilled in fashion design, have historical knowledge of costume design and are experts in predicting fashion trends, while others simply have an innate aesthetic sense and panache for styling. Some fashion designers like to work with stylists to help put together the looks on the models before they go down the runway. They get your clothing, shoes, and accessories on influential people such as celebrities, socialites, news anchors, talk show hosts, politicians, and businesspeople, and they also pull clothing and accessories from your showroom or design studio for photo shoots and editorials.

An Interview with Celebrity Stylist and Television Personality Robert Verdi

Celebrity stylist and television personality Robert Verdi.
PHOTOGRAPHER: FIDEL BERISHA, 2011.

Was there a pivotal moment in your childhood, growing up in New Jersey, or at some point in your life, that led you to pursue a career in jewelry design?

❯ I wasn't a jock, I wasn't a brainiac, I wasn't an incredibly talented artist, but I was a savvy businessperson as a kid, and I had a lot of creative ideas. I was making jewelry in my art class and selling it to my peers, and then I started selling it in a local jewelry store. My art teacher was incredibly supportive and wanted to see me succeed. She brought me to FIT in New York when they had an open house, and the head of the department looked at my portfolio and said he had not seen talent like mine come through their doors since Robert Lee Morris. That was the moment I knew I needed to go in this direction.

Upon graduation from the Fashion Institute of Technology (FIT) in New York, you began selling your jewelry line to what I call the "three B's"— Barneys, Bergdorf's, and Bendel's—and to the department store Bloomingdales. What advice would you give to an aspiring fashion designer who is pounding away at the pavement trying to land his or her first retail account?

❯ Have tenacity without being abrasive or desperate. A lot of it is personality-based, and not being unrealistic. Approach retailers with a business mindset. For example, suggest that you can bring them an additional customer base that they don't currently have, by conducting trunk shows with your collection. The world has already seen Halston, Dior, Lagerfeld, Marc Jacobs, and Donna Karan. You are you and don't emulate what other people are doing. Do what you do.

What advice would you give to an aspiring fashion designer who is trying to launch his or her own collection?

❯ There is strength in numbers. Get together with other designers and do a group show. You have a better chance of being discovered in the digital space, but be sure to present your collection with authority and cultural awareness.

As a stylist, please describe the collaborative process that takes place with a fashion designer.

❯ The designer is so close to the product that they can't sometimes step back and see it through the eyes of others. The stylists help designers speak the language of the consumers by helping them make the look wearable. Stylists translate the language of fantasy to the language of reality.

Why is it important for fashion designers to form relationships with fashion stylists?

❯ The collaborative process between designers and stylists is important because stylists usually have the better relationships with the celebrities who carry a lot of clout. We are like matchmakers who connect the celebrity with the design house. We are the conduit between the designer and the retail consumer, as we make them want to buy the product. As stylists,

we can increase your bottom line. We are all at the front rows of all the fashion shows. We edit the collections for celebrities for award shows and personal appearances, and for advertising and editorial pieces.

In 2000, you co-created and co-hosted Full Frontal Fashion on the WE network, the first television show to air complete coverage of the runway fashion shows. Please describe how this fantastic idea came about.

❯ Judy Licht had just come off her ABC anchor stint and was the brains behind the show. The fashion industry is so privatized and secretive, and no one had been able to really see what went on behind the scenes, and it showed everyone what went on at fashion week. There was no editing, as we showed everything in real time, from the first look to last look. It was a really unique experience for everyone who could see what was going on inside the Tents as it happened.

You have also hosted Fashion Police, *a weekly television show critiquing celerity wardrobes, when it aired on the Style network. You were also a celebrity judge on the TV Land series* She's Got the Look, *in which women competed for a modeling contract and magazine layout. You often serve as a guest on a variety of talk shows such as* Live with Regis & Kelly, The Today Show, *and* The Fabulous Life Of *on VH1. You have appeared on NBC, CNBC, and Fox News commenting on all matters of fashion and style. As if that were not enough pomp and circumstance for one person, you were also featured in* Time Out New York, Ocean Drive Magazine, New York Magazine, *and* The New York Post. *Please describe in a nutshell what all of these amazing experiences were like.*

❯ Each one of them uses a different piece of my expertise. For *She's Got the Look*, rather than it being about fabric and cut, it was about personality and body. *Fashion Police* was an amazing opportunity. I was the only stylist who worked the red carpet and dressed the people who walked the red carpet.

There are so many wonderful but eccentric personalities in the fashion industry, which has so eloquently been illustrated by Gladys Perint Palmer in her book, Fashion People. Do you think that extreme artistic talent plays a part? If not, what is your take?

❭ This is a great question. I think it's about personal expression. So many people are sadly unable to be unique. They are looking for something that makes them fit in.

How do you achieve balance between your career and your personal life?

❭ This is also a great question. Someone told me a long time ago that you can have it all, but you can't have it all at the same time. And this is true for me.

For the longest time, my career was the only thing I was interested in, and then I finally decided that I wanted to have a personal life. But it would have been hard to do it at the beginning of my career.

What would people be most surprised to learn about you?

❭ I'm much more shy than I come across. When you are a big television personality, people don't expect you can turn that off. The kind of person I am is not the person they expect me to be. My life is not all about fashion all the time. I actually subscribe to *National Geographic* magazine.

Describe the ultimate perfect day for you.

❭ Oh my God—I wouldn't have to leave the house. When you stop running around it makes a big difference. I would take a bath and read a stack of books, and I would surrender to bad foods, like homemade macaroni and cheese made by my mom. And the phone wouldn't ring!

OPEN SEES

An open see is a fashion designer casting call, of sorts. It gives a designer the opportunity to show his or her collection to buyers of a store. One of the most well-known open sees takes place at Henri Bendel in New York. For more than forty years, their open see has helped launch the careers of fashion designers: Anna Sui, Pamela Dennis and Todd Oldham, among others.

Illustrated by Izak Zenou for Henri Bendel, "Designer Call," 2007. COURTESY OF IZAK ZENOU.

At this event, held twice a year, buyers see designers on a first come, first serve basis and preview clothing and accessories collections, including handbags, small leather goods, belts, hats, hair accessories, and jewelry. For those who cannot make it to Henri Bendel in person, they occasionally offer an online open see. Sak's Fifth Avenue, Bloomingdale's, and Macy's have held open calls in the past, so check with major department and specialty stores in your area to find out if they participate in these events.

CONTESTS AND GRANTS

There are endless contests and grants all over the world that aspiring designers can enter to help fund their business startups. The CFDA/*Vogue* Fund is a grant whose mission is to provide funding and business mentoring for emerging fashion designers. The winner receives $300,000, and two runners-up receive $100,000 each. Finalists receive a profile fea-

Izak Zenou for Henri Bendel. COURTESY OF IZAK ZENOU.

ture on the Council of Fashion Designers of America (CFDA) website. To check the eligibility requirements, go to the CFDA website at www.cfda.com.

The Ecco Domani Fashion Foundation (EDFF) awards an annual $25,000 grant to seven different emerging fashion designers to present a runway show at Mercedes-Benz Fashion Week in New York. Many past winners have gone on to launch successful companies. Go to www.eccodomani.com/fashion-foundation/ for information on how to apply for a grant.

GenArt is another leading platform for emerging fashion designers in the United States. Since 1995, GenArt has presented more than 500 emerging womenswear, menswear, and accessory designers in various fashion programming venues nationwide. GenArt's alumni include Zac Posen, Rebecca Taylor, Philip Lim, Duckie Brown, Vena Cava, Rodarte, Ohne Titel, Alexandre Plokhov, Raquel Allegra, and several others. Some of these designers have gone on

Delfi beach tunic from Panos Emporio. COURTESY OF PANOS EMPORIO.

to be nominated for and/or received awards from the CFDA. GenArt's fashion program has received publicity in *Vogue* magazine, *Elle*, Style.com, *The New York Times*, and E! News. For more information, contact fashion@genart.com or go to www.genart.com/fashion. Search "fashion grants," "fashion funds" or "fashion contests" on the Internet to find out about these opportunities in your local area.

SOCIAL MEDIA OUTREACH

Twitter, Facebook, and Pinterest—oh my! Social media outreach for companies is all the rage and for good reason—it promotes your brand, generates sales and allows you to connect directly with your customer on a global level, at no cost. Rather than use only one or two formats, it is best to integrate several different social media outlets into one interconnected marketing program.

For starters, you can easily create a Facebook page to share engaging posts, photographs and videos, post photos of your designs to Pinterest, using Instagram, create a LinkedIn account to network and tweet about your latest designs and company milestones on Twitter. Blogs are a great way to show your audience the intricacies of your work and a behind-the-scenes look at your company operations through text, photographs and videos. YouTube is an effective for broadcasting videos showing your design process. Analyze what topics your followers are reacting to and make adjustments as necessary.

Once you've got these basics down pat, you can start using more advanced social media sites. There are several online articles that you can read to learn about the most effective ways to use social media to promote your brand.

PUBLIC RELATIONS

The right public relations strategy can propel your emerging brand into the spotlight and transform it to a top tier label. We will now discover the key components that go into creating a successful public relations strategy.

UNLOCKING THE KEYS TO A SUCCESSFUL PUBLIC RELATIONS STRATEGY, BY AMY ROSI, PRESIDENT OF AROS COMMUNICATIONS IN NEW YORK

For the emerging fashion designer, the decision of when and how to best implement a public relations strategy can be intimidating. Who will I hire? When should I start? How much will it cost? Is it the right time? What should I say to the press? These are questions that, if answered incorrectly, can lead to disappointment and wasted energy with hard-earned funds. With the right approach, you will be famous before you know it! Don't we wish it were that simple.

In my career, I have had the pleasure to handle the branding and public relations for leaders in their fields, including Escada, David Yurman, Barnes & Noble, Jane Seymour brands, A Pea in the Pod, Bergdorf Goodman, the Savannah College of Art and Design, and launching new startups, brands, and labels in fashion, jewelry, home design, and retail. This makes me intimately familiar with the enthusiasm and anxiety aspiring fashion designers feel when they try to handle their own publicity in-house or place themselves in the hands of a professional. In each case, I first asked myself how they are different in their competitive marketplaces and what we can do to establish this credential. Here are some questions you can ask yourself to see if you are ready and able to dive into a PR strategy:

1. What do you want to accomplish? Do you want to make the cover of *InStyle* or *Vogue* magazine? Sell to Bergdorf's or Bloomingdale's? Find an angel investor? Get a write-up in *The New York Times*? Good publicity is about telling your story and strategically getting the message out there where the influencers and your potential customers will find it. You need to have realistic goals to manage your own expectations of what will be accomplished.

2. What is your message, and how will you tell it best? Take the time to write your own press release to help you focus on your special story. Define your brand mission statement and describe your collection and designing inspirations. Decide what is different or unique about you and your collection, and push the envelope creatively with inspirational sketches, images, and even editorial press samples.

3. When do you want your publicity to break? Is it for your runway show or seasonal showroom presentation? Are you exhibiting at a trade show? Are you launching a new line? Are you traveling the country at trunk shows? Are you debuting at a major retailer? Each one of these assignments requires a special strategy that the right PR agency can handle for you.

4. Do you have the funds to support a PR campaign? I have seen too many publicity endeavors fail due to lack of funding. Plan the most effective press day or press outreach, and keep the PR campaign going long enough (6 months minimum) to get results if you are working with an agency.

In-House or Outsourcing?

Your resources in terms of money and time may dictate the decision you will make when it comes to having in-house or outsourced public relations. There will be the scheduling of showroom editorial appointments, editorial requests and the routing and tracking of samples, fittings and appointments for celebrities and special clients, as well as sending out images. Having a dedicated person on staff that can handle the complete responsibility of PR requires a professional with experience and who has editorial relationships in place to successfully contact the press and get results. Best place to look is for editors who are looking for a new assignment, or emerging talent from an established PR firm looking for an in-house opportunity to work with a fashion designer. Even if you hire an outside agency, you will need someone in your office to be the point person for PR.

How to Hire a PR Firm or Publicist

Do your research. Check the results other fashion startups and successful emerging fashion brands are getting, and find out who is handling their PR. The Internet makes it easy. Call the contact on the posted press release. Ask around and get referrals. A recommendation is a great way to pre-vet an agency or publicist and also get an introduction to meet them. Keep in mind that a good publicity agent is interviewing you as well, and wants to accept a client they can promote successfully. Ask the PR candidate to present a proposal which sets goals and objectives, along with the cost of services and estimated out-of-pocket expenses. Ask to see examples of their editorial placements. Be prepared to provide them with the following:

- High-resolution images and/or sketches of your collection
- A press release and bio
- A headshot of you
- A brand mission statement
- A logo and letterhead
- An electronic lookbook that can be e-mailed or uploaded

Timing is everything in PR. The window to being chosen for an editorial can be a matter of hours, or days, in the age of online PR. Before signing on, invite the PR candidate to see your collection, and meet their team. Once you have decided to hire a PR firm or publicist, sign a letter of agreement from the firm spelling out a time frame, responsibilities, and fees. Trust each other and allow time to realistically get results. Be proactive but not overreactive. Each PR assignment has a different timeline and needs a specialist. By example, publicizing a runway show is on the fast track. It typically takes one to three months to get the pre-press, fill the seats with press, retailers, and influencers, wrangle a celebrity, and handle the now almost immediate post-publicity. There are agencies that specialize in fashion show "front of house" publicity, and this is where you need to go to be successful. After the fashion show, don't stop! Even If you have the resources to have a runway show or fashion presentation during Fashion Week, don't expect that explosion of publicity to live on long past the moment of hype and buzz.

Being represented by a reputable agency with established press relationships lends credibility and an implied endorsement to your products and talents. It is important to understand that a publicist cannot make an editor cover you or your collections, but a connected one can get in front of the right press to make those "miracles" happen for the emerging fashion designer.

Costs

Expensive is not always better, and less expensive is not always successful. Find three firms you would like to work with and tell them your budget. If they want to work with you, they will suggest a price to accommodate your needs. You do not want to hire a firm that simply wants your business for cash flow.

Getting Noticed

My mother gave me a great piece of advice that has served me well: "You can't get asked to dance unless you go to the party." One of your more important jobs is to show up at the right events, enter design competitions, connect on social media, and be highly visible to the industry and press. This takes work and energy, but you will be amazed at who you may unexpectedly meet.

Fashion designers are known by the signature look of their clothes. Publicity is the most effective way to get brand recognition. Having a successful public relations program is a key to success. Remember, you are in control of your image. What you send out will come back tenfold if there is continuity in the messaging. A professional, in partnership with the designer, can transform and transport your brand message so that the image in the press reflects who you are and what your clothes look like, to attract and keep your customers. Publicity today is multi-channel and demands a range of skills to get results. A profile in *WWD* is the pinnacle of trade coverage that will attract the manufacturing and retail worlds. Fashion bloggers are on the front lines today of getting the word out on hot designers and collections, but an editorial in a leading fashion or lifestyle publication is still the gold standard of press. To be successful today, you have to target them all.

Establishing a Sales and Order Fulfillment Strategy

With the rise in the variety of technological advancements we see today, fashion designers are constantly challenged to develop new ways in which to sell to their target customer, from online portals and social media outlets to more traditional methods such as brick-and-mortar storefronts and department store partnerships. It is important to develop a year-by-year sales strategy of measurable sales goals and tactics (plan of how to reach your sales goals), including targeted accounts, timelines, and expansion plans to help keep you on target and assess your progress.

Order fulfillment is the basis for earning revenue, but it is how quickly you can fulfill your orders that can make or break your company. The most productive way to carry out this process is to partner with a trustworthy order fulfillment center. However, if your finances are limited, there are various software programs that manage point-of-sale, inventory management, shipping and delivery, and order fulfillment.

The fulfillment process begins when your customer makes a purchase, whether it is through an online portal, on the telephone, in person, or at a showroom or store. This information must then be communicated to your design studio, warehouse, or the facility where your merchandise is stored. Having your inventory organized will improve upon the amount of time it takes to fulfill the order. You will need to decide how your products will be shipped to your customer (Fed Ex, DHL, local post office), and you should also have some form of tracking service to ensure the package was delivered to the customer within the delivery window that you provided.

An Interview with Fern Mallis, Creator of New York Fashion Week and President of Fern Mallis, LLC

You were voted "best dressed" in your senior year at James Madison High School in Brooklyn, New York. Is this when your interest in fashion first began?

❯ I was always in love with clothes. My mother had great style when I was growing up, and my dad and his brothers all worked in the Garment District. I loved going to work with him and seeing the showrooms, meeting the buyers and fashion directors, and observing the energy and vitality on the streets in the district at the time. I somehow knew I always would have a career in fashion.

Prior to starting your own consultancy, you were senior vice president of IMG Fashion. What were your main responsibilities there?

❯ I oversaw Mercedes-Benz Fashion Week in NYC, reviewing all the venue plans, creating all

Portrait of Fern Mallis. PHOTOGRAPHER: TIMOTHY GREENFIELD-SANDERS

the graphic imagery and identity for each season, and generally involved in every aspect of creating a smooth, efficient and successful Fashion Week. In this capacity, I worked closely with all the designers and getting them to show in the Tents, and I collaborated with all the sponsors to develop programs and initiatives to support the industry. I was the key spokesperson, and face of Fashion Week, and was instrumental in creating MBFW Miami Swim and MBFW at Smashbox Studios in Los Angeles. I was integrally involved in the expansion of the fashion division worldwide - bringing Fashion Week to Mumbai, Berlin, acquiring Sydney and Melbourne, consulting in Mexico City, and I traveled extensively to Dubai, China, South America and Europe exploring opportunities for expanding the FW franchise, and other cultural collaborations.

You are credited as the creator of New York Fashion Week and for introducing fashion weeks in several other cities. How did this come about?

❯ When I joined IMG after they acquired 7th on Sixth from the CFDA, it was a logical expansion. IMG as an international event company had relationships and offices around the world, and with my fashion experience and expertise, most major cities wanted to create a version of what we did in NYC, and bring business and exposure to their city, and create a platform for their designers.

What is a typical day like as president of your own consulting firm, Fern Mallis LLC?

❯ I never know what to expect, as each day is a new adventure, and a new opportunity presents itself. I continue to attend a wide variety of industry events and functions. I have new meetings almost every day with someone who wants my advice, to hire me for consulting services, or to join their boards. I am being honored by many different organizations, I am continually asked to mentor, speak, and moderate panels and discussions. Each day, I try to do some research on the designers I am interviewing for the "Fashion Icons with Fern Mallis" series at the 92Y, and making plans for additional interviews for Sirius XM. No two days of mine are ever the same, and I am having a great time at this stage in my career.

You have been featured as a judge and mentor on several fashion design themed television shows, such as **Project Runway** *and* **The Fashion Show,** *among others. What traits did the most successful fashion designer contestants on these shows exhibit?*

❯ They displayed their talent and their creativity. They succeeded in solving the specific theme or assignment of the show, and created garments that were unique and original, well made and had their own unique personality and signature in them. They were always able to communicate and explain their vision. They had a spark that indicated they would persevere and make it. They made me curious to want to see more.

You are the host of **Fashion Icons with Fern Mallis** *at the 92nd Street Y in New York in which you interview various fashion designers such as Calvin Klein, Donna Karan, Tommy Hilfiger, Tom Ford, Diane Von Furstenberg and Marc Jacobs; you have your own radio show on SiriusXM STARS channel, interviewing top designers and celebrities; you starred in an Off-Broadway play and in 2012, launched your jewelry line FERN FINDS: on HSN - all such fantastic accomplishments! What is next for you?*

❯ I am extremely busy with each of these projects and a host of fabulous clients that I consult for.

What advice would you give an aspiring fashion designer who is trying to launch his or her own collection?

❭ Be passionate, and want it more than anything in the world, stay true to yourself, and learn how to communicate and express yourself. Be a sponge and learn and listen. Learn your fashion history, go to museums, and theatres, and absorb the culture - it's what you need to bring to your clothes. Talent in the fashion industry is like truffles in a field in France -fashion editors and retailers will seek you out and find you if the talent is there. But you must create the vision, follow through and work hard.

An Interview with Chris Knott, Founder of Peter Millar

Peter Millar founder, Chris Knott in his office in Raleigh, North Carolina. PHOTOGRAPHER: ROBERT STEY.

You are the founder and creative director of your company, Peter Millar. What led to the formation of your business?

❭ I felt there was a niche out there for a luxury product at an affordable price point.

Please explain the story behind how the name of your company evolved and describe how you came up with your regal crown logo and tag line, Set the Standard.

❭ Growing up my mother had a small antique shop and she gave me an antique lawn ball with the inscription, Peter Millar. I felt the name was timeless and classic and a good representation of my company. We have always wanted to be a company that everyone else is trying to follow from the product we make, to the service we provide, to the type of customers we sell to, so we thought, "Set the Standard" was a fitting description.

How would you define the Peter Millar design aesthetic?

❯ When we first started, it was southern preppy and then it evolved into timeless classic with a twist. We don't want to be too traditional, but rather follow what is going on in Europe and all over the world and put our own spin on it. We do that with pattern work, colors, and fabrics.

How does the design process begin for you? Do you begin with a theme or some form of inspiration, a silhouette or a recently discovered can't-live-without fabric?

❯ It starts with great, sellable color and then we figure out what silhouettes we need to keep the line fresh and forward thinking.

Loro Piana, one of the most well-respected Italian fabric mills in the world, authorized Peter Millar to use its Storm System® waterproof and wind resistant fabric in your collection. Please expand on this.

❯ We are big fans of Loro Piana; we love their fabrics and love what they stand for. Loro Piana is true luxury. We are using some of their fabrics in our outerwear, sport coats, pants and suits and they came to us because they see our product in the right places.

What do you think Peter Millar does best?

❯ We over deliver great product on a timely basis.

Peter Millar design studio, Raleigh, North Carolina.
PHOTOGRAPHER: ROBERT STEY.

What advice would you give an aspiring fashion designer trying to launch their own collection?

❯ Figure out who your customer is and who you are designing for. If you don't know where the finish line is, you can't run the race. You then have to figure out how you are going to get the product to them. If you can't figure that out, it doesn't matter how good you are, it will never get off the ground.

Peter Millar takes great pride in dressing some of the most talented and acclaimed golf professionals on the PGA tour. Who are the golf professionals that are current ambassadors of the Peter Millar brand?

❯ We had a relationship with Timeless for several years and we got about 20 players through them.

Right now, we have 3 players on tour, including Bill Haas, Brent Snedeker, and Harris English.

When product is shipped from the warehouse to the customer, a unique item is included inside the package. Please describe what it is and how this great idea developed.

❯ We put a special mint in every package we ship. We also include a packing list that is in the same order of the products in the box so it is easy to check in. We have specially designed boxes with dividers in it so the product doesn't slide around. It costs more money to do this, but we want our packages to be a present when they show up.

Describe the ultimate perfect day for you.

❯ Cruising around on a boat in 80 degree weather in Wrightsville Beach, North Carolina with my family.

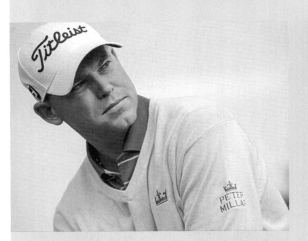

Professional golfer and Peter Millar brand ambassador, Bill Haas. PHOTOGRAPHER: STEVE EXUM.

Peter Millar Spring 2013 Tailored Collection. PHOTOGRAPHER: STEVE EXUM.

An Interview with Manolo Blahnik, Shoe Designer

Portrait of Manolo Blahnik. PHOTOGRAPHER: MICHAEL ROBERTS.

Was there a pivotal moment in your childhood, upbringing in the Canary Islands or at some point in your life, which led you to pursue a career in footwear design?

❯ Maybe subconsciously I was influenced by my mother's love for customizing her own shoes. She used to get her dresses made and there were no beautiful shoes available on the islands, so she would buy materials and customize her own. She used to visit the local cobbler and learned from him how to make shoes. Also, I was always fascinated with the black espadrilles my nanny used to wear.

I thought they were so chic and I was fixated by the way the straps tied around the ankle and how the shoe was attached so firmly to her foot.

You began your career as a theater set designer and on a visit to New York back in 1970, your friend, Paloma Picasso introduced you to the legendary Diana Vreeland, who was editor-in-chief of Vogue at the time. What happened next?

❯ Ms. Vreeland saw my theatre design sketches and advised me to focus on 'extremities' because she liked the way I drew shoes and the ideas I had for them.

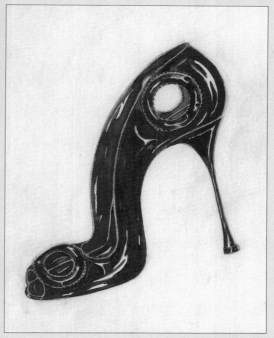

Autumn/Winter 2012/2013 Orlo illustration by Manolo Blahnik of a patent leather peep toe shoe.

What is your design philosophy?

❯ My design philosophy is to stick to what I like and not follow the trends. I design what I like and I never change because of what someone might say.

Aside from having impeccable taste, you are a true artisan of your craft, not only designing each and every handmade shoe, but you are intricately involved with every step in the process. Please explain this further.

❯ I am a total perfectionist when it comes to my shoes. I feel I have to oversee every step of the production process, as it is my name on the label and I want to be happy with every detail on each shoe. So from my sketch to the last, heel and the prototype, to choosing the color and the material, I am there making sure I am happy with the outcome.

Carrie Bradshaw, the loveable character on the "Sex in the City" HBO television show and subsequent movies is obsessed with your shoes, so obsessed, in fact that in one episode, when confronted by a robber, she pleads, "Please sir, you can take my baguette, you can take my ring and my watch, but don't take my Manolo Blahniks." Did you collaborate with their costume designer Patricia Field in any capacity? Did you see an increase in sales during this time and how did this publicity have an effect on your business?

❯ We didn't even know which ones would end up on screen as they bought shoes from the collection at the time. Of course when they ended up in the series, it had a huge impact on our business. It introduced my name to people all over the world who watched the series and through that I got a lot of new customers whom I never had before.

You have said that shoes "transform a woman" and that you don't follow fashion, you just "feel." Please expand on these concepts.

❯ It is difficult for me to define in words what is beautiful and chic, but I know when I see it. When a woman wears beautiful shoes, she walks differently—in a much more elegant and sensual way, especially if the shoes are comfortable; this to me is the most important thing.

How do you successfully design season after season a collection that is both true to your design aesthetic and vision and commercially saleable? Is there ever a conflict?

❯ It is always a challenge to come up with new ideas, as I have been designing only shoes for the last 40 years. When I do come up with something new that I love, it brings me huge joy. As for commerciality, I very often love a crazy shoe and produce it, and if it turns out that it is not very sellable, we just sell it in small quantities to those women who like unique and quirky shoes.

Eufrasia red velvet court shoe with pearl and emerald accessory and leather heel by Manolo Blahnik.

What advice would you give an aspiring fashion designer trying to launch his or her own fashion collection?

❯ Just do it! Don't be scared. It will take time and huge amounts of hard work and patience, but if you believe in it, go for it. Follow your heart.

What three things can't you live without?

❯ Old films, books and chocolate.

Describe the ultimate perfect day for you.

❯ The perfect day would start with me watching an old film and then reading a marvelous book. After that I would go for a walk with my dog through a beautiful garden with amazing plants. Later, I would sit down in my room and sketch new designs for the upcoming collection.

Illustrated by Izak Zenou for Henri Bendel. COURTESY OF IZAK ZENOU.

6 Strategic Business Trends in the Fashion Industry

If you are not in fashion, you are nobody.

—LORD CHESTERFIELD

Outsourcing and Globalization

Outsourcing is the practice of obtaining goods or subcontracting services from an outside source. Outsourcing to overseas countries, primarily in Asia, is a common business custom in the fashion industry, as labor is often less expensive and cost savings can be substantial. According to Shyam Raj, chief executive officer of REACH Sewn Technologies based in Bangalore, India, price is the primary factor in a company's decision to outsource. "At a comparable level of skill sets, a pattern maker in the United States will cost $6,000 a month, while it would cost just $500 in India." However, there can be negative implications for outsourcing. A major benefit of working with a production facility locally is that the designer and sourcing and production executives can monitor the progression throughout each stage of the manufacturing process, enabling them to catch any mistakes that may occur along the way, rather than at completion when it is too late. When a company contracts work out to production facilities overseas, they generally have very little knowledge of the working conditions and may be contributing to the exploitation of underpaid laborers in a third-world country. However, some companies, such as The Gap, have compiled a set of vendor conduct rules for their suppliers, and Gap employees interview factory workers and managers to ensure these rules are in place. They also conduct factory inspections to monitor working conditions. In addition, outsourcing can produce additional costs for the shipping of the garments back and forth until final approval. Each company has to analyze their business model and decide what the best methodology is for them. And it is not just the production aspect of the manufacturing cycle that is getting outsourced. Some companies are farming out aspects of their product development processes, like patternmaking.

Globalization is a cost savings initiative, and is the process by which a company expands their business on an international scale, by relocating their manufacturing, production and distribution functions to another country. Several developing countries offer tax breaks, low-cost land and labor to construct factories in export processing zones (areas in which goods may be landed and re-exported without the interference of customs and customs duties), and low labor production rates, making it attractive for companies to build their operations internationally. According to the International Labor Office, more than 60 percent of world clothing exports are manufactured in developing areas, such as Asia, which accounts for 32 percent of exports. China, in particular, has emerged as one of the world's largest suppliers of clothing. Countries such as Bulgaria, Hungary, Poland, Romania, and the Czech Republic have become substantial suppliers to the European markets. Morocco, Mauritius, Tunisia, and Madagascar have all become important producers exporting their products to industrialized countries. For the past two decades, Germany, Belgium, France, Japan, Hong Kong, China, Taiwan, Korea, and the United States have been major world textile exporters, and Mexico and Brazil have become key players in footwear production.

Corporate Social Responsibility

Corporate social responsibility (CSR)—also known as corporate responsibility, sustainability, and corporate citizenship—is a company's commitment to maximize their positive impact and minimize their negative effect on society and the environment. Companies that incorporate CSR thinking, particularly when it's a key ingredient of the corporate DNA, often realize decreased expenses; increased employee loyalty, retention, and recruitment; increased brand awareness and customer loyalty; improved reputation; product and service innovation; new market penetration; and increased sales.

CSR IN ACTION IN THE FASHION INDUSTRY, BY AMY SPRINGSTEEL, DIRECTOR OF CORPORATE RESPONSIBILITY, ING U.S.

CSR is approached by first analyzing business operations and supply chain policies and practices to determine where the most significant impacts occur. From there, a strategy is developed and employees across the business are galvanized to develop solutions to lessen the negative impacts. Lastly, companies engage various stakeholders (those individuals and organizations who have a "stake" in the success of the business) and experts to provide feedback on the strategy and plans. Once approved, companies take action to implement a CSR plan through channels such as strategic philanthropy, employee volunteering, employee giving, diversity and inclusion, environmental sustainability, supplier engagement, product and service innovation and business ethics. In this way, companies are able to manage impacts in ways that align with their business objectives thereby creating shared value for the business, the community, and the environment.

Case in Point: Ralph Lauren

What: According to information on GreenOrder's website, Ralph Lauren Corporation embarked on a process to understand the company's environmental impact and identify areas of improvement that align with business goals. GreenOrder, an advisory company, performed an eco assessment and life-cycle analysis, developed four company-wide initiatives, and worked with the company to implement and measure progress.

Why: The result of this work led Ralph Lauren Corporation to improve shipping practices, thereby reducing costs and greenhouse gas (GHG) emissions; negotiate the company's first green lease; and implement greener office practices.

The results are reported in an annual CSR report, or in some companies' cases, in an integrated annual report outlining both CSR and corporate performance and highlights. These measures, both the process of incorporating CSR thinking and publicly disclosing it, have a direct effect on a companies' triple bottom line: people, planet, and profits (or performance).

The concept of CSR is new to many companies in the fashion industry, but to others, such as CSR pioneer Timberland, which has been incorporating it for nearly forty years, it has been a part of their corporate structure from the beginning. Wide-scale awareness of CSR and the fact that corporations are increasingly reaping benefits from it, has brought it increased exposure and credibility in recent years. More and more fashion companies are realizing the importance of CSR and implementing programs and even building business models around it within their corporate structure.

Specifically, when a fashion business analyzes their environmental impact, they often discover that toxic chemical use and excessive needs for water are widespread. Because natural resources are not unlimited and polluting water sources will make them even more finite, this poses a great challenge to the longevity of running a fashion business. According to the nonprofit organization Earth Pledge, approximately 8,000 chemicals are used throughout the world to turn raw materials into textiles. The U.S. Department of Agriculture reports that one-quarter of all pesticides are used toward growing cotton, primarily for the apparel industry. According to the report *Well Dressed?: The Present and Future Sustainability of Clothing and Textiles in the UK* from the Institute for Manufacturing at Cambridge University, during the dyeing process, a tee shirt on average will use 4–5 gallons of water, the global textile industry discharges 40,000–50,000 tons of dye into the water systems, and cotton uses 22.5 percent of the world's consumption of insecticides and 10 percent of all pesticides.

Fast fashion, the need for retailers to quickly produce and turn around trendy fashions at affordable prices (aimed particularly at the tween and teen market), is also an environmental cause for concern. Fast fashion leaves a pollution footprint in its wake. Polyester, for example, is the most widely used synthetic fiber and is made from petroleum. The manufacture of polyester and other synthetic fibers is an energy-intensive process, requiring large amounts of crude oil, that releases emissions into the water near manufacturing plants and is an overall hazardous waste generator. The fashion industry, however, has begun to tackle these issues.

In 2005, Earth Pledge launched its FutureFashion initiative to promote the use of renewable, reusable, and nonpolluting materials and production methods for the fashion industry. Another organization, the Ethical Fashion Forum, provides a variety of tools and resources to help facilitate the industry's move towards more sustainable practices. In addition, the Sustainable Apparel Coalition developed an index to measure the environmental and social performance of apparel and footwear products. The index allows companies to analyze products, buildings, materials, and processes against environmental and design driven factors. And, in 2012,The Nordic Initiative Clean and Ethical (NICE), supported by the Nordic Fashion Association and the United Nations (UN), announced the launch of the Chemical Tool for designers, buyers and consumers, which outlines all the chemicals used in textile production and offers worksheets to assist companies in working with suppliers and factories to address chemical content. Additionally, the partnership created the Code of Conduct, launched at The Copenhagen Fashion Summit hosted by the Danish Fashion Institute, the world's largest conference on sustainability and CSR in fashion. The Code includes sixteen principles to guide companies in ensuring ethical, responsible and sustainable manufacturing in fashion.

The International Organization for Standardization defines eco-fashion as "identifying the general environmental performance of a product within a product group based on its whole life-cycle in order to contribute to improvements in key environmental measures and to support sustainable consumption patterns." The International Organization for Standardization is developing standards for a labeling system to identify garments that meet "environmentally friendly" criteria.

There are many factors that constitute the sustainability of the textile process, including the renewability and source of the fiber, the process of making the fiber into a textile, the working conditions of the people in the factories producing the materials, and the carbon footprint of the textile. A company's carbon footprint comes from the total greenhouse gas (GHG) emissions released as a result of its operations. The urgency to reduce GHG emissions is due to the fact that these gases greatly affect the temperature of the earth. This, in turn, affects weather and natural conditions and the ability for human beings and animals to thrive and survive.

In the European Union, the Registration, Evaluation, Authorisation and Restriction of Chemicals (REACH) requires clothing manufacturers to identify the chemicals used in their products, and in some cases, to inform their customers about potentially hazardous

cotton/bamboo blouse

silk/hemp dress

silk chiffon dress

silk crepe skirt

Eco Fashion

In-school women's spring concept sketched by Ricardo Charles, 2009.

chemicals that may be found in their products. Such regulations, coupled with increasing consumer awareness about the importance of sustainable products, may provide some momentum to transform the way the garment industry manufacturers its products.

Beyond familiarizing themselves with industry association guidance and efforts, one approach designers can take to incorporate sustainable fashion is to use recycled or reclaimed fibers that are made from pieces of fabrics collected from clothing factories, which are then processed back into short fibers for spinning into yarn. Examples of fibers that can be classified as eco-friendly include hemp, soy, bamboo and sustainably grown or organic cotton. Hemp does not use extensive amounts of soil since it grows fast and requires no pesticides or herbicides. Soy is made from soybeans and is processed using enzymes rather than toxic agents. Bamboo grows very fast and does not require extensive upkeep, including no pesticides or fertilizers. Organic cotton uses no pesticides, herbicides, insecticides, or chemicals during its growth process.

Organic cotton is grown in at least twelve different countries, and in 2004, America's largest retailer, Wal-Mart, began selling organic cotton women's shirts at its Sam's Club division. Today, Wal-Mart is distinguished as the world's largest buyer of organic cotton. Another approach to sustainable fashion is for designers to use polymers created from plant-based crops. Ingeo (the trademark name of a plant based polymer produced by NatureWorks LLC) is made of a corn by-product that is transformed into a polylactide, which is then spun into fibers and woven into fabrics that can be composted into

Recycled mood board for Ethical Fashion Show in Paris, 2008. COURTESY OF TIERRA ECOLOGIA.

packaging materials. Italian-based couture house Versace has used Ingeo in their runway collections. Additionally, fashion designers such as Stella McCartney, Stewart+Brown, Rogan Gregory, and many others offer socially conscious fashions in their collections. Portland Fashion Week, based in Portland, Oregon, has featured sustainable designers in their shows since 2005, and a number of Hollywood celebrities such as Natalie Portman, Cameron Diaz, Alicia Silverstone, Jennifer Aniston, and Salma Hayek have been associated with the promotion of sustainable fashion.

Other CSR considerations include sustainable packaging materials, fair trade and sourcing raw materials locally to reduce the carbon footprint from shipping goods. When fashion companies analyze their product fulfillment practices, they also look into retail packaging, the way in which customers take the product home after purchase. Landfills are wrought with store bags, which don't disintegrate but rather contribute to increased carbon emissions. Fair trade is a concept whereby farmers and small businesses are guaranteed a fair price for their products as well as a premium that will in turn be used to fund projects in the community. Sourcing raw materials locally not only reduces the carbon emissions from shipping, but also supports local economies.

Case in Point: Gucci

What: As part of their commitment to the environment, Gucci introduced biodegradable bags in all of their global directly operated stores. The bags and boxes, certified by the Forest Stewardship Council (FSC), are made from trees in managed forests.

Why: The bags and boxes are 100 percent biodegradable and thereby do not contribute to waste that takes up space in landfills. The markings on the inside of the bags stating this fact demonstrate to Gucci's environmentally conscious consumer that Gucci is doing its part to reduce its impact on the environment, therefore differentiating this luxury brand from its competition.

A company's environmental impact also stems from its daily operations such as paper use, employee travel, waste production, and water use. Additionally, corporations are seeking ways to address their product's carbon footprint not only from product manufacturing at inception, but also at its disposal, which is often referred to as "cradle-to-grave." For fashion companies, this means thinking through what can be done with a garment, shoe, or accessory once a consumer has made good use of it, so it does not end up in a landfill, adding to the greenhouse gases created through decomposition.

Case in Point: Patagonia

What: Patagonia takes their commitment to reducing their impact on the environment so seriously that they have created a program to educate and inspire their consumers to think of recycling as the last resort. The goal of this program is to encourage their customers to think sustainably by doing the following: 1) Buying only what they need; 2) Fixing what they can before buying something new or discarding it; 3) Sharing and trading what they already have; and 4) Recycling back to the company anything that is left over. With these efforts, Patagonia is taking responsibility for the footprint of its products from inception (cradle) to end use (grave).

Why: Known as the Common Threads Initiative, the company took their initial sustainable concept goals and crafted them into mutually beneficial messaging. The guidance they provide is not only beneficial for their customers, but also positions the company in a positive manner and encourages sales. Taken from the Patagonia website (www.patagonia.com), this is the final result:

1. Reduce: We make useful clothing/gear that lasts a long time.
2. Repair: We help you repair your Patagonia clothing/gear.
3. Reuse: We find a home for Patagonia clothing/gear you no longer need.
4. Recycle: We will take back your Patagonia clothing/gear that is worn out.

Form meets function with the Dewberry Tote, a multipurpose oversized tote that can be used as a beach, yoga, diaper, or travel bag. From Canopy Verde, 2011. COURTESY OF CANOPY VERDE.

Other areas of CSR strategy include community investment and business ethics. Community investment includes the work corporations do to benefit the community—advocating for public policies that affect both the community and the business, working with governments to enact relevant legislation, donating through grants and sponsorships to nonprofit organizations whose mission is in line with the industry or company's business objectives, mobilizing employees to volunteer, raising funds through employee giving campaigns, and supporting nonprofit benefit events. Many corporations maintain a corporate foundation that manages this work. Examples of philanthropy in CSR include The Metropolitan Museum of Art ("The Met") Costume Institute Gala Benefit in New York, the Runway to Green fashion show, and the Acqua for Life Armani–UNICEF partnership.

The Met Costume Institute Gala, known as the Met Ball has become the fashion charity event of the year, with top tables of seats selling for $250,000 and a guest list of the who's who in fashion, film, television, theater, media, music, and politics. It garners interest world-wide with live Red Carpet coverage by numerous television stations and shows such as *Access Hollywood*, *Entertainment Tonight*, and *Extra* and, in 2012, it raised $11.5 million in one evening. As part of the CSR effort to create shared value for the business and community, many corporations participate in this type of event to demonstrate their support for the fashion industry, for the unsurpassed networking opportunities, and positive publicity. In turn, the non-profit raises dollars to support their cause. In these ways, philanthropy aligns with a company's business objectives.

For the Runway to Green fashion show, designers ranging from Balenciaga to Burberry donated clothing for sale to benefit top environmental nonprofits. The 2012 event, in partnership with Christie's Auction House, was hosted by Seth Meyers from *Saturday Night Live* and included a surprise performance from pop singer Nicki Minaj. It too elicited national coverage, including the *New York Times* and *Wall Street Journal*, which is a key component that motivates corporations to participate. The Acqua for Life Armani–UNICEF partnership benefits the UNICEF TAP Project, which helps to improve access to safe, clean water for the world's children. For every person who "likes" Acqua for Life on Facebook, Giorgio Armani will donate $1 to UNICEF, demonstrating another example of shared value.

In the area of business ethics, companies ensure they have policies and practices in place regarding workers' rights, human rights, fair labor, equal opportunity, and codes of conduct to which employees, consultants, and suppliers are required to adhere. For example, fashion companies that operate in California must adhere to The California Transparency in Supply Chains Act of 2010 (SB 657), which requires California businesses to disclose their efforts to address the issues of slavery and human trafficking. This allows consumers to make better, more informed choices regarding the products they buy and the companies they choose to support. Gucci and several other companies address these kinds of issues by certifying their business lines under Social Accountability International's (SAI) SA8000 standard, an approach to ensuring that forced labor is not present in supplier and partner operations. Additionally, companies such as Burberry Group, Gap, H&M, LVMH, Levi Strauss, Nike, Timberland, and PUMA have signed on to the United Nations Global Compact and/or the United Nations Millennium Development Goals to commit to the human rights principles outlined within these programs.

As you can see, corporate social responsibility is a comprehensive business strategy for fashion companies, many of which have created departments solely dedicated to driving these efforts. Integrating CSR within the corporate structure has become a highly effective business tool for companies and has gained momentum in the fashion industry in recent years.

An Interview with Guy Bradford, VP, Corporate Responsibility, of American Eagle Outfitters, Inc.

What areas of corporate social responsibility (CSR) do you believe are critical to the fashion industry?

❯ We believe that CSR initiatives that focus on an organization's impact to people and planet are critical to the fashion industry. For example, one of the most important areas that we focus on is the potential impact that companies like ours can have on stakeholders in our supply chain. These stakeholders may include a variety of people, from workers in our contracted factories to private citizens who live or work near waterways that may contain water discharge from factories. Our impact on the environment is no less important and will be a focus point for our program's growth in the future.

How does American Eagle Outfitters, Inc. address these focus areas?

❯ We have extensive factory-monitoring programs which revolve around inspecting sourcing factories and working towards solutions when we find issues. When necessary, we collaborate with human rights and labor groups, government officials, and other brands in our industry to resolve more complicated and widespread issues. We also continuously aim to improve our wastewater treatment programs, so that fabric mills and denim laundries do not put harmful water back into local waterways.

In what ways does your corporate responsibility department collaborate with design?

❯ Our primary approach to collaborating with design is through frequent engagement with our production and sourcing teams, who work very closely with design teams to plan the manufacturing of our merchandise. Our goal is to ensure our production personnel are aware of challenges that can arise with factory social compliance, and we subsequently work to leverage these internal partners when addressing issues. Additionally, there is true business value in developing sustainable sourcing practices, so we are always looking for ways to incorporate intelligence we've gathered "in the field" and share it with our internal partners to be included as part of their decision-making process.

Last year, your company partnered with Cotton Incorporated for a nationwide denim-recycling program. Please explain what this program entails.

❯ During the month of October in 2011, customers were encouraged to bring any type of denim from any brand to our American Eagle Outfitters stores. The denim was then given "new life" by being converted into UltraTouch™ Denim Insulation (a sustainable building material made out of denim remnants used for insulation in homes) and provided to communities in need. Everyone who recycled their denim at AEO stores received a 20 percent discount on their entire purchase that day. In fact, we've been recycling with the help of Cotton Incorporated and Habitat for Humanity for some time now. Our ongoing program is called "From Blue to Green." This initiative was started in December 2007, and the first shipment was made in December 2008. It takes 500 jeans to insulate one home. So far, we have donated enough ripped and torn denim to insulate approximately 380 homes. Hurricane Katrina victims were the first to benefit from our donation.

What are the most impactful ways that American Eagle Outfitters is making the world a better place?

❯ While we view corporate responsibility as an organization-wide initiative, we feel we have made the most progress to date in our supply chain. Continuously assessing our impact to the various stakeholders we affect and using that information to improve our business practices allows us to ensure that our efforts with improving working conditions, protecting the rights of workers, and taking steps to reduce our impact to the environment are relevant, meaningful, and sustainable.

What goals does American Eagle Outfitters, Inc. have in place to reduce its carbon footprint?

❯ We recognize how important the issue of greenhouse gases is to our customers and our associates. We have included a goal in our 2011 Corporate Responsibility report (www.AEBetterWorld.com) to develop a carbon strategy to identify key opportunities for reducing our footprint. This goal is under way, and we plan to provide updates in future reports.

Sustainable Clothing Company Profile: Izzy Lane

Model wearing Izzy Lane Wensleydale cardigan.
PHOTOGRAPHER: NICKY EMMERSON, 2010.

How do you define an eco-friendly company?

❯ An eco-friendly company is one that is not purely company-centric and looks beyond its own interests, those of its shareholders, and feeding consumerism. It measures the wider impact of its practices and makes appropriate decisions on that basis rather than purely on profit. An ethical company seeks to improve the lives of people, animals, and the health and sustainability of the planet. Ethical or "eco" is subjective, however—what is "ethical" practice from one person's perspective is not necessarily from another's. For example, some may view wool as a by-product from the meat industry and therefore ethical to use, as it is an otherwise wasted resource. Others may argue that it isn't ethical to use the wool from animals which have potentially been kept inhumanely. Some companies use an ethical gesture as a front to the media in attempt to divert one's attention from otherwise unethical practices. Some argue that it is better to be in a third-world

Rescued sheep that were saved from slaughter, Izzy Lane 2011. COURTESY OF IZZY LANE.

country paying low wages than to not be there at all, whilst others believe it is more ethical to produce closer to home.

How is Izzy Lane making the world a better place?

❯ Izzy Lane is a unique case; the ethical aspect of my brand is that it puts animal welfare at its core. When I arrived in the fashion industry, I quickly discovered that there was little traceability of animal fiber back to an animal. You might know where the pork in your sausage comes from and what sort of life that animal had, but certainly not the wool in your socks or the cashmere in your sweater. I discovered that, in some cases, lambswool did not come from a happily bouncing lamb but generally was shaved from the skin of the dead carcass. In the UK, I quickly discovered that farmers are compelled by law to sell their wool to the British Wool Marketing Board, who then would auction it off to registered merchants for the best price. It is therefore impossible and illegal to work directly with a farmer, pay him a good price, and know that those animals are well cared for. As a vegetarian, I decided I would rescue my own flock of sheep. Over several years, I rescued 600 lambs from slaughter. I use their wool in my fashion brand, and this pays for them to live out their lives here in the Yorkshire Dales.

Please describe the eco-friendly textiles and materials that you use in your clothing.

❯ I use the wool from my own rare breed Wensleydale sheep for my knitwear. There are only 1,800 of them in the world, and they produce a long, silky, lustrous yarn. Some of my pieces are hand-knit by ladies from across the Yorkshire Dales. There is a tradition here of hand-knitting dating back to the Middle Ages, and the skills have been passed down through generations. By employing our hand-knitters, we are helping to support our local rural community and keep these skills alive to pass on to future generations. Our rare breed Shetlands produce a soft, fine fleece and come in a multitude of different, natural colors. Much of it we weave undyed into herringbones, hopsacks, and houndstooth cloth for our jackets and skirts. We weave our cloth on traditional Victorian looms in the Scottish Borders. I can ensure the integrity and authenticity of each piece we produce since I am with it on its journey, from the nurture of the sheep through to the finished piece.

Now more than ever, fashion customers are expecting their favorite clothing and accessories brands to engage in business practices that promote a cleaner planet by reducing their environmental footprint. Was this the impetus for the formation of your company? If not, please explain what prompted you to start an eco-friendly company.

❯ What prompted me to start Izzy Lane was a love of fashion, of course, but also discovering that the wool in our country was being burned and buried, as it had such little value. I have pieces of cloth my mother gave me from the 1940s. Holding them always evoked such strong feelings of place, of Britishness—the sheep, the mills, the people of our Isles, you could feel that in their warmth and the texture of the age-old designs. To juxtapose those feelings with the context of today, when wool was being described as a waste product, it prompted me to start my own company. To know that our textile industry was on its knees partly as a result of this, I threw that knowledge and my feelings together, combined with my deep love of animals, and decided to launch Izzy Lane.

Model wearing Izzy Lane Shetland buckle jacket and pencil skirt. PHOTOGRAPHER: NICKY EMMERSON, 2010.

Sustainable Clothing Company Profile: tierra Ecologia

How do you define an eco-friendly company?

❯ An eco-friendly fashion and textile company takes responsibility for its direct impact on the environment in all areas of production and in developing a product that is made with integrity. This includes design concept, type of sustainable fabric sourced (organic and/or recycled), dye choices, choosing manufacturing methods that eliminate waste, and reducing landfill and carbon emissions. Consideration is also given to the office, staff, workplace, machinery, sales, packaging, and distribution.

Why do you feel it is important for companies in the fashion industry to take an environmentally sound approach in their operations?

❯ It is important because it will help our ecological environment as well as human value. The fashion and textile industry is notoriously known for its high usage of chemicals and pesticides that damage natural ecosystems and create imbalance on Earth. The environmentally friendly approach also encourages fair trade relationships, which balances economic power and provides income at grass-root levels, keeping traditional hand skills alive.

How is tierra Ecologia making the world a better place?

❯ tierra Ecologia® (eco earth) enhances the environment through our responsible production methods. Our goal is to practice low-impact environmental production by creating our atelier as a pure and safe workplace using solar energy, rainwater, handcraft skills and techniques, and carefully collected botanicals from our dyers garden for hand solar dyeing. tierra Ecologia's fashion label, eco logika®, incorporates stylish designer wear specializing in combining fashion and conscience,

using natural and environmentally friendly textiles.

Please describe the eco-friendly textiles and materials that you use in your collections.

❯ The collection uses high-quality natural fibers, botanical dyes, eco yarns, and textiles such as sustainable silks, certified organic merino wool, cotton/hemp and linen, recycled remnants, and recycled denim. We invent new yarns and textiles using recycled denim and source only organic cotton, wool, and handloom silks. We dye and print textiles with natural dyes. The handmade eco luxury collection is dyed with Australian botanicals collected off verge-side waste, windfalls, and our own property. Our production methods use ancient hand skills in knit and crochet, supporting global communities. We support skilled artisans as well as our community by providing a range of fashionable products made with integrity.

Now more than ever, fashion customers are expecting their favorite clothing and accessories brands to engage in business practices that promote a cleaner planet by reducing their environmental footprint. Was this the impetus for the formation of your apparel company? If not, please explain what prompted you to start an eco-friendly company.

❯ My key influences were from childhood where I was brought up during the Rhodesian War in Africa. Due to world trade embargo with that country, to survive as a community, everything had to be recycled or grown organically. The products that emerged at that time were totally unique to Rhodesia. It became what we know today as a totally self-sufficient and sustainable environment. This upbringing had planted a seed for future exploration in eco fashion, and so the journey began!

Sustainable Accessories Company Profile: Khepri NYC

How do you define an eco-friendly company?

❯ For me, an eco-friendly company is one that attempts to create solutions for the issues of waste and pollution in all stages of a product's life. I think the ultimate goal of many eco-friendly companies is to create a "closed loop" for the life cycle of a product, meaning from the sourcing, production, and packaging to the disposal of the product, there is zero impact on the environment. For me, of equal importance is the consideration of the social impact of a company. Truly sustainable business practices take into account living wages and humane work environments for employees, as well as environmental factors.

Why do you feel it is important for companies in the fashion industry to take an environmentally sound approach in their operations?

❯ The global fashion trade takes such a toll on the environment, and with the advent of "fast fashion," a return to sustainable business practices, environmentally and socially, is more important than ever. The "race to the bottom" in the fashion industry refers to the increasing pressure on production facilities to create products faster and cheaper, resulting in the abuse and exploitation of laborers around the world. Thankfully, there is a growing movement away from these sorts of practices and towards the "slow fashion" movement focusing on high-quality products made ethically. While the volume of "slow fashion" absolutely pales in comparison with "fast fashion" giants, many companies are doing what they can to increase awareness and participation in a more sustainable fashion industry.

How is Khepri NYC making the world a better place?

❯ I don't have any illusions that Khepri is having a huge impact on the world, but I am of the viewpoint that every little bit counts and what we are doing is providing options that are sustainable, as well as design-driven.

Please describe the eco-friendly textiles and materials that you use in your handbag and tote bag collections.

❯ I use vintage materials and recycled materials, meaning post-consumer clothing and textiles that are cut and remade into new garments. I use leather jackets, skirts, and pants as well as wool blankets, kilim rugs, military tents, vintage laundry sacks, and any other recycled or eco-friendly materials that inspire me and will work for my purposes.

Now more than ever, fashion customers are expecting their favorite clothing and accessories brands to engage in business practices that promote a cleaner planet by reducing their environmental footprint. Was this the impetus for the formation of your accessories company? If not, please explain what prompted you to start an eco-friendly company.

❯ I was motivated by a desire to design, but figuring out how to design sustainably was a natural part of the process for me. It was simply the only way I could move forward in the industry while maintaining integrity. I had personally tried to seek out sustainable accessories, and the lack of options in the market convinced me that there was room for a company like Khepri.

All of your products are made in New York City. How are you able to keep your costs down, since you do not benefit from the lower labor costs of outsourcing your manufacturing operations overseas?

❯ To a certain extent, there will always be a premium on products that are produced responsibly, and the hope is that consumers will understand the value of ethically sound purchases. That being said, I am still able to keep product pricing in the same range as other products of similar market value that are being produced outside of the U.S. By being careful and producing in small volume, I am able to limit mistakes, and I always take cost into account when I design. As the company grows, I hope to innovate and keep the company as streamlined as possible to keep pricing competitive.

What eco-friendly textiles and materials do you use in your collection?

❯ Most of our tees are produced using 100 percent organic cotton and are printed using specially mixed, super low-impact water-based inks that give the prints a soft hand. All of our prints come from artist collaborations. We feel that art in itself holds a spiritual component. We, along with our artists, are avid supporters of social and environmental awareness. So it's only true to the line that we build upon this mindset by using eco-conscious fabrics and donate a portion of sales to a charitable cause each season. If our efforts can positively impact the world in our small way, we are happy.

Polly Baumler, Founder, Des Artistes, Munich, Germany

❯ Our clothes are fully made of linen in a wide range of its natural shades: ivory, ecru, beige, milk, cotton white, or warm brown. Linking fashion with eco and ethic philosophy, we make premium and leisure wear for active women.

Lukasz Caplicki, Owner, Freaky Flax, Lodz, Poland

❯ Estrella Eco-chic's philosophy is to reuse and recycle material that would otherwise have been discarded. My collections reflect the fact that we can create new fashion products with vintage and recovered matter in a chic and innovative style. The recycled fabric comes from vintage silk scarves found in the thrift shops and from unused fabrics of designer's collections. I rarely throw away fabric, even the smallest pieces are reused. Choosing to recycle for me is a creative challenge where my artistic, social, and environmental values are fulfilled.

Tamara Rubilar, Director, Estrella Eco-chic, Montreal, Quebec, Canada

❯ Avni uses all naturally dyed clothing. Natural dyeing is the process of dyeing fabric using natural ingredients, such as flowers and herbs, without the use of chemicals. Not only is the fabric produced in an environmentally friendly manner, but it is also very good for the skin, as some herbs, such as turmeric, impart medicinal properties. Another important aspect to our dyeing is that we try to use waste products as much as possible. For example, we use marigold flowers that are thrown away by temples in India. The flowers are brought in, dried, and powdered to create beautiful yellow/gold hues. Similarly, we use onion peels, pomegranate skin,

Haruka shoe by Hetty Rose, 2011. Heel type: Self covered with kimono fabric. Upper material: Vintage kimono textile fabric. Lining: Leather. Sole: Leather. COURTESY OF HETTY ROSE.

Fall/Winter 2011 Collection by Avni Fashion. COURTESY OF AVNI FASHION.

and coconut shell. Other than natural dyes, I also use eco-friendly fabrics such as bamboo, peace silk (silk yarn made without killing the worms), and organic cotton.

Avni Trivedi, Head Designer and Founder, Avni Fashion, LLC, Boston, Massachusetts, USA

❯ My collection is completely handmade using mainly reclaimed, recycled, and vintage materials. These are primarily vintage Japanese kimono fabrics, each holding different meanings shown by their use of color and design. I hand-select the most exquisite fabrics from Japan to use as uppers for shoes which are then skillfully combined with handcrafted wooden heels, recycled leather, and natural leather soles, creating modern stylish

footwear. Sustainability in the fashion field can be a challenge, so by having a concept which adheres to ethical and ecological sensitivities, I can be free with my designs.

Henrietta Samuels, Founder, Hetty Rose, Ltd., Essex, United Kingdom

❯ My company developed recycled denim yarn for our eco denim collection, which is hand-knitted and crocheted in Vietnam, supporting a local community group. My lifestyle label, eco logika® uses hemp and organic cottons, and the cloth is dyed using natural dyes. I source certified organic textiles and other textiles that have no chemical treatments on them. I usually sight the eco certification in order to check the authenticity of its origin. My current eco couture collection combines raw organic fibers, hand-spun silks, recycled remnants, certified organic Australian merino wool, and luxurious sustainable silks fused with various constructive and embellished techniques to create stunningly elegant, ultra-feminine garments made by hand and machine. The enticing color palette of neutral antique hues, hand-dyed in natural botanicals, is highlighted by vibrant appliqué and beadwork using glass, shell, and semiprecious stone.

Charlene O'Brien, Creative Director, tierra Ecologia, Perth, Western Australia

What eco-friendly textiles and materials do you use in your collection? (Continued)

"Aine" from the Summer 2012 tierra Ecologia Phoenix Collection. PHOTOGRAPHER: JODIE EDOM. MODEL: JESS TRUSCOTT.

❭ When we started to make reusable shopping bags in 2007, we were intent on using an eco-friendly fabric for our line. Our search led us to 100 percent recycled PET (rPET), a relatively inexpensive fabric that mimics the functionality of nylon and polyester, but is made entirely from recycled plastics. It was an exciting discovery because nothing about rPET is a compromise to our vision. We create strong, compactable bags, and this material allows us to make a shopping tote that holds 50 pounds of groceries and then folds down into a little tiny pouch. Repreve, the Unifi yarn in our produce bags, is arguably one of the most environmentally friendly textile products in the world.

Liz Long and Holly Tienken, Founders, Bag the Habit, Jersey City, New Jersey, USA

❭ At Ecolett we seek to build the best products that cause no harm to the planet. We currently use environmentally friendly fibers such as organic cotton, hemp, and lyocell (made from the wood pulp of cellulose).

Irina Holmes, Designer/Owner, Ecolett, Martinez, California, USA

❭ All Canopy Verde bags are developed using 100 percent organic cotton which is dyed using the OEKO-TEX® Standard 100 certified dyeing process. They are then finished with chemical-free embroidery, chrome-free leather, and wooden hardware, which give the bags their signature look. Moving forward, the bags will be finished with synthetic leather rather than chrome-free leather, making them vegan-friendly as well.

Linda Wong, Founder, Canopy Verde, New York, New York, USA

❭ We combine nature's work with human technology and design to create our timeless wellness fashion. All stages of our production cycle are made in Perú under sustainable and fair-trade conditions. Our fibers are obtained from rural artisan and Indian farmers using pre-Columbian techniques to grow naturally pigmented cotton plants in their small farmyard plots. No dyes, chemicals, or other synthetic processes have been used to grow, soften, or color the fibers. The cotton is harvested manually, colors are sorted entirely by hand, and the fiber is mill-spun in small batches. The incredibly soft hand, heathered

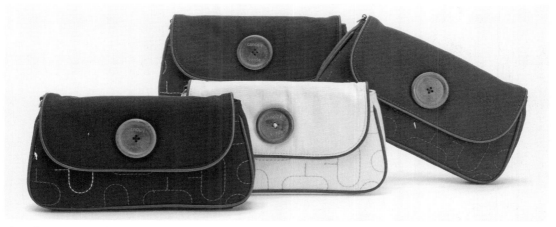

The Calamint is the perfect little clutch for all your essentials from Canopy Verde, 2010. COURTESY OF CANOPY VERDE.

look, and distinctive colors are achieved not only organically, but naturally in every way. We also process undyed baby alpaca hair, which comes in an array of nine shades. At no time are chemical agents or other artificial means employed during the production of these fibers.

Sibi Siebenmann, Founder, eco zona, Bern, Switzerland

❯ Enamore mainly uses organic cottons and bamboo, and all our fabrics are certified by regulated companies. In addition, the factories in which our garments are produced are audited by BCSI, WRAP, and other such organizations. The materials used ensure longevity.

Rachel Braund, Creative Director, Enamore, London, England, United Kingdom

Conclusion

Being a highly effective designer requires a delicate balance between drawing on your own creative ingenuity and utilizing strategic business acumen. Very few professions require such a dichotomy. Additionally, a fashion designer is not only expected to be skilled in his or her craft, but to also have a sense of how each area of the business functions. Furthermore, in our ever changing society, designers must continually adapt their sensibilities to accommodate the evolution of cultural norms, advanced technologies, and sustainable business practices.

By reading this book, you have gained a broad spectrum of knowledge about the inner workings of the fashion industry and what is means to be a successful fashion designer today. Armed with this knowledge, you can better follow your heart and pursue your dreams. There is no greater reward than doing what you love. For any aspiring fashion designer, your fierce determination to succeed will drive you through the journey ahead. No matter what obstacles you face, or how often you are challenged, be open to criticism, while remaining true to your vision.

In fashion design, there will always be a growing demand for individuality and innovation, as well as a thirst for the next big talent. Will it be you? I'm rooting for you!

APPENDIX

The following are professional organizations, associations, councils, and resources that may be of assistance in your journey to becoming a fashion designer.

Professional Organizations, Associations, and Councils

Joining fashion associations and organizations affords you the opportunity to network with hundreds and sometimes thousands of other people who work in the fashion industry. By joining these groups, you can attend networking events, cocktail receptions, and panel discussions with top-level fashion insiders, and be part of the fashion community. It also allows you to expand your professional network and be on the cutting edge of the newest technologies and goings-on in fashion design and the fashion world.

American Apparel & Footwear Association (AAFA)

1601 North Kent Street, Suite 1200
Arlington, Virginia, USA 22209
T: (703) 524-1864
F: (703) 522-6741
www.wewear.org
AAFA was established in the year 2000 after the American Apparel and Manufacturers Association and Footwear Industries of America merged. It is regarded as a national trade association devoted to companies involved in the apparel, footwear, and sewn products trade.

American Institute of Graphic Arts (AIGA)

164 Fifth Avenue
New York, New York, USA 10010
T: (212) 807-1990
www.aiga.org
Founded in 1914, AIGA is the oldest and largest professional membership association for design. AIGA now represents more than 22,000 design professionals, educators, and students through national activities and local chapter programs.

British Fashion Council

Somerset House, South Wing
Strand, London, WC2R 1LA
T: +44 (0) 20 7759 1999
www.britishfashioncouncil.com
E-mail: info@britishfashioncouncil.com
The British Fashion Council helps to advance British fashion designers on a global scale. Their programs reinforce the United Kingdom's fashion design excellence status.

California Fashion Association (CFA)

444 South Flower Street, 37th Floor
Los Angeles, California, USA 90071
T: (213) 688-6288
F: (213) 688-6290
www.calfashion.org
E-mail: info@calfashion.org
The California Fashion Association (CFA) is a forum established to provide guidance and business resources to the apparel and textile industries of California.

Canadian Apparel Federation (CAF)

151 Slater Street, Suite 708
Ottawa, Ontario K1P 5H3, Canada
T: (613) 231-3220
F: (613) 231-2305
www.apparel.ca
E-mail: info@apparel.ca
CAF is the trade association for the apparel industry in Canada. CAF offers its members various programs and services. Working closely with government officials, CAF advocates policies that will positively impact its members.

Council of Fashion Designers of America (CFDA)

1412 Broadway, Suite 2006
New York, New York, USA 10018
T: (212) 302-1821
F: (212) 768-0515
www.cfda.com
The Council of Fashion Designers of America (CFDA) is a not-for-profit trade group founded in 1962, which is made up of over 400 of America's leading fashion, accessory and jewelry designers.

Their mission is to progress the position of fashion design and to cultivate the development of up-and-coming designers with programs that support professional development and scholarships, including the CFDA/*Vogue* Fashion Fund, the Geoffrey Beene Design Scholarship Award, the Liz Claiborne Scholarship Award, and the CFDA/*Teen Vogue* Scholarship. CFDA is also a key participant in the annual Fashion's Night Out global event. They also host the CFDA Fashion Awards, which has been touted as the Oscars of fashion and recognizes top talent in the fashion industry. Through the CFDA Foundation, Inc., they raise funds for various charities, including Fashion Targets Breast Cancer and The CFDA-*Vogue* Initiative for HIV and AIDS, with its 7th on Sale event.

Fashion Center BID

209 West 38th Street
New York, New York, USA 10018
T: (212) 764-9600
F: (212) 764-9697
www.fashioncenter.com
Email: info@fashioncenter.com
Founded in 1993, The Fashion Center Business Improvement District is a not-for-profit corporation whose primary mission is to promotes the strength of the Garment District in New York City. They also formed the Emerging Designers Networking Group to bring similar minded people together to share resources and to facilitate the exchange of ideas. Along with the variety of services they offer, they are well known for the Fashion Center Information Kiosk located in the heart of the Garment District on the northeast corner of 7th Avenue and 39th Street. The award-winning design of the kiosk features the world's largest button, held up by a 31-foot steel needle, and is a resource center offering information and help to visitors and workers in the industry. Walking along the sidewalks of the Garment District, you will come across the Fashion Walk of Fame, a series of plaques honoring New York's most preeminent designers and the world's only monument commemorating American fashion, and was initiated by the Fashion Center BID.

Fashion Design Council of India (FDCI)

209 Okhla Industrial Estate, Phase 3
Okhla, New Delhi, India 110020
T: +91 11 26842180
www.fdci.org
Email: contact@fdci.org
The Fashion Design Council of India (FDCI) is represented by over 350 members and was founded on the principle of fostering the growth of fashion designers in India.

Fashion Awareness Direct (FAD)

10a Wellesley Terrace
London, N1 7NA United Kingdom
Tel/Fax: +44 (0)20 7490 3946
www.fad.org.uk
Fashion Awareness Direct is an educational charity whose goal is to impart a realistic interpretation of the fashion industry to young people aged 13 to 25, through the use of workshops and contests.

Fashion Footwear Association of New York (FFANY)

274 Madison Avenue, Suite 1701
New York, New York, USA 10016
T: (212) 751-6422
F: (212) 751-6404
www.ffany.org
E-mail: info@ffany.org
FFANY was established in 1979 as a nonprofit serving the common interests of footwear manufacturers by organizing trade shows and exhibitions for the footwear industry. Its members include over 300 footwear manufacturers, representing over 800 brands.

The Fashion Group International (FGI)

8 West 40th Street, 7th Floor
New York, New York, USA 10018
T: (212) 302-5511
F: (212) 302-5533
www.fgi.org
E-mail: info@fgi.org
FGI is a global, nonprofit professional organization with 5,000 members in the apparel, accessories, beauty, and home industries. You must be sponsored to join the organization, but once you are accepted, you will be part of a prestigious group of people whose members include the biggest names in fashion. They offer networking opportunities, lectures, seminars, and other events that enable the people of the fashion industry to come together in a variety of forums and venues.

Garment Industry Development Corporation (GIDC)

262 West 38th Street, Suite #506
New York, New York, USA 10018
T: (917) 885-6467
www.gidc.org

The Garment Industry Development Corporation (GIDC) is a nonprofit organization established in 1984 by the Garment Workers' Union, the City of New York, and the New York Skirt and Sportswear Association to help fortify the apparel industry in New York. They offer training and technical assistance, buyer referrals, and marketing to apparel manufacturers and workers in the industry, acting as a liaison between designers and manufacturers.

Gen Art

627 North La Peer Drive
West Hollywood, California, USA 90069
www.genart.com/fashion
Email: fashion@genart.com
Since 1994, GenArt has been an industry leader in introducing some of the most exciting new talent in fashion, including Zac Posen, Rebecca Taylor, Chaiken, Rodarte, Louis Verdad, Milly, Philip Lim, Peter Som, Twinkle by Wenlan, Duckie Brown, and Shoshanna. Through high-profile group runway shows, fashion presentations, and shopping events, GenArt showcases the best new design talent in womenswear and menswear, providing emerging designers with invaluable media and public exposure, and industry insiders with a first glimpse of the next rising stars. GenArt also produces the Business of Fashion seminars with the CFDA as well as numerous networking events, and serves as an authority for industry and resource referrals.

Hong Kong Fashion Designers Association (HKFDA)

Room 216A, 2/F, InnoCentre, 72 Tat Chee Avenue, Kowloon Tong
Kowloon, Hong Kong
Tel: 852-2330 1738
Fax: 852-2330 5015
www.hkfda.org
E-mail: mail@hkfda.org
The Hong Kong Fashion Designers Association (HKFDA) was founded in 1984 to unite fashion designers with the aim of developing and enhancing their careers.

International Council of Shopping Centers (ICSC)

1221 Avenue of the Americas, 41st Floor
New York, New York, USA 10020
T: (646) 728-3800
F: (732) 694-1755
www.icsc.org
E-mail: icsc@icsc.org
Founded in 1957, the International Council of Shopping Centers (ICSC) is the international trade association of the shopping center industry. With more than 50,000 members in over 90 countries, its mission is to advance the shopping center industry, by promoting it as an authority in the consumers and services market.

National Retail Federation (NRF)

325 Seventh Street, NW
Suite 1100
Washington, District of Columbia, USA 20004
T: (800) 673-4692
F: (202) 737-2849
www.nrf.com
The National Retail Federation is the largest global retail trade association, with membership representing retailers in more than 45 countries. The NRF also publishes *Stores* magazine, a monthly magazine dedicated to retail professionals.

Nordic Fashion Association (NFA)

www.nordicfashionassociation.com
The NFA was begun in 2008 by the five Nordic fashion organizations, including the Danish Fashion Institute, Helsinki Design Week, Icelandic Fashion Council, Oslo Fashion Week, and Swedish Fashion Council. The purpose of the organization is its focus on implementing socially responsible ethics within the Nordic fashion industry.

Society of Illustrators (SI)

128 East 63rd Street
New York, New York, USA 10065
T: (212) 838-2560
F: (212) 838-2561
www.societyillustrators.org
E-mail: info@societyillustrators.org
The mission of the Society is to promote the historical evolution of illustration, and to encourage appreciation of it as an art form, through exhibitions, lectures, education, community involvement and networking opportunities.

Fashion Industry Networking Websites

Fashion Industry Network

(www.fashionindustrynetwork.com)
Fashion Industry Network is an online business network for the fashion industry to exchange information regarding fashion design and style.

Fashionising (www.fashionising.com)

> Office 137
> 5 Ebury Bridge Road
> London, SW1W 8QX United Kingdom
> Fashionising.com is an online social networking
> site dedicated to fashionable socializing for those
> who work in the fashion industry

Fashion Networks (www.fashion-networks.com)

> 19925 Stevens Creek Boulevard
> Cupertino, CA 95014
> Fashion-networks.com is an online membership-
> based fashion networking community.

Professional Networking Websites

Professional networking sites are established each day by the dozens. All of them offer networking opportunities, while still allowing you to maintain your privacy. The most popular among them are listed in this section.

LinkedIn (www.linkedin.com)

> LinkedIn is an online professional, no-fee networking website with over 175 million members in over 200 countries, representing 170 industries. You can connect, be introduced to, and collaborate with professionals in the fashion industry who can help you accomplish your career goals. LinkedIn also offers premium memberships with various benefits.

Networking For Professionals

> (www.networkingforprofessionals.com)
> Networking For Professionals is a fee-based business networking group that combines online networking and in-person events.

Plaxo (www.plaxo.com)

> Plaxo is a no-fee online address system that allows you to organize all of your contact information in once place. For an additional fee, you can sync your address book with your iPhone, BlackBerry, mobile phone, or email program or you can receive the services of a Plaxo Personal Assistant who monitors your contact database and makes recommendations to keep it working as efficiently as possible.

Spoke (www.spoke.com)

> Spoke is an online business networking site with a unique twist. While the other networking sites only connect members with other members, Spoke allows you to make new connections using Spoke's Open Network® of more than 40 million people at 2.3 million companies. They offer a variety of membership options ranging from no-fee to $99.95/month.

Talk Biz Now (www.talkbiznow.com)

> Talkbiznow provides a professional no-fee–based networking platform, enabling communication between you and newfound contacts in both the national and international marketplace. Talkbiznow comes equipped with a suite of productivity services that have been developed to help increase your business productivity. With your personal profile, you can choose to publicize your current career position and career history. By building a personal profile, you are then able to search for like-minded business professionals and give them a glimpse of your background before becoming business contacts.

XING (www.xing.com)

> XING is an online global business network that connects people for the purpose of forming business and career opportunities. XING allows you to see how people are connected, which helps in generating new contacts of your own. They offer both free and premium memberships.

Social Networking Websites

There are a plethora of online, no-fee–based social networking sites that allow you to make not only friends, but business connections.

Facebook (www.facebook.com)

> Facebook is an online social networking site that allows millions of people to keep up with friends and family with photos, links, and videos; to connect with old friends from the past, and to learn more about new people that they meet. Facebook's mission is to give people the power to share and make the world more open and connected. If you create a profile on Facebook for the purpose of networking, keep it professional and separate from your personal profile.

Twitter (www.twitter.com)

Twitter is a no-fee online service for family, friends, and coworkers to communicate and stay connected through the exchange of answers to the question, "What are you doing?" It is a great way to promote yourself or your brand.

Professional Trade Publications

The Apparel Strategist (www.apparelstrategist.com)

The Apparel Strategist is the leading online U.S. business journal related to the apparel and textile industry. This publication presents reports about the current trends of the industry, predictions on the future growth of the industry, graphical representations, and vital statistics of the apparel and textile industry business cycles.

Drapers Record (www.drapersonline.com)

Drapers Record is a U.K.-based publication, which provides news and job listings for the British fashion industry.

Fashion Market (www.fmmg.com)

Fashion Market is a U.S.-based monthly publication, which provides all the important news related to the apparel industry.

Images Business of Fashion (www.imagesfashion.com)

Images Business of Fashion is one of the top-selling business magazines, having over half a million readers in the Indian subcontinent and the Middle East. Published monthly, it focuses on the marketing, retailing, branding, and merchandising aspects of the Indian fashion industry and is making a foray in the American and European markets.

Pursuit (www.pursuit.co.za)

Pursuit magazine is one of the most popular fashion trade journals in South Africa. Published every two months, it provides its readers with the latest trends, marketing techniques, interviews with celebrities, and discussions on the South African apparel and textile industries.

Sportswear International (www.sportswearnet.com)

Sportswear International is a German magazine that is published both in English and German,

six times a year. Founded in 1975, it offers pertinent information about jeans wear, sportswear, active wear, outerwear, menswear, casual wear, footwear, contemporary clothing, young designers, and the textile market. The magazine reports on the latest trends, new brands, and issues related to the fashion industry and a special feature is its award-winning fashion shoot and photography section.

Women's Wear Daily (www.wwd.com)

Often called the "fashion bible," *Women's Wear Daily (WWD)* is the professional trade newspaper for the fashion, beauty, and retail industries and has become the go-to reference for the latest breaking news. *WWD*'s in-house online job listing is located at www.fashioncareers.com, and their main website can be accessed at www.wwd.com. If you would like to post a "position wanted" ad, you can go to www.wwd.com/classifieds.

Online Portfolio Websites

A selection of Web-based portfolio websites, both free and paid options, are listed in this section.

BigBlackBag (www.bigblackbag.com)

BigBlackBag.com is a non-flash online portfolio website builder specifically designed for photographers, designers, artists, and other creative professionals. Although they offer a free trial, pricing starts at $8.99/month and includes a free domain name, email address, e-commerce option, and marketing and productivity tools.

Bleidu (www.bleidu.com)

Bleidu.com allows creative industry professionals such as fashion designers, artists, and photographers to create a free online professional portfolio including your own url.

Carbonmade (www.carbonmade.com)

Carbonmade.com allows you to manage your online portfolio with a variety of tools that change how you display your work. The core idea behind the design of Carbonmade is to keep your images or video at the forefront. Their basic plan called Meh is completely free of charge, and their fee-based plan called Whoo! is $12/month. With the free plan, they provide you with up to five projects and

35 images, and with their fee-based plan, they've bumped up those numbers to 50 projects, 500 high-resolution images, including an additional 10 high-quality videos.

Coroflot (www.coroflot.com)

Coroflot.com hosts individual portfolios and also has a database of job openings. For no charge, you can create a portfolio, and you will be assigned a URL. You can also receive detailed traffic reports to monitor views and activity on your site.

Figdig (www.figdig.com)

Figdig.com is an online community that enables talented professionals such as illustrators, graphic designers, creative directors, and fashion designers to upload, manage, and present their portfolios, which are viewable by those seeking to hire these individuals. They offer a zero membership fee structure.

Pixpa (www.pixpa.com)

Pixpa.com is an online portfolio website for fashion designers and artists to display, share, and sell their work, starting at $9.99/month. It includes design options, including video, a domain name, custom email address, webhosting and search engine optimization (SEO).

Qfolio (www.qfolio.com)

The Qfolio.com online fee-based portfolio format been designed to allow you to feature your work in a clean and concise manner. Each individual who signs up for the program will be assigned a Qfolio web designer who will help you create a customized portfolio.

Styleportfolios (www.styleportfolios.com)

Styleportfolios.com gives you a single page portfolio format with a personalized Web address that you can place on a résumé, in a cover letter, or on a business card. You can choose from 3, 6, 12, or 18 of your own images and will be listed in their designer database.

Talentline™ (www.staging.24seveninc.com/talentline/)

Talentline is a monthly newsletter showcasing the work of employment agency 24 Seven's most talented designers. A potential employer can click on the artwork of the designer they are interested in, and 24 Seven may then set up an interview.

Viewbook (www.viewbook.com)

Viewbook enables designers to manage their own portfolio websites on the Web and on iPad and mobile devices, such as iPhone. Prices begin at $4/month.

Color and Trend Forecasting Companies

The Color Association of the United States

33 Whitehall Street, Suite M3
New York, New York, USA 10004
T: (212) 947-7774
www.colorassociation.com
E-mail: info@colorassociation.com
Founded in 1915, The Color Association of The United States is a membership-based organization headquartered in New York City, that operates as the foremost forecasting agent to color professionals whose color decisions have a direct impact on the marketplace.

ColorVoyant

P.O. Box 737
Holicong, Pennsylvania, USA 18928
www.colorvoyant.com
E-mail: info@colorvoyant.com
ColorVoyant is a color-marketing firm that specializes in color directives for the fashion and cosmetic industries.

Cotton Incorporated

World Headquarters
6399 Weston Parkway
Cary, North Carolina, USA 27513
T: (919) 678-2220
F: (919) 678-2230
www.cottoninc.com
The mission of Cotton Incorporated is to ensure that cotton remains the first choice among apparel consumers. They offer agricultural, fiber, and textile research, market information, technical services, advertising and public relations, fashion forecasts, and retail promotions of cotton.

Fashion Snoops

39 West 38th Street
New York, New York, USA 10018
T: (212) 768-8804
F: (646) 365-6013

www.fashionsnoops.com
E-mail: info@fashionsnoops.com
Fashion Snoops is a worldwide trend forecasting company, delivering an online, subscription-based service of style insight to its global clientele of fashion professionals.

Mudpie Ltd.

21–24 Home Farm Business Centre
Lockerley, Romsey Hampshire SO51 OJT, United Kingdom
T: +44 20 3005 1000
F: +44 20 3005 1009
www.mudpie.co.uk
E-mail: enquire@mudpie.co.uk
Mudpie supports creative professionals by providing trend forecasting, trend guides and consulting services for leading brands. They place revenue-building ideas alongside inspiration in their presentations.

Pantone LLC

World Headquarters
590 Commerce Boulevard
Carlstadt, New Jersey, USA 07072
T: (201) 935-5500
F: (201) 896-0242
www.pantone.com
Pantone is known around the world as the color authority and provider of a standardized method of color communication between the designer and manufacturer and the retailer and consumer.

Promostyl

Head Office
853 Broadway, Suite 800
New York, NY, USA 10003
T: (212) 228-8001
www.promostyl.com
E-mail: info@promostylamericas.com
Promostyl analysts, stylists, and designers travel around the globe to provide trend services and consulting to creative people in the fashion industry.

The Style Council (TSC)

242 W. 36th Street, 14th Floor
New York, New York, USA 10018
T: (212) 564-9380
F: (212) 594-2315
www.stylecouncil.com
E-mail: tsc@stylecouncil.com
The Style Council is the leading textile design and trend forecasting service studio for retailers, designers, merchandisers, and manufacturers.

Trendstop

28–39 The Quadrant
135 Salusbury Road
London NW6 6RJ, United Kingdom
T: +44 (0)870 788 6888
F: +44 (0)870 788 6886
www.trendstop.com
Trendstop offers trend and color forecasts in the form of trend reports and webinars for the apparel, accessories, and footwear industries.

TRENDZINE Fashion Information

Gainsborough House
81 Oxford Street
London W1D 2EU, United Kingdom
www.trendzine.net
E-mail: info@fashioninformation.com
Trendzine is a forecasting service company offering precise trend predictions for the apparel and accessory industries.

Worth Global Style Network (WGSN)

Head Office, North and South America
130 Fifth Avenue, 7th Floor
New York, New York, USA 10011
T: (877) 277-9476
F: (212) 201-2830
www.wgsn.com
E-mail: us-sales@4C.wgsn.com
WGSN is the world's leading global trend analysis, forecaster, and research service, providing creative and business intelligence for the apparel, style, design, and retail industries. They have offices throughout the United States, Europe, Asia, the Middle East, South Africa, and South America.

Broadcast and Cable Television Programming with a Fashion Theme

America's Next Top Model (The CW)

America's Next Top Model (ANTM) is a reality television show, hosted, judged, and produced by supermodel Tyra Banks, in which several women compete against each other for the title of America's Next Top Model and a chance to launch their modeling career.

Fashion Police (E! Entertainment Television)

Fashion Police is a television show whose co-hosts, Joan Rivers, Giuliana Rancic, Kelly Osbourne, and George Kotsiopoulos, critique celebrity fashion on and off the red carpet.

The Fashion Show Ultimate Collection (Bravo TV)

Known as *The Fashion Show, The Fashion Show Ultimate Collection* is a television show hosted by fashion designer Isaac Mizrahi and model Iman, in which designers compete for a cash prize and the opportunity to have their fashions sold to a retailer.

Fashion Star (NBC)

Fashion Star is a reality television series hosted by supermodel Elle Macpherson, and featuring Jessica Simpson, Nicole Richie, and fashion designer John Varvatos who, together, act as mentors to unknown fashion designers competing for the chance to win a multimillion dollar prize and the opportunity to launch their collections in either Saks Fifth Avenue, Macy's, or H&M. The winning designs will be available for immediate purchase by the public at the end of each episode.

Project Runway (Lifetime Television)

Project Runway is a reality television show hosted and judged by model Heidi Klum, Michael Kors, and Nina Garcia, in which fashion designers compete against each other to create clothing within a restricted timeframe. Tim Gunn acts as their mentor throughout the process. Their creations are featured on a runway and judged, until the elimination process concludes with one remaining contestant. Prizes have included cash, mentorships with fashion companies, editorial spreads in major fashion magazines, and the chance to show the winning collections during New York Fashion Week.

The Rachel Zoe Project (Bravo TV)

The Rachel Zoe Project is a reality television show that follows celebrity stylist Rachel Zoe as she balances her celebrity stylist and fashion designer roles with her personal life.

Tim Gunn's Guide to Style (Bravo TV)

Tim Gunn's Guide to Style is a reality television series hosted by mentor Tim Gunn and style expert Gretta Monahan, in which they complete a makeover on guests who then are given specific style guidelines to follow.

What Not To Wear (TLC)

What Not To Wear is a reality television series, hosted by Stacy London and Clinton Kelly, in which everyday people receive full makeovers, including wardrobe, hair, and makeup.

Full-Feature Movies with a Fashion Theme

Clueless, Paramount Pictures (1995)

Director Amy Heckerling's adaptation of Jane Austen's novel *Emma, Clueless* follows the misadventures of Beverly Hills high-schooler Cher (Alicia Silverstone) as she gives a fashion-challenged student a makeover.

Confessions of a Shopaholic, Buena Vista Pictures (2009)

With dreams of writing for a top fashion magazine, shopping addict Rebecca (Isla Fisher) struggles with her shopping obsession and inadvertently begins working for a financial magazine. As she comes close to landing her dream job, she ponders whether overcoming her addiction will actually make her happier. Based on a novel by Sophie Kinsella.

The Devil Wears Prada, 20th Century Fox (2006)

After taking a job in New York as assistant to powerful fashion magazine editor Miranda Priestly (Meryl Streep), small-town girl Andrea Sachs (Anne Hathaway) is ecstatic, until she gets a taste of what it's like to work for one of the most infamous fashion editors in the high-stakes world of fashion publishing. Based on a novel by Lauren Weisberger.

Zoolander, Paramount Pictures (2001)

The fashion world is turned upside down when an utterly flaky male model, Derek Zoolander (Ben Stiller), discovers that fashion mogul Jacobim Mogatu (Will Ferrell) is behind a plot to assassinate the prime minister of Malaysia.

Documentaries with a Fashion Theme

Chanel, Chanel (1986)

Directed by Elia Hershon, this documentary profiles fashion icon Coco Chanel, depicting an exploration of her life, work, and sudden rise as a designer in the 1900s. Archival footage is presented, along with a series of interviews with her successor, Karl Lagerfeld, and others closest to her.

Jack Taylor of Beverly Hills (2007)

For over sixty years, Jack Taylor has dressed many of the legendary stars of the past, including Cary Grant, Frank Sinatra, Dean Martin, Sid Caesar, and Elvis Presley. This inviting documentary, directed by Cecile Leroy Beaulieu, brings the viewer up close and personal with the still-working 90-something Taylor whose exhilarating passion for custom tailoring is contagious (www.jacktaylorthemovie.com).

Lagerfeld Confidential (2006)

For the first time, Karl Lagerfeld, the man behind the House of Chanel and one of the most enigmatic style legends of all time, is filmed for this documentary portraying his professional and private life. After three years of trekking the globe, director Rudolphe Marconi uncovers the day-to-day life of this most forthright and outspoken fashion icon (www.lagerfeldfilm.com).

Marc Jacobs and Louis Vuitton (2007)

With unprecedented access to one of the world's most popular fashion designers, Loïc Prigent offers an enlightening depiction of the reserved and worshipped Marc Jacobs through his daily life. Whether in the offices and workrooms of Paris and New York, the back of his car, or backstage at a fashion show, we see his talent on display. Jacobs endures unimaginable pressure as he balances both the demands of putting together the Louis Vuitton collection and his eponymous Marc Jacobs line.

Ralph Rucci: A Designer and His House (2008)

Martha Stewart narrates this David Boatman documentary following fashion designer Ralph Rucci during the creation of his spring 2008 ready-to-wear and fall 2008 couture collections. It also features interviews with a number of the fashion industry's top insiders.

Seamless (2005)

Director Douglas Keeve takes a look at the intensely competitive world of the fashion industry with this gripping documentary, which follows ten fashion designer hopefuls as they compete in a contest created by Vogue magazine and the Council of Fashion Designers of America. Anna Wintour, Vera Wang, and Isaac make cameo appearances.

The September Issue (2008)

Dubbed as the real Devil Wears Prada by Vanity Fair magazine, The September Issue goes where no camera crew has ever been allowed to go before: behind the scenes into the world of Vogue's legendary editor-in-chief, Anna Wintour. The viewer learns how the editorial team puts together and completes their largest issue of the year, the September issue, with a glimpse into closed-door staff meetings at the Condé Nast headquarters, as well as various scenes filmed during photo shoots and fashion week (www.theseptemberissue.com).

Starz Inside: Fashion in Film (2008)

This documentary looks at the influence contemporary fashion has had in films and how films have inspired fashion trends. Jean Paul Gaultier, model Tyson Beckford, and others discuss films such as Bonnie and Clyde, Annie Hall, The Devil Wears Prada, and Sex and the City.

Unzipped (1995)

Shot primarily in black and white, Douglas Keeve's intriguing documentary about fashion designer Isaac Mizrahi explores his creative process from beginning inspirations to completed runway show. It features the original '90s supermodels, Cindy Crawford, Naomi Campbell, Linda Evangelista, and Christy Turlington.

Valentino: The Last Emperor (2008)

Produced and directed by Matt Tyrnauer, this is a fascinating documentary providing a peek into the life of one of the most famous fashion designers of all time: Valentino. Filmed over the course of two years, it culminates with the last runway show of Valentino's illustrious career, complete with floating red ethereal dresses, Valentino's signature design. His longtime partner, Giancarlo Giammetti, is by his side throughout most of the documentary (www.valentinomovie.com).

Yves Saint Laurent: His Life and Times and *5 Avenue Marceau 75116 Paris* (2004)
This DVD provides two separate documentaries. *His Life and Times* provides in-depth interviews with the private, Algerian-born, French designer, who is considered one of the most influential haute couture designers of all time. *5 Avenue Marceau 75116 Paris* is a look inside Yves Saint Laurent's famed atelier during the creation and completion of his final spring line.

Major Fashion Magazines

Allure—America (www.allure.com)

Allure—Korea (www.style.co.kr/allure)

Brides—America (www.brides.com)

Brides—United Kingdom (www.bridesmagazine.co.uk)

Collezioni—Italy (www.logos.info/en)

Cosmopolitan—America (www.cosmopolitan.com)

Cosmopolitan—Armenia (www.cosmo.am)

Cosmopolitan—Australia (www.cosmopolitan.com.au)

Cosmopolitan—France (www.cosmopolitan.fr)

Cosmopolitan—Germany (www.cosmopolitan.de)

Cosmopolitan—Italy (www.cosmopolitan.it)

Cosmopolitan—Mongolia (www.cosmopolitan.mn)

Cosmopolitan—Russia (www.cosmo.ru)

Cosmopolitan—Serbia (www.cosmopolitan.rs)

Cosmopolitan—South Africa (www.cosmopolitan.co.za)

Cosmopolitan—Spain (www.cosmohispano.com)

Cosmopolitan—Sweden (www.cosmopolitan.se)

Cosmopolitan—United Kingdom (www.cosmopolitan.co.uk)

Details (www.details.com)

Elle—America (www.elle.com)

Elle—Belgium (www.elle.be)

Elle—Brazil (www.elle.abril.com.br)

Elle—Canada (www.ellecanada.com)

Elle—Czech Republic (www.elle.cz)

Elle—China (www.ellechina.com)

Elle—Denmark (www.elle.dk)

Elle—Finland (www.elle.fi)

Elle—France (www.elle.fr)

Elle—Germany (www.elle.de)

Elle—Hong Kong (www.ellehk.com)

Elle—Hungary (www.ellemagazin.hu)

Elle—India (www.ellenow.com)

Elle—Italy (www.elle.it)

Elle—Japan (www.elle.co.jp)

Elle—Korea (www.elle.co.kr)

Elle—Netherlands (www.elle.nl)

Elle—Norway (www.elle.no)

Elle—Quebec (www.ellequebec.com)

Elle—Russia (www.elle.ru)

Elle—Slovenia (www.elle.si)

Elle—South Africa (www.ellemagazine.co.za)

Elle—Spain (www.elle.es)

Elle—Sweden (www.elle.se)

Elle—Taiwan (www.elle.com.tw)

Elle—Thailand (www.elle.co.th)

Elle—Turkey (www.elle.com.tr)

Elle—United Kingdom (www.elleuk.com)

Essence (www.essence.com)

Glamour—America (www.glamour.com)

Glamour—Germany (www.glamour.de)

Glamour—Greece (www.glamourmagazine .gr)

Glamour—Hungary (www.glamouronline.hu)

Glamour—Italy (www.glamour.it)

Glamour—Mexico (www.glamour.mx)

Glamour—Netherlands (www.glamour.nl)

Glamour—Paris (www.glamourparis.com)

Glamour—Poland (www.glamour.pl)

Glamour—Russia (www.glamour.ru)

Glamour—Spain (www.glamour.es)

Glamour—South Africa (www.glamour.co.za)

Glamour—United Kingdom (www .glamourmagazine.co.uk)

GQ—America (www.gq.com)

GQ—Australia (www.gq.com.au)

GQ—Brazil (www.gq.globo.com)

GQ—China (www.gq.com.cn)

GQ—France (www.gqmagazine.fr)

GQ—Germany (www.gq-magazin.de)

GQ—India (www.gqindia.com)

GQ—Italy (www.gqitalia.it)

GQ—Japan (www.gqjapan.jp)

GQ—Mexico (www.gq.com.mx)

GQ—Russia (www.gq.ru)

GQ—Spain (www.revistagq.com)

GQ—South Africa (www.gq.co.za)

GQ—South Korea (www.style.co.kr/gq)

GQ—Taiwan (www.gq.com.tw)

GQ—Turkey (www.gq.com.tr)

GQ—United Kingdom (www.gq-magazine .co.uk)

Harper's Bazaar—America (www .harpersbazaar.com)

Harper's Bazaar—Argentina (no official website)

Harper's Bazaar—Australia (www .harpersbazaar.com.au)

Harper's Bazaar—Brazil (no official website)

Harper's Bazaar—Bulgaria (no official website)

Harper's Bazaar—Canada (no official website)

Harper's Bazaar—China (no official website)

Harper's Bazaar—Czech Republic (no official website)

Harper's Bazaar—Greece (no official website)

Harper's Bazaar—Hong Kong (www .harpersbazaar.com.hk)

Harper's Bazaar—India (no official website)

Harper's Bazaar—Indonesia (www .harpersbazaar.co.id)

Harper's Bazaar—Japan (no official website)

Harper's Bazaar—Kazakhstan (no official website)

Harper's Bazaar—South Korea (no official website)

Harper's Bazaar—Latin America (no official website)

Harper's Bazaar—Malaysia (no official website)

Harper's Bazaar—Romania (www .harpersbazaar.ro)

Harper's Bazaar—Russia (www.bazaar.ru)

Harper's Bazaar—Singapore (no official website)

Harper's Bazaar—Spain (no official website)

Harper's Bazaar—Taiwan (no official website)

Harper's Bazaar—Thailand (no official website)

Harper's Bazaar—Turkey (no official website)

Harper's Bazaar—United Arab Emirates (no official website)

Harper's Bazaar—United Kingdom (www.harpersbazaar.co.uk)

Harper's Bazaar—Ukraine (no official website)

Harper's Bazaar—Vietnam (no official website)

In Style (www.instyle.com)

Lucky—America (www.luckymag.com)

Lucky—Greece (www.glamourmagazine.gr/lucky)

Marie Claire—America (www.marieclaire.com)

Marie Claire—Australia (www.marieclaire.com.au)

Marie Claire—Brazil (www.revistamarieclaire.globo.com)

Marie Claire—China (www.marieclairechina.com)

Marie Claire—France (www.marieclaire.fr)

Marie Claire—Hong Kong (www.marieclaire.com.hk/index1.htm)

Marie Claire—Italy (www.marieclaire.it)

Marie Claire—Japan (www.marieclaire.co.jp)

Marie Claire—Malaysia (www.marieclaire.com.my)

Marie Claire—Spain (www.marie-claire.es)

Marie Claire—Taiwan (www.marieclaire.com.tw)

Marie Claire—Turkey (www.mcdergi.com)

Nylon—America (www.nylonmag.com)

Vogue—America (www.vogue.com)

Vogue—Australia (www.vogue.com.au)

Vogue—Brazil (www.vogue.globo.com)

Vogue—British (www.vogue.co.uk)

Vogue—China (www.vogue.com.cn)

Vogue—Germany (www.vogue.de)

Vogue—Greece (www.voguehellas.gr)

Vogue—India (www.vogue.in)

Vogue—Italia (www.vogue.it)

Vogue—Japan (www.vogue.co.jp)

Vogue—Korea (www.style.co.kr/vogue)

Vogue—Mexico (www.vogue.mx)

Vogue—Paris (www.vogue.fr)

Vogue—Portugal (www.vogue.xl.pt)

Vogue—Russia (www.vogue.ru)

Vogue—Spain (www.vogue.es)

Vogue—Taiwan (www.vogue.com.tw)

Vogue—Turkey (www.vogue.com.tr)

W—America (www.wmagazine.com)

W—Korea (www.style.co.kr/w)

Wallpaper—United Kingdom (www.wallpaper.com)

INDEX OF INTERVIEWS

INDEX